God Wants a Relationship Not a Performance

Don Anderson

First Printing of Second Edition, 2003.

God Wants a Relationship Not a Performance
By Don Anderson

First Printing of First Edition, April 1989 by Loizeaux Brothers, Neptune, NJ.

Printed in the United States of America.

ISBN 1-591609-35-6

References noted "DAV" are taken from the author's personal translation of the Greek text.

References noted "NIV" are taken from the HOLY BIBLE, NEW INTERNATIONAL VERSION®. Copyright © 1973, 1978, 1984 by International Bible Society. Used by permission of Zondervan Publishing House. All rights reserved.

The "NIV" and "New International Version" trademarks are registered in the United States Patent and Trademark Office by International Bible Society. Use of either trademark requires the permission of International Bible Society.

References noted "NASB" are from the *New American Standard Bible,* copyright The Lockman Foundation 1960, 1962, 1963, 1968, 1971, 1972, 1973, 1975, 1977 and are used by permission.

References noted "Phillips" are from *The New Testament in Modern English (*Revised Edition), translated by J.B. Phillips, copyright J.B. Phillips 1958, 1960, 1972 and are used by permission of Macmillan Publishing Company.

Library of Congress Cataloging-in-Publication Data
Anderson, Don, 1933-
God Wants a Relationship Not a Performance.
p. cm.
Bibliography: p. 317
ISBN 0-87213-005-3 (***Previous ISBN # from 1st printing***)
1. Bible N.T. Romans V-VIII—Commentaries. 2. Bible. N.T. Romans V-VIII—Meditations. II. Title.
BS2665.3.A53 1989
227'. 107—dc 19

88-30847
CIP

The author wishes to acknowledge the editorial assistance of M. Jane Rodgers.

Xulon Press
www.XulonPress.com

Xulon Press books are available in bookstores everywhere, and on the Web at www.XulonPress.com.

Other Titles by Don Anderson

Abraham: Delay Is Not Denial

Ecclesiastes: The Mid-Life Crisis

Song of Solomon: Make Full My Joy

A Gift Too Wonderful for Words

Joy Comes in the Morning

James: Running Uphill into the Wind

Joseph: Fruitful in Affliction

Drawing Closer Growing Stronger

Keep the Fire!

A Great While Before Day: Issue 1

A Great While Before Day: Issue 2

Acknowledgments

The message of relationship over performance has been the passion of my heart during all our years of ministry. What a privilege is mine to finally see this work in print a second time. A publishing venture is not a lone ranger project. The sacrifices of many have brought this book to fruition. Jane Rodgers, word artist and editor *par excellence* has done it again. We have worked on ten books together and Jane is the editor of our *Grapevine* magazine. Jane, thanks for being there, always available to take on another one. You are a wonderful sister in our Lord.

Bill Lawrence, Tammy Lively, and Genevieve Martin: the Lord knows of your sacrificial service in this project.

Pearl Anderson, my lover, confidante, and best friend: thanks for 50 wonderful years of marriage and ministry together.

Dedication

To a divine piece of work—with whom I have shared so much: Pearl O. Anderson, my wife and sweetheart. Honey, you are beginning to look a lot like Jesus!

Contents

Foreword

Performance counts. Employees have annual performance reviews. Salesmen have their performance measured by sales quotas. Shareholders review the performance of a company through quarterly and annual reports. We have been conditioned to the idea that we must perform well to achieve our desires. We may even wonder if there is anything meaningful that doesn't require a performance! But we needn't wonder.

In *God Wants a Relationship Not a Performance*, Don Anderson explains with characteristic clarity that God is vitally interested in what we *are*, not necessarily in what we *do*. As we see in this fresh look at Romans 5-8, the Lord longs first for a personal relationship with us through his Son; then, his desire is for this relationship to become richer and more intense. Only God can grant us fulfillment in life; this satisfaction comes from an ever-deepening relationship. We cannot hope to perform on our own to gain his favor. The notion that it's relationship, not performance, which truly counts with God may be surprising to employees and executives such as those who work with us at State National Companies. But I like to think that maybe the message might startle us a little less here than at other companies.

For many years now, our employees have had the opportunity to participate in a weekly morning Bible study taught by Don Anderson. One summer while attending a Colorado family camp led by the Ministries, I asked Don to consider adding this class to his annual schedule. I wanted those I worked with to have the chance to hear someone teach God's word as accurately, clearly, and practically as Don does. He graciously agreed, and the results have been tremendous. Some have accepted the Lord as savior; others have learned how to deal with difficult situations in their lives; others have been regularly refreshed and encouraged through hearing God's word and letting it do its work of growth in them.

God Wants a Relationship Not a Performance won't disappoint you. After you read it, I imagine you'll be relieved as you learn that God isn't in the business of reviewing our performance, but instead waits on us, desiring that we come to know him better and better. The book has shown me that as my relationship with the Lord deepens, so does my desire to grow, and my conduct becomes more consistent with the principles laid out in scripture. With God, there is no pressure to perform!

Terry Ledbetter
President & CEO
State National Companies
Fort Worth, Texas

I Never Got to Know You

"Sixty-four years!" Jack exclaimed. "Sixty-four years I have been performing for God, and tonight I have come into relationship with him through his Son!"

Bettie's story was similar. As she poignantly put it, "How could I have been deceived through all these years, playing out on the stage of life what I thought was an acceptable performance, while God was standing by waiting for a relationship with me through his Son, Jesus Christ?'"

What joy such forthright statements of faith bring to our heart, and to God's heart! But with the crescendo of gladness echo a few notes of regret. Why did it take Jack so long to find the savior? Why was Bettie deceived for many years as well? Both were frequent churchgoers. Both, practically till the very moments of their salvation, would probably have told you they were Christians. They gave money to churches and charities. They served on committees and councils and sang in choirs. They were decent, law-abiding people. Yet the reality of Jesus Christ had not pierced their hearts. For decades, succumbing to the lure of service for its own sake, they were dead in their trespasses and sins because they never got to know the savior. It took each nearly a lifetime to discover the truth Bill Butterworth expresses in his song, "What Does It Take?"

> What does it take to get to heaven?
> I've heard many ways.
> I've heard God wouldn't let you in
> Unless you died on certain days;
> I've heard you gotta work and join
> And pay and do and don't
> With all the requirements to make it to heaven,
> I guess I won't.
>
> Son, where ya' been all o' your life?
> Ain't ya heard of the Golden Rule?
> Son, come on now, get it straight:
> Ya gotta go to Sunday School!
> Son, don't listen to them, listen to me:
> Ya gotta keep those Ten Commands!
> My Mommy told me I wouldn't go to heaven
> If I didn't wash my hands!
>
> Boy, don't ya know that God will like you
> If you put money in the plate?
> Boy, ya just gotta go to church
> And, of course, never be late!
> Kid, ya gotta do your best
> And build up lotsa good deeds!
> My Mommy told me I wouldn't go to heaven
> If I didn't eat my peas!
>
> Then someone showed me somethin' diff'rent,
> They showed me what the Bible said;
> It was simple, not like opinions

Swimmin' around in my head.
When I saw it wasn't by workin',
But faith in Christ alone,
Then I believed Jesus died for me,
And heaven will be my home.

What does it take to get to heaven?
I have found the way!
I heard that God really loves me,
And for my sins He's paid;
I saw heaven was a free gift,
Just by simple faith.
With trustin' Christ to take me to heaven,
I couldn't make a mistake.[1]

What does it take to get to heaven? The answer is *faith*—not some confidence in our own ability, but instead a wholehearted trust in the Lord Jesus Christ and his finished work at Calvary. It's a relationship *with us*—not a performance *from us*—that God desires. But so often we, like the subject of Butterworth's song, choose to believe that we're saved by churchgoing, rule following, money giving, or commandment keeping. It isn't so.

And once we do enter into a relationship with God through faith in Jesus Christ, how incredibly easy it is for us to turn around and strive to perform all the more to somehow try to keep God's favor. The institutional church often encourages this. When the shift in organized religion goes from relationship to ritual, pulpits proclaim performance and the result is meaningless motion. What's left are programs without power and people prideful or frustrated by failure. That's not what God intends. We can be neither saved nor made holy by what we do. God is concerned with what we *are*—in him and to him!

FROM THE BEGINNING ...

The simple truth is that from the days of creation, God has been vitally interested in establishing, maintaining, and sustaining a growing relationship with his creatures, humankind. Relationship with him was—and is—the Father's primary purpose in creating us. A journey through the pages of scripture should convince us of that. God's word teems with examples which make it clear that he desires for us to walk in fellowship with him. He longs for us to know him better and better and, in the process, to become more like him.

Genesis 1:27 states, "God created man in his own image, in the image of God he created him; male and female he created them" (NIV). Adam was formed first, then God with compassion fashioned a suitable companion, Eve, when he saw Adam's need. We read that the "man and his wife were both naked, and they felt no shame" (Gen. 2:25 NIV). There was perfect freedom, beautiful fellowship, a marvelous three-way communion between God and his children which we cannot completely comprehend. Only after Adam disobeyed the one rule God had given him, was this perfect unity marred. Then the man and woman hid in shame from the Lord God as he walked in the midst of the garden in the cool of the day (Gen. 3:8-10). The relationship between humankind and God was changed for all time.

But just because Adam's sin altered the relationship between creator and creature doesn't mean the Lord stopped desiring communion with men and women! The Bible is filled with accounts of God's outstretched arms reaching to embrace sinners—open, longing for restoration and fellowship. A changeless, constant God, he is ready and waiting for us to turn to him. He deeply desires that we love him and respond to him. He has even provided, through the sacrifice of his own Son, the means by which we can enjoy such a relationship today. Then and now, God is a God of relationship.

God is also a God of second chances, and then some! After Cain disobeyed directions and offered a sacrifice of the fruit of the ground rather than an animal sacrifice, God said to him, "Why are you angry? Why is your face downcast? If you do what is right, will you not be accepted? But if you do not do what is right, sin is crouching at your door; it desires to have you, but you must master it" (Gen. 4:6-7 NIV). Although the Lord, in his infinite wisdom and foreknowledge, knew that Cain would sin by becoming humankind's first murderer, God still reached out with a gentle promise of acceptance and forgiveness. Even Cain was invited to fellowship with the Father!

Others didn't resist God's overtures of relationship. In fact, the Lord so enjoyed the rich friendship he had with Enoch, who "walked with God," that he whisked him directly into heaven, bypassing the gateway of physical death (Gen. 5:24).

Noah also "walked with God," and the Lord handed him blueprints of an ocean liner and instructions for rain. The Father plucked Noah and family and two of every creature from the threshold of disaster, preserving a remnant of the human race when he rightly could have wiped the slate clean of sinful man and started over.

In time, God began a plan to restore fellowship between his children and himself. To Abraham, he gave promises concerning a specific land and people, and the promise that through Abraham's seed, through a special descendant, "all peoples on earth will be blessed" (Gen. 12:3 NIV). This promised seed, Jesus Christ, would come to earth as God in human flesh—his death on the cross God's provision to permanently end the separation begun in the garden. In the words of the hymnist, "Oh, the mighty gulf that God did span / At Calvary!"

The same God answered Isaac's prayers about Rebekah's barrenness, and he appeared to the fugitive Jacob at the top of a ladder in a dream, promising to watch over the patriarch and fulfill his promises to him. The same God accompanied Joseph from a position of privilege in his father's house to the dry, dusty pit where his brothers tossed him, to slavery in Potiphar's house, to prison, and eventually to the palace of pharaoh. The same God spoke to Moses and Joshua, assuring them of his abiding presence and constant protection.

This God empowered Gideon, inspired Samuel, and anointed David. He spoke to his people through Elijah and Elisha. He opened channels for Ezra and Nehemiah and granted success to Esther. He sustained Job in time of horrendous trial. He communicated through the prophets, revealing his will and his intentions to Isaiah, Jeremiah, Ezekiel, Daniel, and others. He is pictured in Hosea as a faithful husband of an unfaithful wife, loving unconditionally and never giving up. He is, in the words of Nahum, "a refuge in times of trouble. He cares for those who trust in him" (Nah. 1:7 NIV).

In the New Testament, where we uniquely see God in the person of Jesus Christ, interacting with men and women, we notice Christ's ministry was characterized by relationships. He concerned himself with the twelve, with Martha, Mary, Lazarus, the rich young ruler, Zaccheus, Nicodemus, Mary Magdalene. He cared about a small boy who carried five loaves and a couple of fish. He loved lepers, the lame, tax-gatherers, prostitutes, promiscuous women, the diseased and dying, the bleeding and frail, the helpless and hopeless, the blind and the broken. No one was excluded from his invitation of relationship.

The books of the New Testament are chronicles of the Lord's undying love and unending faithfulness, and his desire to fellowship with us:

> "I am the vine, you are the branches; he who

abides in Me, and I in him, he bears much fruit; for apart from Me you can do nothing" (John 15:5 NASB).

"I do not ask in behalf of these alone, but for those also who believe in Me through their word; that they may all be one; even as Thou, Father, art in Me, and I in Thee, that they also may be in Us; that the world may believe that Thou didst send Me" (John 17:20-21 NASB).

"So when they had finished breakfast, Jesus said to Simon Peter, 'Simon, son of John, do you love Me more than these?' He said to Him, "'Yes, Lord; You know that I love You.' He said to him, 'Tend my lambs'" (John 21:15 NASB).

"For you have not received a spirit of slavery to cause you to fear, but you received the spirit of adoption by which we are crying out, 'Abba! Father!'" (Rom. 8:15 DAV).

"God is faithful, through whom you were called into fellowship with His Son, Jesus Christ our Lord" (1 Cor. 1:9 NASB).

"Husbands, love your wives, just as Christ also loved the church and gave Himself up for her; that He might sanctify her, having cleansed her by the washing of water with the word, that He might present to Himself the church in all her glory, having no spot or wrinkle or any such thing; but that she should be holy and blameless" (Eph. 5:25-27 NASB).

"As you therefore have received Christ Jesus the Lord, so walk in Him" (Col. 2:6 NASB).

"Faithful is He who calls you, and He also will bring it to pass" (1 Thess. 5:24 NASB).

"But the Lord is faithful, and He will strengthen and protect you from the evil one" (2 Thess. 3:3 NASB).

"Since therefore, brethren, we have confidence to enter the holy place by the blood of Jesus, by a new and living way which He inaugurated for us through the veil, that is, His flesh, and since we have a great priest over the house of God, let us draw near with a sincere heart in full assurance of faith, having our hearts sprinkled clean from an evil conscience and our bodies washed with pure water. Let us hold fast the confession of our hope without wavering, for He who promised is faithful" (Heb. 10:19-23 NASB).

"Draw near to God and He will draw near to you. Cleanse your hands, you sinners; and purify your hearts, you double-minded" (James 4:8 NASB).

"What we have seen and heard we proclaim to you also, that you also may have fellowship with us; and indeed our fellowship is with the Father, and with His Son Jesus

Christ" (1 John 1:3 NASB).

THE NEW BIRTH—A REBORN RELATIONSHIP

Relationship is always the Father's objective. As Christians we look forward to rich fellowship with him for eternity, as we're presented to him in the marriage supper of the lamb (see Rev. 19). But how must it begin?

As Jesus tells Nicodemus, a very religious man, a Pharisee, "You must be born again," the relationship God so deeply desires to have with us begins when we experience a spiritual rebirth and come to faith in Christ (John 3:7, 1 Pet. 1:23, John 1:13). Paul writes to the Corinthians "Therefore if any man is in Christ, he is a new creation; the old things passed away; behold new things have come" (2 Cor. 5:17 DAV). Physical birth is followed by hunger for milk, then meat. Likewise, spiritual birth is attended by a healthy hunger for the milk and then the meat of the word of God. In the words of the apostle Peter: "like newborn babes, long for the pure milk of the word, that by it you may grow in respect to salvation, if you have tasted the kindness of the Lord" (1 Pet. 2:2-3 NASB). A daily, disciplined diet of the word of God is the key to spiritual growth and development. As the Spirit of God guides us into all truth, the fruit of his work is that we become more and more like Jesus.

The changes wrought in the lives of the disciples testify to the power of the Spirit to work in a person's life. Peter becomes a preacher at Pentecost. John, the son of thunder, quick to anger, is transformed into the apostle of love. Saul of Tarsus, chief of sinners and persecutor of the saints, is so filled with Christ's love that he is willing to pay any price to spread the gospel. It is time for us to join them in singing: "What a wonderful change in my life has been wrought, since Jesus came into my heart."

Are there dangers in resisting the relationship? Yes. For some, like Judas Iscariot, who chose silver over the savior, it means suicide. For others, it means emptiness and misery on earth. For all, it means spiritual death: separation from God for eternity unless the step of faith is taken before earthly life is ended.

For those who receive Christ as savior, yet insist on continuing to perform all the more, the danger is different. The results may be stress, bitterness, jealousy, strife, competition; and the absence of peace, satisfaction, and fulfillment. When the focus is on *us* instead of the savior, we do not bring God pleasure. There is so much more to the Christian life, as we'll see in the book of Romans.

TO A FRIEND

It is the desire of God's heart that you come to know him, that you accept his provision of salvation. Why don't you stop reading right now and do business with God? Acknowledge your need of a savior because of your sin. Accept by faith the glorious gift he is offering you in his Son. Thank him for coming into your life. When the transaction is completed, you get some great news! The heavenly Father takes full responsibility for all that happens from here to glory. The Spirit of God has come into your life, too, and he will guide you into truth, providing power for peace, contentment, and victory over sin. You could sing: "It is well with my soul," because it finally is.

Remember, God longs to be close to you. What you try to do to impress him, won't. He's concerned with what you allow him to make of you, not with what you attempt to make of yourself. As Paul vividly shows us in Romans 5-8, the doing cannot be ours—it's got to be God's! And whatever our circumstances, the Lord is waiting to make things right when we are willing to turn to him.

Many years ago, one of our children brought home the following letter from a friend. I do not know the author, but I suspect that he or she had learned from experience that

God is waiting for an opportunity to be with us. Our heavenly Father longs to save us; once we've received his gift of salvation, he longs to reveal more and more of himself to us. He is our matchless, priceless, precious friend.

> Dear Friend,
>
> I just had to send a note today to tell you how much I love you and care about you. I saw you yesterday as you were walking with your friends. I waited all day, hoping you would want to talk with me also. As evening drew near, I gave you a sunset to close your day and a cool breeze to rest you, and I waited, but you never came. It hurt me, but I still love you because I am your friend. I saw you fall asleep last night, and I longed to touch your brow, so I spilled moonlight on your pillow and your face. Again I waited, wanting to rush down so we could talk. I have so many gifts for you, but you awakened late that next day and rushed off to work and my tears were in the rain.
>
> Today you looked so sad, so all alone—it made my heart ache because I understand. My friends let me down and hurt me so many times, but I love you. Oh, if you would only listen to me; I really love you. I try to tell you in the blue sky and in the quiet green grass. I look for it in leaves on the trees and breathe it in the colors of the love song that you sing. I clothe you with warm sunshine and perfume the air with nature's scent. My love for you is deeper than the ocean and bigger than the biggest want or need in your heart. If you only knew how much I want to help

you. I want you to meet my Father. He wants to help you too. My Father is that way, you know. Just call me, ask me, talk with me. I have so much to share with you, but I won't bother you. I'll wait because I love you.

Your friend,
Jesus

CHAPTER 1

Rethinking the Reason God Made Us

I'd like you to meet some friends of mine: Joe, Daniel, Sondra, Frank, and Julia. Perhaps you know them already, or maybe you know others just like them.

Joe is a businessman. He is highly driven, fiercely competitive, and very successful. Although Joe will be the first to admit that he tries to beat out his competitors almost any way he can, he is relatively ethical in his professional dealings. His methods to gain the upper edge may sometimes be questionable, but they are never illegal. Do it unto others before they do it unto you is the corporate creed by which he operates. Tough as nails in the marketplace, Joe savors the sales charts when the numbers are good and aggressively answers the challenge when the quarter is poor. He is committed to doing whatever it takes—working overtime, offering incentives, switching strategies—in order to ensure that his division turns in a stellar annual performance. Swimming with the sharks is the name of his game.

As far as personal conduct goes, you might say Joe is

relatively moral, by the world's standards. He drinks, but he's no alcoholic. Conventions? He may have an out-of-town fling once in a while, but he stays away from long-term affairs. He won't steadily cheat on his wife, and he doesn't cheat his customers, his employees, or the IRS either. A self-sufficient and, as he likes to put it, a self-made man, Joe's crusty independence permeates his entire philosophy of life, extending to his attitude toward God.

Another thing about Joe: everything in his life is compartmentalized. Work makes up the largest segment, then community service, then golf. Joe is a *bonafide* civic leader—a member of the rotary club, chamber of commerce, and regional hospital board. His wife is involved with the Junior League, the local chapter of her sorority, and the museum society.

Family is next on the list of Joe's priorities, then God. Not that you could call Joe religious ... actually, what he is spiritually, he is on his own terms. He'll admit there's a God out there, but institutional churches turn him off. He figures he keeps the Ten Commandments and lives by the golden rule. "Do you know the sermon on the mount, Mr. Anderson? Well, I live by that," he'll tell me, without ever understanding the implications of his words. God helps those who help themselves, he also firmly believes. Heaven? To be honest, Joe isn't really worried about heaven and hell. Like everything else, Joe approaches on his own terms the subject of where he'll spend eternity. He figures he's done enough good in his life to earn whatever, if any, eternal reward is out there. He reasons that hell is the place for the Hitlers and Stalins, not the guys like he is ... guys who do their best to stand on their own two feet.

Now that you've said hello to Joe, meet Daniel. What a contrast ... in some ways. Daniel became a Christian during his freshman year in college. After his conversion to Christ, his hunger for God's word was insatiable. With encouragement from other Christians, Daniel pored over scripture. He also plunged into a campus ministry organization, working his way into a leadership position. He witnessed for Christ just about wherever he went. In his dorm alone, he spoke to nearly two hundred students by graduation day, and at least a third expressed interest in learning more about Jesus. Many accepted Christ outright, with Daniel there to lead them in prayer to mark that decision. Daniel was a *do-er*, and his college years flew by as he continued to *do* for God, all the while soaking up God's word and spending ample amounts of time in prayer. Shortly before graduation, Daniel was offered a chance to join the staff of the Christian organization with which he'd been involved. But his parents were against it—they thought he needed some time in the "real world" first. And Daniel was convinced that he didn't need to work in a Christian organization in order to serve the Lord. So he declined the offer.

Now, Daniel is in his thirties. Ten years have passed since college, and he is in a mid-level management position of a large corporation. He is married to a fine Christian woman; she stays home to take care of their two preschoolers. He is a deacon in his church and serves on the local board of a citywide youth ministry. He leads a Bible study in his home and teaches Sunday school. Yet there is an emptiness. A feeling gnaws at him that tells him he's missed the boat in his spiritual life. He's beginning to believe he blew it in college by not opting for "professional Christian service," and now, with family and financial obligations, it seems too late for him to do what God may have really wanted him to do. Daniel figures he's missed God's will and, though life is nice enough, it's not what it ought to be.

Then there's Sondra. She attended church while growing up, a religious denomination which taught her that obeying the Ten Commandments was the right thing to do and the way to please a distant, harsh, but just God. She learned that she needed to ask God's forgiveness regularly. Even though Sondra confessed her sins daily, doubts about whether or not she'd make it into heaven plagued her. Had she remembered to mention every sin? Had she really done enough? Worry was her constant companion; guilt was a problem, too. How could she ever make up for the mistakes she'd made in the past? It just had to be too late for her.

When Sondra hit her early thirties, she heard about the need to have faith in Christ, decided she did, prayed a prayer confessing her sins and asking Jesus to be her savior. She felt better for a month or so, then she began to worry again. Was it really for real? Was she truly going to heaven? What about that white lie she'd told yesterday? What about the gossipy remark she'd made about a co-worker last week? What about the angry words she'd exchanged with her older sister? And just like Daniel, Sondra wasn't, and isn't, too happy either.

Next, meet Frank. We became close friends when I was pastoring a church in his community. He owns a large real estate firm bearing his name. He has made it big, so now he figures it's time to enjoy the fruit of his labor. Frank is a family man. He married his high school sweetheart, and they have had 45 wonderful years together. They have three children: two girls and a boy, all married. Six grandchildren round out the family. Frank's son is heir apparent to his dad's company. Frank is a great guy, honest, generous—but talking to him about a relationship with Christ is tough.

Frank and the family attend church regularly, but only because it's the thing to do. Very early, Frank became involved with a Masonic organization. Today he prides himself on being a master Mason and a Shriner. I tease him about that Shriner bit: joking that he is involved mainly so he can drive those mini-cars in the parades. He responds, "Come on, Don. We are famous for taking good men and making them better. Isn't that what you do, too?" My reply goes something like this, "Frank, I applaud you for your ambition but my call is quite different: I bring sinners to a savior who shed his own blood that he might cleanse and forgive them. He then places them in his family with an inheritance reserved for them in heaven when they die." Sad to say Frank usually turns me off at that point. We are still good friends but Jesus is one part of our friendship that is off limits.

Finally, here's Julia. She isn't at all concerned about her eternal destiny. She figures she has heaven all sewn up because of the sort of person she is. She attends church every Sunday. She does volunteer work at a local children's shelter supported by her congregation. She boycotts the products of companies with questionable Third World practices. She sponsors a foster child with monthly contributions to a relief organization. She occasionally marches for animal rights, AIDS awareness, and the preservation of the rain forest. At least once a year she holds hands with strangers in a vast line to symbolically promote world peace. As Julia likes to put it, she lives her religion. Since God is a God of love, he'll honor her commitment and dedication. She tries to model herself after that great moral teacher, Jesus, but doesn't think she needs any of this salvation-by-faith stuff she often hears about from her more "narrow-minded" friends.

What do these five have in common? Joe, Daniel, Sondra, Julia, and Frank, have messed up their spiritual lives by falling into essentially the same trap. They're tangled in the snare of trying to perform to please God and, so far, they are either finding that performance alone doesn't satisfy or they are temporarily deluded into thinking it does.

Frank feels very comfortable in what he believes. He is popular with friends and family. He does all the *right* things. He is an encourager and supporter. Just stay off that Jesus thing and the cross and the blood and we will get along just fine. Frank is most vulnerable when we are at funerals together. Death makes him feel awkward and uneasy. You can see fear and uncertainty in his eyes when I ask him if being a master Mason and a Shriner alone is what God requires at heaven's entrance.

Sondra, on the other hand, is a Christian. She believes that Christ took the punishment for her sins at Calvary. But thanks to her rigid upbringing and natural inclination to worry, she doesn't feel easy about the situation. She feels somehow that she'll make God angry at her, that he'll slam shut the gates of heaven, and she'll lose out on her eternal reward because of some unconfessed sin. Her life is plagued by worry and doubt. She is missing out on the peace and rest she should have as a believer.

Daniel is definitely a Christian—no doubt about it. Eternal security is not an issue with him. He understands that he has been saved by God's grace alone, through faith alone, and that nothing will ever separate him from the heavenly Father. He doesn't lie awake at night wondering if he's confessed every sin. But he still doesn't have the sense of inner peace that he would like. He attributes this to the theory that he is not doing what God wanted him to do with his life, and that it is too late for him to cut through the roadblocks of urban professionalism and return to the right path. He just isn't accomplishing things for God like he did in college! He is frustrated and, though his wife is wonderful and his kids are great, there's got to be more.

And then there is Julia. Dangerously smug, she feels good about herself and about her behavior toward God. She enjoys doing what she believes a Christian should do. The social and political activism is rewarding. She is positive that a new age of enlightenment will be ushered in because of her actions and the actions of others like her. She's plugging along, doing the best she can, living a relatively moral, socially responsible, religiously open-minded existence. She's consumed with causes and confident that it will all be good enough to get her into heaven someday. Tragically, her self-righteousness makes her difficult to approach with the truth of Jesus Christ, the truth that people are not basically good and everyone desperately needs the savior. Julia's days of disillusionment are coming, however. Ultimately some of her causes will fail; her optimism will wane; her heroes will prove themselves human and vulnerable. It is inevitable. Someday she may even ask herself, "Is this all there is?' and start a search for something deeper and more meaningful in life.

Finally, let's not forget our businessman, Joe. The epitome of the self-made man, his concept of God is limited. Like Julia and Frank, Joe is terribly hard to reach with the message of the gospel, the good news that Jesus Christ died for his sins because he could never be good enough to get to heaven otherwise. Joe does so many things so well that it is hard to conceive of his ever admitting his inadequacy and need of a savior. His life is wrapped up in quotas; the questions of eternity don't bother him because the best he can do has always been good enough. It'll likely take some crisis over which he has no control—some financial fiasco or family tragedy—to drive Joe to his knees in search of the Lord Jesus. And in reality, that moment of honest seeking and surrender may never come. Joe may well die as he has lived, to the very end singing with Frank Sinatra, "I did it my way," only to find out too late that his way wasn't God's way at all.

Joe, Daniel, Sondra, Frank, and Julia are not real people, but they are realistic. They are based on actual men and women I know. The biblical knowledge and understanding of the five range from practically nil to nearly immense, but they all have yet to learn the same crucial lesson: genuine satisfaction comes only from relationship. Lasting peace and contentment are by-products of a deepening union with the Lord Jesus Christ, and any actions we take should grow out of that friendship and fellowship. First and foremost, God desires to establish a relationship of unconditional love and acceptance with us. He's not interested in exacting a performance from us. He isn't in the market for *do-ers* but *be-ers*! That is perhaps the central issue of the book of Romans.

LOOKING AT THE BOOK

Paul's letter to the Romans is a finely crafted theological masterpiece. When journeying through it, one must plan for a slow trip with plenty of time for contemplation and meditation. The book clearly communicates why God created us. It should cause some of us to rethink our reasons for being. We may figure we're put here to do things for God, but in the pages of Romans, Paul shows us there is so much more to the Christian life.

Back in the days when televisions were only black and white and I was attending seminary, we were warned by our professors not to attempt to preach on Romans till we'd been in the ministry at least twelve years. I played it safe and waited twenty before tackling the book. Now that several more decades have swept by, I am convinced it's time to revise the book you are reading, which first appeared in print about ten years ago.

Why? Each year at many churches, camps, conferences, and Bible classes, God gives me the tremendous privilege of meeting and ministering to hundreds of folks interested in learning more about his word. If there's one misconception to be singled out as the major cause of breakdown in the Christian life, it's the idea that a human being is capable of performing to please God. The desire to perform infects both the saved and the unsaved. It wraps its tentacles around the Joes, Daniels, Sondras, Julias, and Franks of the world and renders them spiritually useless. The results can be devastating.

PLAYING TO AN EMPTY HOUSE

As men and women, our natural tendency is to desire to *do* for God. It's only human to want to accomplish things to please him. So, many of us fill our lives with works of worth, which we hope will outweigh the bad stuff and get us into heaven when we die. We stake our eternal destiny on the theory that we can work our way to glory.

The belief that we can perform in certain ways in order to get right with God is why cults and non-Christian religions flourish. The cult leader subtly and satanically substitutes himself in the place of Christ and exercises total control over his followers. So many others are caught up in health-wealth-and-prosperity because they are taught that when you do for God, he will do for you. Performing to please Allah is why radical Moslems volunteer for suicide missions. It's why Hindis choose to pacify the gods by starving themselves rather than consuming sacred cattle. The ultimate irony is that God does not respond to such efforts. Followers of false religions may give virtuoso performances, but the tragic reality is that they're playing to an empty house because the Lord will not acknowledge that which is done apart from Jesus Christ (Rom. 1:20-25; Titus 3:5-6). We can never be smart enough, pure enough, kind enough, generous enough, humble enough, affectionate enough, or religious enough, by ourselves, to earn God's forgiveness and reward.

Still, we fool ourselves. Even in mainstream America, hundreds of thousands of well-meaning souls flock weekly to churches. Many have never heard the gospel—a sad possibility given the spiritual condition of many churches today. Or perhaps they have heard the truth of Christ, but its beautiful simplicity has never pierced the heart. So, like Julia, they plop their checks in the collection plate; they volunteer to work for blood drives, food banks, telethons, and assorted charities; they sign up as foster parents for underprivileged kids. All these are good things, mind you; the difficulty develops when the doers figure that because they've lived basically good lives, God will be merciful and save them a place in glory come judgment day. The Bible teaches us that it doesn't work that way. Isaiah 64:6 tells us that everyone's works of righteousness are as "filthy rags" to our heavenly Father (see also Eccles. 7:20). We're never good enough, on our own, to meet his holy standards. Our human performance doesn't cut it with God. Our acceptance of Jesus Christ as savior is the only thing that does. The tragic result of trying to work our way into heaven is that we end up buying our way into hell.

As I write this, I can't help but think of Bubba. What a special man—He almost made it to the triple digits in age. We shared so many things together, including our common enthusiasm for the Dallas Cowboys. But we did not share the savior. Bubba was a sparkling example of a man who lived a good, upright life. He and his wife celebrated their sixtieth wedding anniversary. He had many friends—-he went out of his way to do much good for others—but he did not feel that he needed to be born again and start a relationship with Jesus Christ. We talked and prayed about these matters, but he never quite saw it. I loved the man; his hugs and affirming words brought such joy. But he died not knowing Jesus. Does God cancel his rules recorded in the Bible and make an exception for a case like this? My heart says, "Yes, please!" and my head and holy scripture say, "No." Bubba died without the savior.

CREATED FOR A RELATIONSHIP, NOT A PERFORMANCE

We thrive on performance in our society. We expect our kids to behave, our dog to do tricks and not to bite the neighbors, our employees to complete their assignments accurately and on time. We withhold or dish out pats on the back, privileges, raises, incentives, and approval, based on how others perform. How natural it is, therefore, that even when an individual recognizes that belief in Christ is the only way to please God and receive eternal life in his presence, performance often still proves to be a problem, as it does for Daniel and Sondra. Many a Christian becomes right with God through faith, and then turns around and performs all the more—spinning his wheels in every semi-spiritual direction. The thinking goes something like this: Attend the church board meeting ... donate big bucks for the new playground ... serve on the missions committee ... volunteer to be president of the women's association ... lead a Bible study ... recruit twelve new members a year ... worry about everybody you know ... do, do, do, and you're guaranteed to become a spiritual giant. You'll accomplish big things for God! The fact is, you'll probably die serving and, although you will be in heaven because of your faith, at your funeral a few of us may be wondering if you've done with your life what the Lord really wanted. We'll wonder if God was really pleased by all your busyness, or if, as the mourners file quietly past the casket, he too silently grieves over what might have been ... what should have been.

We in the Christian community are often to blame for the emphasis on performance. Our churches are structured to suit the do-do-do mentality. We take new believers and involve them on committees, corral them into the choir, train them to teach Sunday school, elect them to leadership, and constantly commend them for fine performances. Sometimes the externals become so important that we don't even realize when one of the players has missed the whole reason for the part! "I was an all-American acolyte," mused my friend Ken one evening as we visited together. His wife, Judy, and he invited Jesus Christ into their lives hours later at midnight and, as the old clock down the hall struck twelve, it tolled the beginning of a truly brand new day—and a brand new way of life—for this precious couple. As they wrote later, "Jesus Christ is our savior now! Through all of our trials and sorrows, we never imagined what a powerful and loving friend we could have in him."

The Bible reveals that from the very beginning we members of the human race were created for the express purpose of having that brand new existence in relationship with the Lord. God desired this fellowship, and he breathed life into Adam, Eve, and their descendants not because of what they could *do* for him, but because of what they could *be* to him (Gen. 2:18-24; 3:8-9).

As we'll see in our study of Romans 5-8, the original relationship between God and man was altered because of the disobedience of the pair in the garden. God responded to the sin of humankind by offering Jesus Christ as the means by which individuals can still enter into a relationship with him. And today the Lord remains more concerned with what we *are* to him than with what we *do* for him. His message to us is simply this, "Stop! Be still and know that I am God. Take the time to learn of me. Let me take over. I'll do the doing."

If relationship with him is the Father's primary objective for us, then it ought to be yours and mine, also. First we must get to know him as savior. Next we must commit ourselves to deepening the relationship. That means being careful never to let anything, no matter how good it is, stand in the way of our getting to know him better every day and, as a result, becoming more like him. It means we must, like Martha's sister, Mary, choose the good part and find our place sitting at his feet, learning from him the principles of his word, communicating to him the anxieties of our heart (Luke 10:38-42; 1 Pet. 5:7). It means finding our total adequacy in Him. Chapters 5-8 of the book of Romans tell us how it can happen, and much, much more.

A MESSAGE TO BABY BELIEVERS

When approaching the study of any book of scripture, I try to read nearly everything in print about it. Doing so is next to impossible with the book of Romans. Paul's letter to the church in Rome has inspired hundreds to write volumes of commentaries. The epistle is a rich mine laden with gems of wisdom for understanding God's plan and purpose, a treasure trove of insight into the *how* of practical Christian living.

Before we dive into the priceless wisdom of Romans 5-8, let's discuss the background and structure of the book. First of all, the writer of the letter clearly identifies himself as the apostle Paul in Romans 1:1, and there is no legitimate reason to doubt him.

As far as we know, Paul had not yet visited the church in Rome when he penned his epistle. In 58 A.D. the apostle was in the city of Corinth. His interest in the Roman Christians piqued, he evidently took advantage of the fact that Phoebe, a deaconess in the church at nearby Cenchraea, planned to make a trip to Rome, and wrote a letter that she would carry to the young church there (Rom. 16:1-2).

Why was Paul interested in the Roman Christians? It seems he was acquainted with many of them (Rom. 16). We read in Acts 18 of the start of his friendship with at least two of these believers, Aquila and Priscilla, who had been temporarily driven from Italy (Acts 18:2). Evidently Paul was, in a sense, the spiritual father of the church in Rome. Although he had not actually traveled to Rome to establish the church, many of the Roman Christians, like Priscilla and Aquila, had heard the gospel from him in other parts of the empire. As these new Christians returned to Rome one by one, some maybe recalled by the "home offices" there, it was only natural that they should begin meeting together for worship, sharing their testimonies, bringing friends and family members into the fold. And so in Rome there was a church but no authority and little Christian maturity—just a group of baby believers badly in need of instruction in the true faith. Sensing their need, unable as yet to make the trip to Rome himself, the apostle, under the inspiration of the Holy Spirit, produced the manuscript we know as the book of Romans.

In an earlier letter to the church in Galatia, Paul explains that "when the fulness of time was come, God sent forth his Son" (Gal. 4:4 KJV). The establishment of the Roman empire in all its glory created an environment ripe for the spread of the new religion; in Paul's day the "fulness of time" had come for Christianity. At the time of Christ and in the decades following his death and resurrection, peace generally reigned within the borders of the empire. Roads facilitating military and merchant travel were constructed. Legions marched and fleets sailed, resulting in the spread of not only the Latin language, but also new ideas and religious concepts. Perhaps even more significant than all of these, corruption had seeped into almost every area of human life. Sin was an undeniable realty—a festering malignancy infecting an entire civilization. The infant church of Rome existed in an environment rife with immorality and decadence—the sin city of its day. The inability of man to redeem himself was obvious, as was his need of a savior.

OF DOCTRINE, DISPENSATION, AND DUTY

It was from his study of Romans that Martin Luther was fired with the concept, "the just shall live by faith," the catch phrase which became the battle cry of the Protestant Reformation. As Paul tells us in Romans 1:16-17, where he quotes the prophet Habakkuk:

> For I am not ashamed of the gospel, for it is the power of God for salvation to everyone who is believing, to the Jew first and also to

> the Greek. For in it the righteousness of God is revealed from faith unto faith; even as it has been written, "But the righteous man shall live by faith." (DAV; see also Hab. 2:4)

These verses are the key to understanding Romans. Basically, Paul's objectives in writing his letter to the Romans were three in number:

First, he desired to communicate the fundamental doctrine of salvation, and he does so in chapters 1-8. There he explains the truth of the "gospel ... the power of God for salvation to everyone who is believing" (1:16). He leaves his readers with no doubt about how to get right with God through faith.

Second, Paul intended to explain the situation regarding the nation of Israel, and to reveal the Lord's dealings with Jew and gentile. Because the gospel was sent "to the Jew first and also to the Greek" (1:16), Paul's readers probably wondered about the specific position of Israel now that the church had been formed. Where did the Jews fit in, since Christ had come? This he reveals in chapters 9-11, dealing with what Bible scholars call *dispensationalism.*

Third, Paul wanted to present a discourse on practical Christian living: the manner in which "the righteous man ... live[s] by faith" (1:17). He accomplishes this in chapters 12-16 of the text, offering God's wisdom on dealing with the questionable issues in life, the nit-picky items on which believers might disagree. The text focuses on how to handle the gray areas.

If you'd like a short outline to help you remember, here is one:

I. Doctrine: Romans 1-8
II. Dispensation: Romans 9-11
III. Duties: Romans 12-16

A PRODUCT TO SELL: ROMANS 1-8

As a college kid, I paid for school by working as a door-to-door encyclopedia salesman. The challenge was to convince customers that they couldn't get along without my product. With my memorized sales pitch and transparent enthusiasm, I made a killing, writing dozens of orders. It paid the bills.

In the first part of Romans, Paul uses a sales strategy similar to what I followed when selling encyclopedias. The apostle begins by convincing his readers, his "customers," of their need of God's righteousness, the "product" he is pushing. The difference between is that, unlike a luxury set of books, Paul's product, the righteousness of God, is an absolute necessity for us all.

Remember Romans 1:17, where Paul says of the gospel of Christ, "For in it, the righteousness of God is revealed from faith to faith." God's standard is perfection. This means that in order to come into his presence, we must theoretically be completely righteous, totally obedient to his holy law, spotless, blameless. But being perfect is impossible for us, because our nature is sinful. What we do may look good on the surface, but God reads our heart. And, as Christ puts it in Luke 16:15, "that which is highly esteemed among men is detestable in the sight of God" (NASB). Why? God knows we were born in sin. He knows that however we strive and struggle we'll never be good enough to earn his righteousness because there will always be some shortcoming, some character flaw, some dishonorable desire, some disobedience.

To put it plainly, we need help getting to heaven. Showing his readers this is one of Paul's primary aims in Romans. The master salesman, he convinces his customers of their need of God's righteousness. In chapter 1 he speaks of the sin of the gentiles: although the invisible attributes of God are clearly seen in the workings of the universe, men and women still reject him. Their need of God's righteousness is obvious (1:18-32). In Romans 2, the apostle turns his attention to the Jews, God's special people. They too are sinners, falling short of his standards despite their greater knowledge and the history of his dealings with them (2:17-3:8). The clincher comes in chapter 3, where Paul sums up his case with these words, "for all sinned and are falling short of the glory of God" (Rom. 3:23 DAV). That says it all, doesn't it? Jew and gentile alike—you, me, and everyone else—have *all* fallen short of God's standard of perfection. The bar is too high. The stopwatch has stopped before the race has started. There's no way any of us, by ourselves, can produce a righteousness that is acceptable to a holy God. We need outside help: *his* help.

With his readers on the edge of their seats, Paul delivers his final sales pitch, explaining the closing of the deal. God's righteousness *cannot* be bought. It cannot be earned by paying 48 installments on a contract. It comes only through faith in the substitutionary sacrifice of Christ. Because we cannot achieve perfection on our own, God graciously provides the means by which we can become righteous in his sight. He offers his righteousness to us freely, through the single condition of faith in Jesus Christ. All wrapped up and ready, the gift of the Father's Son is ours for the taking, truly a gift too wonderful for words. Keith L. Brooks puts it this way, "That righteousness which the Father requires, the Son became, the Holy Spirit convinces of, and faith secures." On the cross, Jesus, himself sinless, himself God incarnate, God-made-man, took the punishment for our sin. Our only option is to believe, to place our trust in his finished work. And as Christians we are, as Paul says:

> Being made righteous as a gift by His grace through the redemption which is in Christ Jesus; whom God displayed publicly as a

> propitiation in His blood through faith for a proof of His righteousness, because in the forbearance of God He passed over the sins previously committed." (Rom. 3:24-26 DAV)

It's faith, only faith, that literally delivers us from the jaws of hell and enables us to have an ongoing relationship with God through his Son. And this wasn't a new idea, even in Paul's time. Even in Old Testament days, men were reckoned righteous because of their faith. Steering his argument to address this point, the apostle describes the life of Abraham in Romans 4, showing us that the patriarch was made righteous because of his faith, not because of his works.

By now we should all be asking ourselves the question: Do I have it? Do I have the righteousness of God? Have I come to terms and established a relationship with him? Romans 5 begins to answer that question.

A RADICALLY REVISED RELATIONSHIP

In Romans 5-8, the section we'll be chiefly dealing with in this book, the apostle explains the new situation, under something called grace, for those who stand acquitted before God by faith. *Grace* means God's "unmerited favor," and, as Christians and recipients of that favor, we find ourselves in a unique position we neither deserve nor earn. By God's grace alone, we are not only forgiven, but are also brought into a radically new relationship with him as a result of our faith in Christ. In this new relationship, we have peace with God, as we see in Romans 5. We also, as chapter 6 reveals, have union with Christ. Romans 7 tells that we are free from the law. And chapter 8 explains the mysteries of the life we can now be empowered to lead, a life controlled by God's own Spirit.

Romans 5-8 is among the most glorious sections of the

entire New Testament. The chapters clearly convey the truth that it is by grace alone, through faith alone, that we enter into a relationship with God. As we make our journey through chapters 5-8, we'll be taking a mostly verse-by-verse look at the biblical text. Scripture itself—intact, in context, and unaltered—fully ministers to our needs by conveying God's messages to us with a precision and clarity inspired by him alone. We'll notice that Paul often repeats principles and concepts in the passages; our conclusion must be that these are the areas the Lord especially desires to emphasize for us. God knows what we need to hear!

Will our relationship with the Lord last? Does our salvation continue to the end? Will our relationship with God enable us to handle the complexities and agonies of life? Can it withstand the wear and tear of human needs? The answers are given in the chapters before us. I invite you to read on and discover the miracle of friendship with God.

And as we travel the pages of Romans 5-8, let's remember these words of encouragement from Jesus himself in Matthew 11:28-30:

> Come unto me, all ye that labour and are heavy laden, and I will give you rest. Take my yoke upon you, and learn of me; for I am meek and lowly in heart: and ye shall find rest unto your souls. For my yoke is easy, and my burden is light. (KJV)

Relationship with God through Jesus Christ is a light burden, an easy yoke. As an older gentleman who came to know Christ so eloquently exclaimed, "O the wonder of it all! So this is what I've been missing for the last thirty-five years!"

Questions to Consider

1. Do you know anyone like Joe, Daniel, Sondra, Frank, or Julia, described at the beginning of the chapter? Do you resemble any of them? Whether or not you're a Christian, is there some way in which you feel you are wrapped up in performing to please God? If so, how so?

2. Read 1 Corinthians 3:12-15. If you're a believer, think about the ways in which you are investing your time. Are the works you are accomplishing those of eternal value, or are they only of the "wood, hay, stubble" perishable sort described in verse 12 (KJV)? Explain.

3. Genesis 5:24 and Hebrews 11:5 give the account of Enoch. Read the verses and describe what Enoch's relationship with God must have been like.

CHAPTER 2

"For great is your love, higher than the heavens; your faithfulness reaches to the skies" (Ps. 108:4 NIV).

The Results of the Relationship

Romans 5:1-11

Relationships don't develop overnight. They may begin in a single moment of time, but it takes time to flesh out a friendship.

I think of when I first met the woman who was to become my wife, Pearl. It all began over 50 years ago. When I first caught a glimpse of that beautiful, godly girl, issues of time and convenience suddenly receded in importance. Our relationship became uppermost; little else seemed to matter. Our priorities changed to allow for time together. Projects were postponed. My grade of "D" in summer school Greek reflected this new center of affection. My encyclopedia sales even began to wane! Everything in my life revolved around Pearl, and this led to a commitment that has now lasted almost half a century.

Even today the relationship between Pearl and me continues to change and to become richer. We long ago reached the point where we often think the same thoughts, pray the same prayers, even jump to the same conclusions! It's taken decades of love and hard work and determined commitment for us to get this far. We haven't grown closer effortlessly—there have been plenty of bumps and chuck-holes in the road. But every step of progress has been marked by cooperation, consideration, and—what is vital to real togetherness—communication.

I haven't come to know Pearl as well as I do merely by touching base with her weekly or having a heart-to-heart talk with her only once a year. We've committed ourselves to spending both quality and quantity time with each other. We've determined to verbalize our concerns, fears, joys, and sorrows together. We've made it a habit to share the good, the bad, and the ugly. We are committed to keeping short accounts and talking through issues. We even reserve every Friday night as date night.

Our marriage hasn't always been like this. Several years ago, as I was going back to school to pursue a doctorate of ministry in marriage and family counseling, one of my courses required that Pearl and I spend 50 hours evaluating our relationship. I learned that I eat too fast and I drive too fast, and I learned several other things, too. I've been working on them since. As I tell young couples whom I have just married: you came to the altar with a four-letter word and you are leaving with one. When you came in, the word was L-O-V-E, and now as you leave, it is W-O-R-K.

Marriage, or any close human relationship, can prepare us to relate to our heavenly Father. As we discussed in the last chapter, relationship with God is possible if we have faith in the atoning sacrifice of his Son, Jesus Christ. Couples whom I marry enter the marriage relationship at a point in time. That moment comes following their vows and the giving of the rings, when, by the authority of the State of Texas, I pronounce them husband and wife. Our relationship with the Lord begins at a specific moment in time, too: the minute we make the decision to believe in Christ and in what he has done for us, and thereby receive him as our savior (John 1:12). That's the start.

While friendship with God begins at a certain moment, like any human relationship, closeness takes time. We can't expect to grow a whole lot closer to God if we only talk to him once a week at Sunday services. We can't expect to have much of an in-depth relationship with him if the only time we earnestly pray is during a time of crisis, or if we rarely read his messages to us found in his word. An occasional psalm, hymn, or rote prayer may calm the conscience, but won't intensify the relationship.

Growing closer to God has got to be a day-by-day, moment-by-moment thing with us. Seeking to know him better and better should become a pulsating, tangible, overwhelming desire of the heart and mind. The psalmist describes it in Psalm 42:1-2: "As the deer pants for streams of water, so my soul pants for you, O God. My soul thirsts for God, for the living God. When can I go and meet with God?" (NIV). It means devoting ourselves to developing our relationship with the Lord with the same fervency with which we pursue earthly affections. Coming to know him fully is the top priority in his program for us.

The fringe benefit of coming to know God better is that we become more like him. We begin to see the result of our relationship with the Lord manifesting itself in our life. We begin to bear fruit for him (John 15:5).

HAVE YOU GOT IT?

Remember that in Romans 1-4 the apostle Paul builds a case for the righteousness of God. A master salesman, he first convinces us that we need that righteousness. Then, as we're ready to sign on the dotted line, he delivers the amazing news that God's righteousness is free. It's a gift that we receive by faith. Too good to be true? Not at all. It's just too good to be true apart from God!

All believers have a relationship with the Lord. But what sort of a relationship is it? What about you? If you believe in Jesus Christ as savior, you are a child of God, but what kind of a child are you? Do you barely know your heavenly Father, or are you growing closer to him? Do you see little tangible change in your life, or are you in the steady process of becoming more like him? Do you find yourself climbing mountains in your spiritual life or wallowing in the mud and muck at the bottom? These are questions we ought to all ask of ourselves as Christians. The apostle Paul supplies us, in the first part of Romans 5, with a means to gauge our spiritual growth. He shifts gears from chapters 1-4, moving from convincing his readers that they need God's righteousness and that it is available through faith, to describing the implications of the relationship Christians may experience with God.

In Romans 5:1-11, we learn of eight *results* of having a relationship with the Lord Jesus Christ. If you're a Christian, you ought to be seeing some of these results manifesting themselves in your life. They're the proof of the pudding—the evidence that your relationship is real. Some you'll experience as soon as you are saved. Others come with time and growth and maturity in the Lord.

Let's look at Paul's message to the Romans and ask ourselves these questions: Do I have a relationship with Christ? If so, what kind of a relationship is it? Am I becoming like the one whose child I am? Or am I like the plane circling the airport—burning fuel but getting nowhere?

ONE: PEACE—ROMANS 5:1

Paul begins Romans 5 with these words, "Therefore,

having been made right by faith, we are having peace with God through our Lord Jesus Christ" (5:1 DAV). The first result of a relationship with the Lord is peace with God. Notice Paul doesn't say that as Christians we have the peace *of* God, but peace *with* God. They are two entirely different things.

The peace of God is temporary, transitory; it comes and goes, depending on how much we're willing to trust the Lord in present circumstances. We can pray to receive the peace of God; Philippians 4:6-7 gives us the formula and the promise: "Be anxious for nothing, but in everything by prayer and supplication with thanksgiving let your requests be made known to God. And the peace of God, which surpasses all comprehension, shall guard your hearts and minds in Christ Jesus" (NASB). When we stop trusting in God's ability to order a situation, we lose that peace. We lose it because we take our eyes off the Lord and instead focus on our resources and ourselves.

A young Christian woman told me of a time her father faced critical surgery. There was some question as to her dad's ability to withstand the rigors of the surgery, and the pre-op pressures had eaten away at the whole family. On the eve of the operation, my friend phoned one of the doctors for test results and received a curt, insensitive reply from his associate. Something snapped. Tears welled up and poured out in a flood of emotion she didn't know she had been restraining. "Dear God, please handle this! Please take care of it!" she cried aloud, all the while heaving deep sobs. Within minutes her spirit was quieted. She was calmed, from the inside out. It was as if God had laid his gentle hand on her shoulder and said, "It's all right. I'm here now. I'm going to take care of everything." That's the peace of God. It comes when we cast all our cares on him, because he cares so deeply for us (1 Pet. 5:7). My friend had to give up on her own strength and lean totally on the Lord in the situation.

He answered with his peace.

The peace of God comes when we trust that God is God. We depend on his goodness, power, love, mercy, and control. Sometimes we experience the Lord's peace in a vivid and personal way. But other times our life seems far too tied up in knots for God's peace ever to help unsnarl the mess. We're just like the sign I saw in a shop the other day: "I'm so tense that when I get calm, it makes me nervous." But the peace of God is always there for the asking. It's available when we trust, but it is also temporary, leaving us when we forget to rely on its source, our heavenly Father.

Peace *with* God is another matter entirely. I'm sure that you have heard someone say, "I've made my peace with God." Yet peace with God doesn't work that way. It is a gift. We don't *make* it; we *are given* it the moment we receive Christ as savior. It is permanent, an unchangeable change in our position from sinner to saved. It marks a cessation of hostilities: our movement from enemy of God to ally and friend. The war is over; the treaty of peace is signed in the blood of his Son, and the white flag of surrender flies atop the castle of the human heart. Christians are positionally at peace with God, permanently reconciled to the one who is the judge of all the universe, the moment they come to faith in Christ. As Paul says in Romans 5:1, "We are having peace with God *through our Lord Jesus Christ*" (DAV). Only the Lord can declare us righteous, and his condition is that we accept the sacrifice of his Son as the payment for our sin.

Tragically, many in the world live with a false sense of peace concerning their relationship with the Lord and their eternal destiny once they exit this life. I know lots of folks like that; in fact, some of them are in my own family. "It's going to be all right, Don," they say. "You're just too concerned about me. God is a God of love, after all. When I die, he'll understand I did the best I could. I don't need any of this Jesus business. I don't have to get right with God by faith." It tears your heart out to see someone you love talking and living like that, speeding spiritually blindfolded through the few short years we call earthly life (2 Cor. 4:4).

Make no mistake—our years on earth are all too few and far too short. We can easily lull ourselves into thinking we're in good shape physically ... and then without warning a heart attack hits, bringing disability or even death. Very much the same thing can be true spiritually. We can delude ourselves into thinking everything is okay because we're nice people and God is going to understand how hard we tried to live a good life. Then comes the moment we leave the temporal for the eternal, and we are unpleasantly surprised to find that we do not have peace with God because we've never come to him on his terms. We haven't come to grips with the truth of Colossians 1:19-20, where we read of Christ that it was the "Father's good pleasure for all the fulness to dwell in Him, and through Him to reconcile all things to Himself, having made peace through the blood of His cross" (1:19- 20a NASB). Peace with God is a reality that so few truly grasp.

In the front of my prayer notebook are the following words, which say it all: "And now I have a captain; he'll guide I know he will; I've given Jesus full command, since he said, 'Peace, be still.' He whispered, 'Peace, be still,' to me; my heart obeyed his will; his word made calm the rolling sea when he said: 'Peace, be still.'"

TWO: ACCESS—ROMANS 5:2

Christians also receive an introduction—access—into God's very presence. Paul puts it this way in Romans 5:2, speaking of Jesus as the one "through whom also we have obtained our *introduction* (entree) *by faith* into this grace in which we stand" (DAV).

The word *introduction* in the verse may also be translated as *entree*. The original Greek suggests two definitions.

First, it means introduction into the presence of royalty. Second, it suggests what happens when a ship, which has been out on the storm-tossed sea, finally arrives safely at its desired harbor. There the ship at last rests in calm and peaceful surroundings.

Non-believers are much like ships bantered and buffeted about by the raging winds and vicious waves of the world. Human solutions offer little real comfort to the problems we face. But as Christians we find ourselves in a position of safety—ships safe from the storm. Oh, we'll still be knocked around by the winds and waves; we'll lose our jobs, bury our loved ones, suffer illness, but we have available to us the peace of God. And not only that but our ultimate destination, heaven, is the safest harbor imaginable!

Believers have access to their royal heavenly Father that previous generations never experienced. After Adam and Eve sinned in the garden, the Lord placed cherubim at its gates so that the man and the woman and their descendants might never reenter (Gen. 3:24). The open and direct relationship shared between humankind and God was dramatically altered forever. Where God once walked alongside man, now there was separation. Sin had erected a Berlin Wall, severing humankind from creator (Isa. 59:1-2).

In the Old Testament, we view the results of this separation. In the centuries before the crucifixion, God manifested himself in the *shekinah* glory: a cloud containing his divine presence, which appeared in the tabernacle of the Jewish people. A great veil separated the ark of the covenant, where the *shekinah* rested, from the Hebrews. Only the anointed high priest could enter into the presence of God, and then only once a year, on the day of atonement. Even before this could happen, the priest had to be ceremonially cleansed and specially dressed in holy garb. As he entered the holy of holies, where the ark was, he carried with him an animal sacrifice. Any carelessness on his part in adhering to the prescribed ritual could mean death for the high priest as he approached the ark. The jingle of the small bells sewn onto the hem of the high priest's robe told those waiting tensely outside that the priest still lived after entering the holy place, and that God had accepted the sacrifice.[1]

When Christ died on the cross, as the ultimate sacrifice, the same hand which wrote the message that Belshazzar was weighed in the balances and found wanting, reached down from heaven and tore the temple veil from top to bottom (see Dan. 5:24ff). As believers we do not have to shed the blood of animals and birds on the altar in order to come into the presence of the Lord. Instead, as the writer of the book of Hebrews says, "we have confidence to enter the holy place by the blood of Jesus, by a new and living way which He inaugurated for us through the veil, that is, His flesh" (Heb. 10:19-20 NASB). Because of Christ's work upon the cross, we can communicate freely with God. No longer do we get the message, "Access denied." We cry, "Abba, Father!" (a term that means "Daddy") and he hears. The Berlin Wall of sin and separation crumbles the moment we come to faith.

Often I am busy in my office, preparing studies, poring over books and texts, writing new material. I don't like to be disturbed. In fact, my secretary sometimes holds my calls and turns away unscheduled visitors (unless there is some sort of urgent need). But no matter how busy I am, there are certain people I stop everything in order to see. These are my wife, kids, and grandchildren. They can approach me at any moment. Their access to me is unlimited. So it is with us and our heavenly Father when we come to believe in his Son. As John 1:12 puts it, "But as many as received him, to them he gave the right to become children of God, even to those who believe in his name" (NASB, see also Rom. 8:12). At the cry of a child of God, everything stops as the Father stoops to wipe away a tear, to hug and to hold until the hurt subsides.

How fantastic it is to be a child of God. What an incredible sense of well being it is at the end of the day to know we are at peace with the Lord. We can sense his smile; we know that when we talk to him in prayer, he's listening. We can read his word and from it hear his answers. There's nothing like it, and as we grow closer to God, we should become ever more conscious of the great privilege it is to have such access to him.

Our access to the Lord is a part of the "grace in which we stand" (Rom. 5:2 DAV). Grace, remember, is God's unmerited favor. We don't deserve his good will, and yet, praise God it is ours in Christ! Remember, it's whose you are and whom you know that will get you to the throne room of the Father in heaven.

THREE: HOPE—ROMANS 5:2

As believers, we are at peace with God; we have access to him, and, as Paul continues in Romans 5, we are "rejoicing (exulting, glorying) in hope of the glory of God" (5:2 DAV). What is the glory of God? Ultimately, it is when the enemies of Christ will become but a "footstool" to him (Heb. 1:13 NASB). For believers, it's the fantastic continuation of the relationship with the Lord begun in faith on earth, a relationship with a king who will soon rule and reign unrivaled. As Christians, we're going to be Christ's subjects in an eternal kingdom. Many do not recognize Jesus as savior now, but the clock of prophetic events is ticking down to the time when Christ's kingdom will be instituted on the earth. Then "every knee should bow ... [and] every tongue should confess that Jesus Christ is Lord" (Phil. 2:10-11 KJV).

Heaven is part of the domain of the Lord's kingdom. Should we suffer physical death before the events described, we'll be immediately ushered into the presence of God's glory in heaven. The earth as we know it, with all its glitter, gold, and gore, is not our last hurrah. The glory of God is our final destination—and what a way to go! If we don't die first, we'll be claimed in an event known as the rapture, when believers will be snatched directly home by Christ (1 Thess. 4:16-18; 1 Cor. 15:51-55). Meanwhile, we should be rejoicing in the hope of God's abundant glory.

The word for rejoicing, which Paul uses in Romans 5:2, also means "exulting" or "glorying." The prospect of God's glory should excite us. We should be looking forward to our homecoming with eagerness. Paul did. "But I am hard pressed from both directions, having the desire to depart and be with Christ, for that is very much better," he writes to the Christians at Philippi (Phil. 1:23 NASB).

Most of us would probably admit that we don't look forward to going home to be with the Lord with Paul's obvious enthusiasm. Heaven may seem like a welcome retreat to the man who is losing a painful battle with cancer or to the woman whose joints are twisted and gnarled with arthritis. But for most of those of us who are alive, kicking, and relatively healthy, staying around the planet Earth seems preferable to leaving. We are way too accustomed to second best.

One of the reasons many folks, even Christians, dread dying is that their priorities are fouled up. They spend so much time down here wrapped up in materialism—cash, credit, cars, and condominiums—that when they prepare to die, they realize they're leaving behind everything they've lived for. It's scary! It's painful! How much easier death is when we've lived life looking up, with our focus on heaven. When we've invested time in getting to know the Lord, then dying really is like going home. The words of L. E. Singer and Don Wyrtzen capture the wonder of what's ahead for the Christian:

> Just think of stepping on shore and finding it
> heaven!

Of touching a hand and finding it God's!
Of breathing new air and finding it celestial!
Of waking up in glory and finding it home![2]

Having a joyful expectancy of that homecoming is what it means to rejoice in the hope of the glory of God. So special is our heavenly home that Christ himself longed for his disciples to experience the glory of eternity with him. "Father," he prayed in John 17, "I desire that they also whom Thou hast given Me be with Me where I am, in order that they may behold My glory" (17:24 NASB).

Think of Stephen, the first martyr of the Christian church. Acts 7 tells us that, after Stephen had preached a powerful sermon surveying Bible history before the Sanhedrin, the Jewish leaders came under intense conviction. Acts 7:55, 56 records that as he was stoned, Stephen, "being full of the Holy Spirit...gazed intently into heaven and saw the glory of God, and Jesus *standing* at the right hand of God; and he said, 'Behold, I see the heavens opened up and the son of man *standing* at the right hand of God'" (NASB, italics mine). Why was Jesus standing instead of sitting? You got it: To welcome his faithful child home! O, Lord, haste the day when my faith, too, shall be sight!

You know you're a growing Christian if you're beginning eagerly to anticipate the glory of heaven, the Son, the Spirit, the Father. And this joyful hope will be evident just by looking at you too! You'll reflect God's glory in your countenance. "But we all, with unveiled face beholding as in a mirror the glory of the Lord, are being transformed into the same image from glory to glory," writes the apostle Paul in 2 Corinthians 3:18 (NASB). I will always remember Miss Lucy from our former church. In her nineties, encountering physical difficulties that would soon usher her into the Lord's presence, Miss Lucy looked directly into our eyes and with a smile of peaceful confidence said, "I'm going to heaven." Shortly, she did.

God's glory is real. We have the scriptural account of Stephen's final moments. We have the testimony of Christ himself. "Let not your heart be troubled; believe in God, believe also in Me," says Jesus in John 14:1 (NASB). "In My Father's house are many dwelling places; if it were not so, I would have told you; for I go to prepare a place for you. And if I go and prepare a place for you, I will come again, and receive you to Myself; that where I am, there you may be also," the Lord continues in that same passage (John 14:2-3 NASB). We also have the testimony of the apostle Paul who, preparing for his own homecoming, writes these words to Timothy:

> For I am already being poured out as a drink offering, and the time of my departure has come. I have fought the good fight, I have finished the course, I have kept the faith; in the future there is laid up for me the crown of righteousness, which the Lord, the righteous Judge, will award to me on that day; and not only to me, but also to all who have loved His appearing. (2 Tim. 4:6-8 NASB)

Are you scared to die? Check out your priorities down here. Death should mean you're going to your everything—not that you're leaving it all behind.

There's an old story about a private in a foxhole on the front lines in World War II. German bullets whizzing about him, the soldier stayed dug in. Morning of the first day melted into afternoon; evening came, then night fell. The dawn of another day broke to find our hero munching K-rations. At lunch it was more of the same. Dinner brought nothing new. After 48 hours, a buddy scrambled into the foxhole with him. "Pete," he exclaimed, "I'm here to relieve you. You're going home!"

"What?"

"Home! Back to fried chicken, mom's apple pie, a hot shower, your family, your sweetheart!"

Now what do you imagine that soldier's response was? Do you think he said, "No! Forget it! I'm staying in this foxhole. I like these enemy bullets. These K-rations are delicious"? Of course not! But you know, you and I often do that very thing. Death to the Christian means the continuation of eternal life, but this time the existence is one of incredible beauty. In heaven there are no enemy bullets, no pain, no lousy food! Despite this, we do almost anything to hang onto another breath of life. We're afraid of the glory of God! And yet it really shouldn't be that way. A sign that we've grown up in our faith is when we are able to view death in a positive light, anticipating all of the future—especially our going home.

FOUR: TROUBLE—ROMANS 5:3-4

So far we've seen that as Christians our faith has a past, a present, and a future. In the past, we received peace with God. Presently, we have access to his throne. In the future, we'll dwell with him in all his glory. To put it another way, we are able to look *back* on the cross and its peace; we look *up* to the Father with whom we are reconciled; we look *ahead* to heaven. Maybe you're ready to go home to be with God right now! But if you're a Christian, there's something else you can anticipate in the meantime.

The fourth result of having a relationship with Christ is voiced by Paul in Romans 5:3-4, "And not only this, but we also are rejoicing (exulting, glorying) in our tribulations; knowing that this tribulation is producing endurance; and this endurance, character; and this character, hope" (DAV). Guess what? As my dad used to say when we kids approached, "Here comes trouble!" We can anticipate a healthy share of hassles as we walk with Christ (see also Rom. 8:17).

I know what you're thinking: Thanks a lot! But the fact is that being a believer involves enduring the disappointments and heartaches of human existence. The mark of Christian maturity is how well we persevere—and whether or not we are able to rejoice or exult in these emotional, physical, and sometimes spiritual trials.

I'm not suggesting that we are to be ecstatically happy because we suffer a pay cut, lose an election, find out we have cancer, or get rear-ended at an intersection. We aren't made that way. Even the godliest and saintliest among us are not thrilled *because* trouble hits. But we are called to rejoice in the midst of our difficulties. Ours is the joy of anticipation, knowing God is going to accomplish much in our lives through the painful experience.

When we have a relationship with God, everything that touches us does so with his knowledge and permission. Wherever we go, whatever we do, whomever we hear—every single facet of our life is designed by the Lord to make us more Christlike (James 1:2-3; 1 Pet. 1:6-7, 4:12-13). Trouble is part of the package (1 Thess. 3:3-4). As we joyfully endure trials, we find ourselves conformed to the image of the Christ who relinquished his heavenly throne to come humbly to earth as a man, the savior who spilled his blood on Calvary's cross for us. What we glory in, as tough times hit, is not the fact *that* tough times hit, but that the tough times *are making us more Christlike*. Now that's worth shouting about!

Think about the life of Joseph in the Old Testament (Gen. 37-50). The favorite son of a doting dad, Joseph at age seventeen is given visions of grandeur by the Lord. His future is brighter than the noonday South Texas sun (believe me, that's bright). What happens next? Ten of his brothers toss him in a pit and sell him as a slave. After serving in the Egyptian Potiphar's house for a decade, a gross miscarriage of justice lands Joseph in prison for three more years. He spends thirteen years on the human trash heap before God miraculously delivers him from prison to the palace of pharaoh and the leadership of the land. During Joseph's thirteen years of enslavement and imprisonment, God prepared him for that ascension to the palace. Joseph learned to serve, to depend on the Lord, to give God the credit and glory for everything. It was God who gave him the dreams in the first place, God who promised to take him through times of difficulty, and God who kept his word.

When we come to the Lord Jesus in faith, he promises an abundant life (John 10:10). While we're on earth, it's a life in which the spiritual vacuum of our heart is filled. When we die, it's heaven in all its glory. The Lord doesn't tell us about the deep valley we'll have to traverse in the meantime. He doesn't tell us about the difficulties we'll face, the traumas, the trials. Why? He wants us to learn to trust him, to trust in the promises he's given, to trust in his sovereign control of everything.

Why doesn't he make the road we travel in life straight, smooth, and neat? A trip on automatic pilot wouldn't do much to strengthen our faith, would it? God lays down the ruts and curves so we'll learn to lean not unto our own understanding, as Proverbs 3:5-6 tells us. And the Lord knows what he's doing. The unpredictable events, the things that hit us from our blind side, all come down the pike for the purpose of making us people more like him. I have witnessed time and time again, through an accident, divorce, death, job loss, or other traumatic event, the hand of God at work molding a richer, deeper, fuller life in the wake of disaster. God is near to the broken and contrite heart. His presence is real in the valley of the shadow.

The proper response to trouble is not to ask: Why me? Why this? Why now? Instead, it's to say, Father, thank you that you've permitted this difficulty in my life. I don't understand what you're trying to teach me. Please show me! With that kind of attitude, you're on your way! Answering him with submission and cooperation is the heart of rejoicing in trouble. Trust leads to triumph.

When we are submissive and obedient to God in the midst of turmoil—and we quickly learn the lessons he desires to teach us—our troubles often become less troubling. I remember when my own dad used to discipline me with the razor strop. When I crowded in close, it didn't hurt nearly as much as when I struggled and tried to tear myself away. Dad never could get a good swing at me when I snuggled up to him!

I am not suggesting that God is taking potshots at us by permitting trouble to enter our life. But there is truth in the notion that the quicker we catch on to what he is trying to teach us, the quicker life will become beautiful. God may not have to take us to the woodshed so many times. If we're slow learners, then he'll pile one learning experience on top of the other. It is the distance between the *why* and the *what* of an unforeseen trial that measures our maturity. When we stop asking, "Why me? Why this? Why now?" and start asking, "Lord, what do you want to teach me?" then growth has taken place. The sooner we learn to rejoice in the trouble, to discover what he's trying to teach us, to quietly and obediently submit and learn our lesson in wisdom, the better it is for everyone. But don't get discouraged. Take it from me, the original stubborn saint: people in the crucible don't often learn quickly! What is encouraging is that whatever happens, in the end there's always heaven to look forward to. As Paul puts it in 2 Corinthians 4:17, "For momentary, light affliction is producing for us an eternal weight of glory far beyond all comparison" (NASB). The psalmist agrees: "Before I was afflicted I went astray, but now I obey your word. You are good, and what you do is good; teach me your decrees" (Ps. 119:67-68 NIV). "It was good for me to be afflicted so that I might learn your decrees" (Ps. 119:71 NIV).

REMAINING UNDER STRESS

There are fringe benefits to the journey through the trauma and trial of human existence too. Paul tells us in Romans 5:3 that the "tribulation is producing endurance" (DAV). Webster's dictionary defines the word *endurance* as "the ability to last, continue, or remain; the ability to stand pain, distress, fatigue; fortitude." The Greek word for *endurance* which Paul uses in verse 3 is *hupomone*. That means "a remaining under" as in remaining under stress. It could be better translated "perseverance." It suggests the struggle of living with the pain, the hurt of hanging in there.

Perseverance is a key component of Christian growth. The writer of the book of Hebrews says: "For you are having need of perseverance, in order that, having done the will of God, you may receive what was promised" (Heb. 10:36 DAV). Commending the church at Ephesus in Revelation 2, our Lord uses the word twice: "I know your deeds and your toil and perseverance, and that you cannot endure evil men, and you put to the test those who call themselves apostles, and they are not, and you found them to be false; and you have perseverance and have endured for my name's sake, and have not grown weary" (Rev. 2:2-3 NASB).

Are you feeling a little weary and weak right now? Are you short of passionate desire to see the struggle through? Paul says in Romans: "Now may the God who gives perseverance and encouragement grant you to be of the same mind with one another according to Christ Jesus" (Rom. 15:5 NASB).

Why does God place us under stress? As the Outward Bound organization philosophizes, when we're under stress, our true character is revealed. Under the gun, I see the real me; you see the real you.

Our society is soft and comfortable. Oh, we have job-related stress, mental fatigue, but the only physically demanding thing that most of us do is to mow the lawn. This has become evident to us as our ministry has offered Christian camping opportunities over the past several decades. For years, we sponsored a camping/rafting trip for local doctors and their children. The guys both loved and hated that trip. They hated the hard work: cutting wood, building fires, cooking, scrubbing pots with steel wool, hauling water, expending a great deal of physical energy in order to manage the basics of life. The trips revealed us to us. We didn't always like what we discovered about ourselves, our ability to rough it, our temper, our weaknesses, and our attitudes. Men who could withstand the rigors of performing twelve-hour surgeries buckled under the pressure of a week's worth of river rafting in the wilderness. I was no exception.

On one expedition, the raft leaked, soaking my sleeping bag and Living Bible. To make it worse, all the food got wet, too. We lived on soggy sandwiches and orange soda the rest of the day. When night fell, and I lay on my still-sopping sleeping bag, I remember feeling sorry for myself and breathing a pitiful prayer: "Lord, all it has to do is rain, and I'll know you are there." Guess what? The drops began to fall!

Under pressure, we get a good picture of ourselves, and we begin to see and deal with areas of need. That's precisely the reason God allows stress. The challenge from scripture is, as Hebrews 12:1 puts it, to "lay aside every encumbrance, and the sin which so easily entangles us, and *let us run with perseverance the race lying before us*" (12:1b DAV). The only way we can develop the quality of perseverance is if we are given something to persevere. And that something often involves either small-scale or large-scale suffering. "For unto you,' Paul writes in Philippians 1:29, "it is given in the behalf of Christ, not only to believe on him, but also to suffer for his sake" (KJV).

I always tell folks in my classes, "When you become a

Christian, you can plan on suffering. Suffering 101 is a required course in the divine curriculum for your life." We can all say that we have been there, done that and got the scars! Or when you reach my age, it is: "I've been there, done that, and can't remember most of it." What should encourage us is that we're not alone in the suffering. God is there to sustain us. He knows exactly what it is going to take to get the job done in making us like Jesus. We have the hope of his glory to hang onto. Bearing the cross now reminds us that we'll wear the crown later!

God even expects believers to put themselves under healthy doses of stress. Paul says, "But I am treating my body roughly and making it serve me, lest when I have preached to others, I myself should be disqualified" (1 Cor. 9:27 DAV). That's the chief reason I took up running many years ago. Running gave me the energy to travel to five or six cities, teach twelve Bible classes, and preach two sermons each week. Nowadays, my new joints (a hip and knee replacement) won't allow me to run, so I cycle. The stress of exercise produces energy.

God gives us a promise to accompany the stress. As Paul says in Romans 5:4, the perseverance we develop produces "character," and this character generates "hope."

What is that hope? The hope is simply that God, who has begun a good work in us, "will perfect it until the day of Christ Jesus" (Phil. 1:6 NASB; see also 1 John 3:2-3). When something happens to us, we can look for God's hand in it. We know he'll continue working on us until he completes what he desires to do in our life. As the children's song goes:

> He's still workin' on me,
> To make me what I ought to be;
> It took Him just a week
> To make the moon and stars,
> The sun and the earth and Jupiter and Mars.

How loving and patient He must be!
He's still workin' on me.

There really ought to be a sign upon my heart:
"Don't judge him (her) yet,
There's an unfinished part."
But I'll be perfect just according to His plan,
Fashioned by the Master's loving hand.[3]

The hope for believers is that when things get rough, the Father sees potential. I'm reminded of the old story about the man who lost his fortune, his wife, his home, and was destitute except for his faith. He wandered aimlessly about the streets one afternoon and happened to pass a church where a bell tower was being added. The man paused to watch a stonemason work. The mason chipped away at a piece of granite, fashioning it into the form of a triangle.

"Sir, may I interrupt you a minute?" asked the man.

"Certainly," replied the mason.

"Why are you making that stone like that?"

"That's easy," replied the mason. Pointing to a small hole in the bell tower above, "See that little hole way up at the top? I'm shaping this stone down here so that it will fit up there."

Tears rolled down the face of the man who had lost so much, because he realized that everything coming his way was a sign that God was shaping him down here on earth so that he'd fit up there in heaven. Trouble produces perseverance, which generates character, which results in hope. That we'll fit *up there* is the hope we can all hold onto. God is going to finish the job he has started with us.

All that is going on in your life *down here* is so you'll fit *down here*, too. God is glorified by much fruit. The pruning and cutting will produce a great crop.

To sum it up, the process of "remaining under" involves three stages:

Stage one: suffering produces perseverance.

Stage two: perseverance produces character.

Stage three: character produces hope, the confidence of final glory.

FIVE: LOVE ... AND SIX: GOD'S SPIRIT—ROMANS 5:5-8

Peace, access, the hope of God's glory, tribulation—each is a result of living the life of faith in Jesus Christ. And there is more. Paul tells us in Romans 5:5, "and this hope does not disappoint; because the love of God has been poured out in our hearts through the Holy Spirit who was given to us" (DAV). We hang onto the hope that God will not forsake us, that he'll continue to work in us till we're called home to glory. The reason we'll not be disappointed by this hope is that God's love literally fills our hearts with passionate desire for him.

God's love ... its reality in us is a fifth result of our relationship with him. The Holy Spirit, who comes to dwell within us at the moment of our salvation, is the badge, the sign, a sixth indicator that we truly know Jesus Christ. We worship a God who is three-in-one: God the Father, God the Son, and God the Spirit. The Holy Spirit is the third person of that trinity, and Paul reveals more about him in Romans 8. For now, let's just recognize the wondrous truth that the Holy Spirit—God's own Spirit—is given to every Christian. In fact, he comes to indwell us the very millisecond we receive Christ as savior. He is our comforter, the tangible assurer that God will do exactly as he has promised. He empowers us to act as we ought to act, think as we ought to think, speak what we ought to speak. He convinces us of the presence of God's love, and as we become grown-up believers, we ought to be increasingly aware of his impact in our life. I pray every morning: "Spirit of God cleanse my heart and fill me with yourself."

What a love God's love is! If you're a Christian, growing in your trust, you should be aware of the presence of the Lord's abiding love for you. As John writes in 1 John 4:16, "And we have come to know and have believed the love which God has for us. God is love, and the one who abides in love abides in God, and God abides in him" (NASB). God's Spirit can sensitize you to his love for you. The process is an indicator that you're getting to know your heavenly Father better and better. It surely was for Bettie.

When she first came to see me for counseling, Bettie was angry over the tragic death of her husband. As she spoke of the evening he died, her voice rang with bitterness: "I was on my knees saying my prayers. 'Please, God, bring Sam home safely,' I begged. And God let him die in a car accident that very night. He should have been walking in the front door when they rolled him into that ambulance!"

"Bettie," I said, "did it ever occur to you that God did bring your husband home?"

"What do you mean?" she stammered in reply.

"Was Sam a Christian?"

"Oh, yes!"

"Then God the Father answered your prayer, and brought him safely home."

That insight sparked a love affair between Bettie and her heavenly Father that touched many lives until she, too, was called safely home with Sam.

God's love transcends our shortcomings, reaching down to blot them out. "For when we were still helpless," Paul writes, "at the right time Christ died for the godless. For one will hardly die for a righteous man; though perhaps for the good man someone would even dare to die. But God is demonstrating his own love to us, because while we were yet sinners, Christ died for us" (Rom. 5:6-8 DAV).

Circle the word *helpless* in those verses. We were completely helpless, totally incapable of saving ourselves, and Christ gave himself for us. As Paul reminds the Christians at Ephesus of their position *before* knowing Christ: "Remember that you were ... separate from Christ, excluded from the commonwealth of Israel, and strangers to the covenants of promise, having no hope and without God in the world" (Eph. 2:12 NASB). Note the word *godless* in Romans 5:6. Christ did not *live* for the ungodly—he *died* for them! The Lord Jesus sacrificed himself for people who knew no God, whose sins were disgusting and vile, who deserved no such sacrifice. Consistent awareness and gratitude for this incredible gift and amazing affection will signal that you're growing up in the Lord ... that you're becoming like Bettie. The sweet, submissive spirit is the soil in which the Father's greatest work begins to grow.

SEVEN: SAFETY—ROMANS 5:9

We were helpless in our sins and Christ made the sacrifice to rescue us. "Much more therefore, having been justified now by his blood, we shall be saved through Him from the wrath," writes Paul to the Romans (5:9 DAV). No matter how bad it gets in this world, believers are in a position of safety. We'll be saved from the wrath that is to come. That safety is the seventh result of having a relationship with the Lord.

The year 1998 marked the fiftieth anniversary of the birth of modern Israel. In the wake of the Nazi holocaust, in which over one-third of the world's Jews tragically perished, public sympathy swelled to support the establishment of a modern Israeli state in Arab-occupied Palestine. After the United Nations General Assembly's approval of a plan of partition, the longing became a reality. On May 14, 1948, David Ben-Gurion proclaimed Israel's statehood: Since then, the Israelis have been embroiled in conflict. The wars of '67, '72, and more recent clashes and terrorist bombings, have claimed the lives of thousands. Few Israeli families have escaped unscathed, and even the young have suffered and died in scores. I recall standing in the national cemetery in Jerusalem some years ago and noting the graves of many, many teenagers, casualties of the ongoing conflict.

The sad thing is that despite all they've endured, the Israelis are in for more. The time of Jacob's trouble is coming. God has allowed the nation of Israel to survive for a purpose. One day, perhaps very soon, the Lord will fulfill his promises to that nation, the descendants of Abraham, by ushering in the eternal kingdom we've discussed earlier. In that day, Jesus Christ, the son of David, will assume his proper throne. Before Christ is established on his throne, the birth pangs of his coming kingdom will be dramatically manifested in a seven-year period known as the tribulation. Revelation 6-19 describes the tribulation as a time of economic collapse, famine, bloodshed, and cosmic upheaval. It will be the wrath of God poured out on sin.

But as believers, we'll be saved from all of this. We won't be around to suffer in the tribulation. God's wrath on our sins has already been poured out on our substitute, Christ! In the words of the poet:

> On Him almighty vengeance fell
> That would have sunk a world to hell.
> He bore it for a chosen race,
> And thus becomes our hiding place.

God's judgment has already been rendered for us, and because of Jesus Christ, we've been pronounced not guilty. If we don't suffer physical death first, then in a moment, in the twinkling of an eye, we'll be taken up to be with the Lord in the event we've discussed previously known as the rapture. According to 1 Thessalonians 4:16-18, the Lord will descend from heaven with a shout. The trumpet of God will sound and first the dead in Christ will rise, then the living Christians will be caught up with the savior in the clouds. Then God's wrath will begin to be poured out on a wicked world (see also 1 Cor. 15:51-54).

Christians will escape this terrible judgment. Revelation 3:10 says that we shall be kept "from the hour of testing, that hour which is about to come upon the whole world" (NASB). We'll not have to endure God's wrath! Our safety is assured, thanks to the savior.

EIGHT: JOY BECAUSE OF THE RECONCILIATION—ROMANS 5:10-11

Peace, access, hope, tribulation, love, the Spirit, safety from wrath—each of these seven is an indicator, a result of the most important relationship in life now and forever after. The final indicator that we're making progress in our relationship with God is the joy we feel just knowing Christ. "For if while being enemies, we were reconciled to God through the death of his Son, much more, having been reconciled, we shall be saved by His life. And not only this, but we also rejoice in God through our Lord Jesus Christ, through whom we have now received the reconciliation" (5:10-11 DAV), writes Paul to the Romans.

We were actually enemies of God, but through the blood of Christ we can be his friends. "And although you were formerly alienated and hostile in mind, engaged in evil deeds," Paul tells the Colossians, "yet He [Christ] has now reconciled you in His fleshly body through death, in order to present you before Him holy and blameless and beyond reproach" (Col. 1:21-22 NASB). Our about-face from foe to friend of God should make every Christian ecstatic. What joy we should be feeling as we but think of the tremendous sacrifice God made by sending his Son, just for us, just so we could have a relationship with him! Our Christian life ought to be marked by a genuine rejoicing in God, for who he is, for what he has done, for what he is going to do.

Note that Paul tells the Romans that we "shall be saved by his [Christ's] life." Let's not forget that Jesus *arose* from the grave. Christianity is the only religion in the world that worships a divine *living* leader. God is alive and taking care of his interests, not the least of which are we who are his children! What is more, the Lord is a leader who lives in us, through his Spirit. He protects, he intercedes, he directs. Truly we are saved by his life, and the power of the resurrection is available to us as we submit to the Spirit. As we'll find out as we continue our study of Romans 5-8, holy living is a potential for every Christian; victory over sin through God's power *is* possible for us in our day-to-day living. We have so much to be grateful for—and that is something to shout about!

WHEN WE ALL GET TO HEAVEN

The anticipation of God's glory puts a song in my heart and a spring in my step! What about you? What fabulous things are in store for those of us in a relationship with the Father through faith in the Son. As the hymnist, Eliza E. Hewitt, writes:

> When we all get to heaven,
> What a day of rejoicing that will be!
> When we all see Jesus,
> We'll sing and shout the victory.

And what more heartfelt desire can be expressed than that of the apostle John in the concluding verses of the Bible's final book?

"Amen. Come, Lord Jesus" (Rev. 22:20 NASB).

Questions to Consider

1. Romans 5:1 tells us that as Christians, we "are having peace with God." What does it mean to have peace with God? How may we also experience the peace *of* God? (see Phil. 4:6-7.) Recall and share, if you wish, an episode in which the peace of God has become vividly real to you.

2. What is the glory of God? Are you rejoicing in the hope of God's coming glory? Why or why not?

3. Suffering is an inevitable part of the Christian life. Using Romans 5:3-5 as a basis, explain why God sometimes permits suffering to enter our lives. What are some of the positive results that can come from trial and trauma? Have you seen any positive results of suffering in your own life?

CHAPTER 3

"That I may know Him, and the power of His resurrection and the fellowship of His sufferings, being conformed to His death" (Phil. 3:10 NASB).

The How of the Relationship

Romans 5:12-21

Flying home from Los Angeles to Dallas one Friday evening, I was exhausted. The preceding week had been spent in the classroom, attending 40 hours of lecture for my doctoral program. The course I'd taken had dealt with biblical counseling, and after that intense week, I didn't care about counseling ... all I wanted were peace and quiet! My frequent flyer card automatically ensures me of an adjacent empty seat when a flight isn't crowded. Most of the time I don't care about this perk, but on that evening as I boarded the 727, I breathed a quick prayer. "Lord, could I have a break to read and relax on this flight? I don't want to practice what I've learned today!" No sooner were the words out of my mouth than a young lady, burdened with bags, stopped in the aisle beside me.

"That's my seat," she said, motioning to the window seat next to me. I couldn't believe it! I looked around to see if the plane was full. It wasn't. I muttered, "Are you sure?"

She was. I stood up to let her in.

She dragged her bags with her and plopped down next to the window, then began shoving some of her things under the seat in front of her. Some books spilled out on the floor, and as I picked them up for her, I noticed all of the titles concerned prayer. Two and a half hours of conversation later, we landed in Dallas.

Within a few weeks the Ministries received a letter from that young lady. She ordered some tapes and assured us that her relationship with Christ was real and meeting her needs. I could tell from the comments she made that some of the results of that relationship were already beginning to manifest themselves in her life. The void was being filled by the only one who can: God himself. Was I grateful that God had overruled my selfishness and allowed me the privilege of talking about him with her on that plane!

In our look at the first eleven verses of Romans 5, we saw eight results of having what that young lady had: a relationship with God through Jesus Christ:

1. Peace with God
2. Access to God
3. Hope in the glory of God
4. Rejoicing in tribulation
5. Love
6. The residence of God's Spirit
7. Safety from wrath
8. Joy in Christ

Our reconciliation with God involves a new standing with him. We become God's allies and instruments. The feud is finished. The fight is over. How does this miracle happen? What is God's logic behind it? By continuing in Romans 5, we can come to understand the outworking of God's plan of salvation for us. We learn the *how* of it all as the apostle Paul opens a door into the very mind of God.

Romans 5:12-21 is not for the light reader. It is heavy theological traffic, tough to navigate in places. The encouraging thing is that once you grasp the major truths of this passage, much of the rest of scripture seems easy by comparison—smaller seas as opposed to the vast ocean of Romans 5.

In verses 12-21, Paul presents two basic truths about becoming a Christian:

1. All men and women are born into the family of Adam and must be reborn into the family of Jesus Christ in order to experience salvation.
2. The action of one man can affect the entire human race.

Throughout the passage, we see contrasted Adam, the original earthly father of us all, and Christ, the head of the new family of believers we enter when we come to know him as savior. We're not born "children of God," but are instead children of Adam, born into his family. This means we enter the world as kicking, squalling sinners guaranteed to live up to our sin potential. Before we meet human death, it is vital that we be reborn by the Holy Spirit into the family of Christ. That is the only way we'll experience eternal life in the presence of the Father. That's the plan, plain and simple.

THE REIGN OF DEATH—ROMANS 5:12-14

"Therefore," Paul states in Romans 5:12, "Just as through one man sin entered the world, and through this sin, death, and so death spread to all men because all sinned" (DAV). When you encounter the word *therefore* in scripture, the old rule to find out what it's *there for*: Wrapping up his comments about the eight results of having a relationship with Christ, Paul has already said the following in Romans 5:10-11:

> For if while being enemies (with God) we were reconciled to God through the death of his Son, much more, having been reconciled, we shall be saved by His life. And not only this, but we also rejoice in God through our Lord Jesus Christ, through whom we have now received the reconciliation. (DAV)

Like the estranged couple who reconcile before the final divorce decree, man becomes reunited with the Lord through faith in Christ's finished work. With the eight results of that relationship in mind, Paul begins in Romans 5:12 to explain how it all works.

Through "one man," says Paul in Romans 5:12, "sin entered into the world" (DAV). That one man was Adam, our forefather. Sin had existed before Adam; Satan and the anointed cherubim fell from their lofty positions because of their rebellion against God long before Adam was created (Isaiah 14). But with Adam, sin infiltrated the human race, the world of humankind. Stealing subtly into the lush garden—that perfect, spotless world created for man—Satan seized the opportunity to capitalize on man's desire for independence and offered the forbidden fruit. Adam bit, and the rest is history. Sin blackened the garden and the souls within. The intimate relationship with him, which God had intended man to share, was shattered, and Satan seemed triumphant (Gen. 3).

From this sin, Paul continues in verse 12, death came

into the world and this death "spread to all men, because all sinned" (DAV). Anyone who has buried a loved one knows the agony that physical death brings. It wasn't supposed to be that way, but Adam's disobedience opened the floodgates of divine judgment. Paul is also referring to another kind of death here. Not only did physical death spread to all men after Adam, but spiritual death—meaning separation from God—also pervaded the creation.

To put it simply, we're dying twice. Physically, our body is in a state of decline and we speed irrevocably toward that day of physical demise. Every time we pay our respects at a funeral, we're reminded of that fact. But until we accept Christ as savior, we're also spiritually dead. If we physically die before we come to know Christ as savior, that spiritual death will be permanent. According to the Bible, there are no second chances to get into heaven. By the sin of Adam, all men are alienated from God. We're born in sin, and if the Lord doesn't call for us, we are going to die. Many, too many, will lie in their caskets twice dead—physically useless and spiritually separated from God for eternity.

Why did Adam sin in the garden? He was just like any of us. He wasn't content with all that he'd been given. The Lord had created an incredibly beautiful, serene, satisfying environment for him, and it wasn't enough. Adam had only been forbidden one item, and still, he proved easy prey for Satan's temptation. He probably reasoned things this way: "This is my garden. I have a right to everything that's in here. Really, it's not what I possess and have experienced that bothers me, but what I don't possess and haven't experienced that is driving me to despair. It bothers me that there is a tree I can't approach. I dream of it at night, and the desire for it consumes me. I don't care what God says; I'm going to take of that tree!"

We men, women, and children share Adam's arrogance. We all share his thirst for independence from God. We share his desire to disobey. We can't help it—that's the way we are, stuck with what theologians call the adamic nature. It's what makes millions of us resist God's provision of salvation by grace. We'd rather think of ourselves as the masters of our own fate and the captains of our own salvation.

We're stubborn. We want to be independent. How we must remind God of our own kids who cry, "No, I do it myself!" as soon as they can toddle. In God's eyes, we must appear so like my daughters who, when they were very young and impatient for their mother's cooking lessons, decided to prepare a meal themselves. Pans were blackened, food scorched, and water boiled away in the effort, when it would have been so much easier, neater, and safer to have done it Mom's way and in Mom's time! (By the way—all our girls are great cooks now, thanks to Mom.)

ENTER, THE LAW

The actions of one man, Adam, affected the entire human race. Because of his sin, we are all doomed to follow in his footsteps. Just try to be perfect on your own. You'll be the first since Jesus Christ to make it.

Paul continues his message to the Romans with these words, "For until Law sin was in the world; but sin is not put to one's account where there is no law" (5:13 DAV). The law to which he refers was the law given to Moses. Paul discusses the Mosaic law in later chapters of Romans, but this is a good place to learn about it.

The Mosaic law was the revealed will of God regarding human conduct. It included the Ten Commandments, but also encompassed over 600 regulations governing the Israelites' social life and ordinances concerning their worship. It was a way of life, an entire system of do's and don'ts, yeses and noes, given to God's people for a specific reason. It was a conditional covenant, demanding rigid, total obedience.

"For until Law sin was in the world; but sin is not put to one's account where there is no law," states Paul in verse 13 (DAV). What does this mean? Even before the giving of the law in the time of Moses, Adam's sin affected the entire race. Sin had entered the world of man through Adam, despite the fact that the "thou shalt nots" had not yet been given. The fact that people died was proof that they were sinners. They died physically because they were dead spiritually; it was a condition resulting from Adam's first sin.

"But sin is not put to one's account where there is no law." How does this fit in? First of all, it does *not* mean that the law is designed as a standard we must strive to live up to. I remember attending a banquet. When the speaker was introduced, the emcee had this to say about him, "And the greatest thing about Henry is that he tries to live by the Ten Commandments." Applause. Everyone at the banquet thought that was wonderful. What a great guy Henry was!

We all think living by the Ten Commandments is good, don't we? But when we focus on doing that before we accept Christ, we're living our life on a performance basis. And when we focus on keeping the top ten, living by the golden rule, *independently* doing things to please God through the keeping of the law *after* we accept Christ, then we're essentially basing our Christian life on performance, too. We're acting like Sondra, from chapter one. We come into a relationship with Christ joyfully and gratefully, yet before too long we enter the vicious cycle of performance, failure, guilt ... performance, failure, guilt. We don't do very well; guilt nibbles at us; then we do pretty well; then we slip up again; guilt jabs us; then we have a small success; then we fail again and feel guilty all the more. If you're stuck in that vicious cycle, it's probably because you're misreading the reasons for the law. You've placed yourself on the performance treadmill, depending on yourself rather than on God's Spirit to give you victory. It's time to throw off the chains of performance and experience the triumphant freedom of the relationship of unconditional love and acceptance God desires for you.

Pearl and I have been married 49 years now and we both must confess that a lot of those years were based on performance. We would dole out love to each other based on performance. Now the freedom and joy of unconditional love, forgiveness, and acceptance has brought our married life to new heights. I told her on our anniversary: "Come along with me, the best is yet to be." Tenderness and kindness have replaced bitterness and critical spirits.

Besides, we can't fulfill the law anyway! It's impossible to be perfect. What the law does is to put sin to our account. When the law comes in and tells us, "Thou shalt not," it shows us, basically, that we already have. The law brings sin out into the light of day. It makes us aware of the specific ways in which we fail to measure up to God's perfect holiness. It expands on Adam's original disobedience, clarifying to us God's convictions concerning right and wrong. And as Paul will discuss later in Romans 5:20, it even stimulates sin.

Think of it this way. Perhaps Norm L. figures he has it all together. He's a good fellow—nice to his wife, kind to his kids, friendly to his neighbors. Oh, he may fudge a little on his expense reports and take a few deductions on his income tax that don't seem exactly kosher, but really, he's a good guy. He'd do anything for you. In fact, Norm himself figures he's a pretty good guy. He's all right. But then in comes the law, saying, "Thou shalt not steal," and Norm is forced to realize that he's been padding his expense reports. Maybe he rationalizes it: the company ought to give him a raise anyway, with all he does around there. But then Norm remembers the time he looked twice at his secretary at the company Christmas party. "Thou shalt not commit adultery," the law reminds him, and although he hasn't actually done it, it has crossed his mind. "But I say unto you, That whosoever looketh on a woman to lust after her hath committed adultery with her already in his heart" (Matt. 5:28 KJV), says Jesus, and Norm realizes he is a sinner. A pretty nice guy, but a sinner anyway. The law proves it. It's a mirror revealing our unrighteousness. It puts sin to our account. There's nothing like having a law around to show us that we've broken it! As Paul puts it in Romans 3:19-20:

> Now we are knowing that whatever the Law is saying, it is speaking to those who are under the Law, in order that every mouth may be closed, and all the world may become accountable to God; because by the works of the Law there shall not be declared righteous any flesh in His sight; for through the Law comes the knowledge of sin. (DAV)

CHRIST, THE ANSWER

"But," continues Paul in Romans 5:14, "death reigned from Adam to Moses, even over those who had not sinned in the likeness of Adam's offense, who is a type of the One who was to come" (DAV). Sin infected humanity as soon as Adam disobeyed God. The men and women who followed Adam did not sin in exactly the same way he did, for God had sealed the garden and no one could approach the forbidden fruit, but people sinned in other ways. We know this because Genesis 6:5 tells us, "The Lord saw how great man's wickedness on the earth had become, and that every inclination of the thoughts of his heart was only evil all the time" (NIV). In response to that great wickedness, God ordered the one faithful man around to build a boat and get ready for rain. And so Noah constructed the ark, loaded up his family and two of every living creature ... and the world experienced a devastating divine judgment (Gen. 6-8).

Paul also says that Adam is a "type of the One who was

to come." What he means is this. As we've discussed, Adam was the first head of the human family. Another "head" was going to come, a man who would bring righteousness and life rather than death and sin. That man would be Jesus Christ, whom Paul elsewhere calls the "last Adam" (1 Cor. 15:45-49).

Christ was first spoken of to the serpent in the garden in Genesis 3:15. "And I will put enmity between you and the woman, and between your offspring and hers; he will crush your head, and you will strike his heel" (NIV), said the Lord God to Satan, the spirit possessing the power behind the serpent. The promised offspring of the woman, who will crush the evil one's head, though Satan might "strike his heel," was none other than Jesus Christ. In God's plan of salvation for mankind, this special holy one, this "last Adam," would be brought into the world as a member of a chosen race, the Jews or Hebrews. In Genesis 12:1-2, we read of the Lord's call of Abram, later known as Abraham, and God's promises to him that he would be the forefather of the nation through which the people of the earth would be blessed by the coming of the holy one.

From Abraham to his son Isaac, to Isaac's son Jacob, to Jacob's son Judah, to Judah's descendant David, the line of the promised seed continued (Gen. 49:10; Isa. 11:1). The prophet Isaiah 7:14, writing 700 years before the birth of Christ, predicted that a virgin would give birth to a child and would call that child Immanuel, or "God with us." Another prophet, Micah, a contemporary of Isaiah, wrote that this amazing birth would occur in the one-horse town of Bethlehem (Micah 5:2). The familiar Christmas story in Luke 2 tells us that it all came about as predicted (see also Luke 1:26-37; Matt. 1:18-2:1). Jesus Christ, the promised seed of Abraham, the greatest descendant of David, was born of a virgin named Mary in a small village called Bethlehem. He was "God with us," God-made-man. He lived the flawless life that only God could accomplish, and as Isaiah also prophesied, he was despised by men and rejected by his own people (Isa. 53:3; John 1:11, 7:5,48). He died a hideous death on a cross in order to pay the purchase price of our redemption when we could not free ourselves. As Paul writes in 1 Corinthians 15:3, "For I delivered to you as of first importance what I also received, that Christ died for our sins according to the Scriptures" (NASB).

What does it all mean to us? On this side of Calvary, we recognize that the actions of one man, Adam, affected the entire human race, and that the actions of another, Christ, have the potential to affect the whole race, too.

"You mean," inquired a skeptical college student attending one of my university classes, "that when Adam bit the apple, or whatever it was, back there in the garden, he made me a sinner too? And that some man called Jesus died on a cross 2000 years ago to take the punishment for that sin? And that my faith in what he did 2000 years ago will make a difference in my life?"

"You'd better believe it," I answered. "You have spoken theology. That's Romans 5 in a nutshell. At the moment you are born, you are born into sin. Little babies are born with a sin nature; it's their inheritance from Adam. You've got to do something about yours and be born again by the Spirit of God into God's family or you won't be ready for eternity."

Paul told the Corinthians: "Therefore, we are ambassadors for Christ, as though God were entreating through us; we beg you on behalf of Christ, be reconciled to God. He made Him who knew no sin to be sin on our behalf, that we might become the righteousness of God in Him" (2 Cor. 5:20-21 NASB).

THE GRACIOUS GIFT—ROMANS 5:15-19

> But the gracious gift is not like the transgres-

> sion. For if by the transgression of the one the many died, much more did the grace of God and the gift by grace of the one man, Jesus Christ, abound to the many. And the gift is not like that which came through the one who sinned; for on the one hand the judgment was out of the one transgression resulting in condemnation, but on the other hand the gracious gift was out of many transgressions resulting in justification. For if by the transgression of the one, death reigned through that one, much more those who are receiving the abundance of grace and the gift of righteousness will reign in life through the one, Jesus Christ.
>
> So then as through one transgression to all men there resulted condemnation, so also through one act of righteousness to all men there resulted justification of life. For just as through the disobedience of the one man the many were constituted sinners, so also through the obedience of the one the many will be constituted righteous.

JUSTIFIED BY THE GIFT

The perfect gift ... how many hours do we comb the malls for just the right item, just the right size, just the right color, to delight our loved one at Christmas? How many of these so-called perfect gifts last long past Christmas day? CDs gather dust, sweaters shrink, and perfume bottles are soon emptied. Indeed there is only one truly perfect present, only one gift that will last forever.

What we do in order to prepare for eternity involves accepting "the gracious gift" Paul speaks of in Romans 5:14. "But the gracious gift," says the apostle, "is not like the transgression. For if by the transgression of the one the many died, much more did the grace of God and the gift by grace of the one man, Jesus Christ, abound to the many" (5:15 DAV). Jesus Christ is that gracious gift. In 2 Corinthians 9:15, Paul exclaims, "Thank God for his Son—a gift too wonderful for words" (NLV). The one by whose transgression the many died is, of course, Adam. The gracious gift of Christ far surpasses what the human race lost thanks to the sin of our human forefather. Christ's actions were superior to those of Adam. His sacrifice "much more" superceded the original sin; his obedience on the cross provided an unfailing and completely sufficient solution for mankind.

The word *abound* in verse 15 denotes liquid overflowing a container. Christ is that vessel whose blessing of salvation overflows, saturating the many who had formerly been dead in sin. "If any man is thirsty, let him come to Me and drink. He who believes in Me, as the Scripture said, 'From his innermost being shall flow rivers of living water,'" Jesus promises in John 7:37-38 (NASB).

"And the gift is not like that which came through the one who sinned; for on the one hand the judgment was out of one transgression, resulting in condemnation, but on the other hand the gracious gift was out of many transgressions resulting in justification," continues Paul in Romans 5:16 (DAV). Again we see that because of one transgression (Adam's sin in the garden) condemnation fell on the entire human race. Yet out of many transgressions—in other words, after centuries of disobedience between the time of Adam and that of Christ—Jesus, the gracious gift, was offered on the cross. Whereas the blood of animals had been repeatedly spilled on sacrificial altars as payment for the sins of men, the sacrifice of Christ was a one-time-only, all-sufficient offering. Christ potentially paid the penalty for every past, present, and future sin. All that any man, woman, or child has to do is to accept his incredible gift through faith. *Justification* means being declared guiltless and being clothed in the righteousness of Christ. He justifies us with his shed blood. The slate is wiped clean by the blood of the lamb, Christ, of whom John the Baptist exclaimed, "Behold, the Lamb of God who takes away the sin of the world" (John 1:29 NASB). As Paul writes to the Colossians about Christ, the ultimate sacrificial lamb:

> And when you were dead in your transgressions and the uncircumcision of your flesh, He made you alive together with Him, having forgiven us all our transgressions, having canceled out the certificate of debt consisting of decrees against us and which was hostile to us; and He has taken it out of the way, having nailed it to the cross (Col. 2:13-14 NASB, see also Isa. 1:18).

What a glorious, liberating truth! The full responsibility for our salvation is on the shoulders of our savior.

Pearl and I were traveling with some friends in the Northwest some years ago. I had planned the itinerary and made all the arrangements. On the fifth day, Bob spontaneously exclaimed, "It's so wonderful to just relax and let you carry the responsibility!" That's exactly what Jesus has done for us for all eternity. He has made all the arrangements for our trip to heaven. The reservations are confirmed, the seats reserved. And unlike me on our tour to the Northwest, he has even paid for the whole trip!

REIGNING IN LIFE, THANKS TO THE GIFT

The statistics on death are impressive. One out of one dies. Thanks to Adam's sin, death is a dictator. Paul reiterates that thought in Romans 5:17, where he says, "For if by the transgressions of the one, death reigned through that one" (DAV). And yet there is more! Paul continues with a fabulous promise, "much more those who are receiving the abundance of grace and of the gift of righteousness will reign in life through the One, Jesus Christ" (5:17b DAV). Without Christ, death is our absolute monarch. With Christ, we are able to "reign in life." That's amazing!

Reigning in life involves an attitude. When Christ enters your heart, you have the option of allowing him to rule there, and when he does, you begin to rule in life. "'Not by might nor by power, but by my Spirit,' says the Lord Almighty" (Zech. 4:6 NIV). You cannot be permanently nailed to the wall by circumstances, hassles, and heartaches. No matter what happens, you'll be given the amazing ability to rebound, as you learn to depend on God. It's a promise. If you don't believe me, look elsewhere in scripture.

"For we do not want you to be unaware, brethren, of our affliction which came to us in Asia, that we were burdened excessively, beyond our strength, so that we despaired even of life; indeed, we had the sentence of death within ourselves in order that we should not trust in ourselves, but in God who raises the dead" (2 Cor. 1:8, 9 NASB). "But they that wait upon the Lord shall renew their strength," writes Isaiah the prophet. "They shall mount up with wings as eagles; they shall run, and not be weary; and they shall walk, and not faint" (Isa. 40:31 KJV). Paul states in 2 Corinthians 4, "we are afflicted in every way, but not crushed; perplexed, but not despairing; persecuted, but not forsaken; struck down, but not destroyed" (4:8-9 NASB). J.B. Phillips translates those verses this way:

> We are hard-pressed on all sides, but we are never frustrated; we are puzzled, but never in despair We are persecuted, but are never deserted: we may be knocked down but we

> are never knocked out! (2 Cor. 4:8-9 Phillips)

Life for the Christian has the capacity to be a constant pageant of "triumph in Christ," writes Paul in 2 Corinthians 2:14 (NASB). We're promised that God will empower us to rise above the rubble, to pick up the pieces, to conquer the crises. Things may not turn out as we expect or hope, but we'll endure, and even learn to glory in our troubles, if we respond properly. Remember, Paul tells us that glorying *in spite* of trouble is one of the outcomes of knowing Christ as savior (Rom. 5:3). When we hit the stresses and the skids in life, the Lord is at work. He'll take us through, as we learn to depend on him. The process may be painful, but we'll emerge from it knowing that the trauma was only temporary. "This too shall pass," applies to even the worst of circumstances ... and in the wake of disaster, the shout of ultimate victory is certain.

The Lord's mission statement for our lives can be summarized with these words: Develop Christ-like character by whatever means to ensure faithfulness and fruitfulness. When we come to Christ, we learn through a deepening relationship that the Lord delights in three things:

1. Submission to his sovereignty
2. Study of his word
3. Sacrificial service in his Spirit

We glorify Christ by what we give rather than by what we get. We don't come to depend on God by *doing* but by *being*. Spending time in his word and in prayer should be our goals. The whole idea of *being* over *doing* contrasts with the so-called prosperity gospel hurled at us from high tech pulpits and the multi-million-dollar sets of Christian television programs. Many modern preachers exhort us to look at what we're going to get in exchange for our sacrificial giving. This is contrary to the whole tenor of scripture. Our service and giving must be the by-products of hearts overflowing with love for God. We give and serve because we want to—out of loving gratitude, not because we have to or because we believe we'll be given some tangible desire. May God keep us from ever becoming complacent, cold-hearted, or calculating about Calvary!

Just in case his readers haven't understood the truth, Paul repeats his major points in verse 18: "So then, as through one transgression to all men there resulted condemnation; so also through one act of righteousness, to all men there resulted justification of life" (DAV). Get it? It's "one transgression" bringing destruction, "one act of righteousness" bringing justification. It's Adam with the apple and Christ with the cross, the perfect life of the latter atoning for the direct disobedience of the first. We stay under condemnation until we come to know the one sent to set us free.

The *how* of it all is concisely summed up in verse 19: "For just as through the disobedience of the one man the many were constituted sinners, so also through the obedience of the One the many will be constituted righteous" (DAV). Note the verb tenses Paul uses. Adam's behavior made sinners of us all; the many *were constituted* sinners (past tense). Yet through Christ, there is a hope; the many *will be* constituted righteous (future tense). Sin and death have one source: Adam. Life, righteousness, and peace spring only from Jesus Christ, and Christ's obedience.

Christ's obedience—think of it. God clothed himself in human flesh, permitting himself to be born in blood and tears like any man. He placed himself under the authority of earthly parents, although he was their savior too. Philippians 2:5-8 puts it well:

> Have this attitude in yourselves which was also in Christ Jesus, who, although He

> existed in the form of God, did not regard equality with God a thing to be grasped, but emptied Himself, taking the form of a bond-servant, and being made in the likeness of men. And being found in appearance as a man, He humbled Himself by becoming obedient to the point of death, even death on a cross. (NASB)

Jesus temporarily traded the sparkling mansions of heaven for the dusty hovels of earth. His journey here was one of increasing humiliation unto the greatest humiliation of them all: the cross. Can you conceive of it? God, hanging on a cross, the creator of the universe dangling from wooden beams, the nails tearing at his flesh! Crucifixion was an unspeakable form of execution; Roman citizens were exempted from it because it was considered too degrading. And yet Christ allowed the soldiers to pierce his hands and feet and nail him on the rough-hewn instrument of scorn. He suffered the death we all deserve, that we might never taste the bitterness of separation from God. How can we not cry, with Charles Wesley, "Amazing love! How can it be that Thou, my God, shouldst die for me!"[1] Hallelujah! What a savior!

OUR NEED—ROMANS 5:20-21

From Adam we inherit death; from Christ we can potentially inherit eternal life in the presence of God. Again Paul turns his attention to the law, and its place in this new relationship experienced between the Christian and Christ. "Now Law entered in alongside in order that the transgression might multiply," writes the apostle, "but where sin multiplied, grace was present in greater abundance" (Rom. 5:20 DAV). We learn in verse 20 that one reason why the law was given was so that the sins of men and women might multiply, might actually increase!

Paul talks about this principle again, in Romans 7, but to put it simply, the presence of the law acts as a catalyst for sin. As soon as human nature hears "No, you don't," the natural response is "Oh yes, I do!" We don't like to be forbidden anything. Just think about your kids. One of the surest ways to get a preschooler to do something is to tell him not to do it. See if the following scene between three-year-old Jimmy and his mother doesn't ring a few bells:

Mom: "Do not play with Mommy's glass pitcher, Jimmy. Do not even touch it. It is a no-no. Do you understand?"

Jimmy: "Yes, I understan' Mommy."

And within a few short minutes there arises from the kitchen such a clatter that Mom jumps up from the laundry to see what is the matter. There's Jimmy, standing with shards of splintered glass surrounding him and a look of sheer surprise on his face.

Jimmy: "I didn't touch it, Mommy! I didn't!"

If you want a preschooler to leave something alone, don't breathe a word of its importance. Don't set a limit, for that limit will light a fire under Jimmy or Jill that will only be quenched by disobedience. Believe me, I know whereof I speak because I've raised five of my own. Anyone who figures kids don't have Granddaddy Adam's sin nature has never had kids! Even as precious as my grandchildren are, they, too, have the same nature. I tease my kids when one of theirs manifests it: "It's so fun to see you getting what you deserve."

Parents should never be shocked when the boundaries they establish are crossed, for the law multiplies sin. Ask any highway patrolman who regularly clocks motorists doing seventy-plus when the speed limit is sixty-five. Rules are made to be broken.

The law was really a love gift from God, to show us our need. Our heart tells us when we cross his boundaries. We know when our thoughts are evil, our intentions dishonorable, our motives questionable. No one who is completely honest with himself has any doubt about how sinful he is. Oh, we may figure we're pretty good, but we surely know that we are not perfect. And when we find out that, from God's perspective, pretty good isn't good enough, we realize we need help—fast.

Perhaps this will help you remember the principles of the second half of Romans 5:

> Adam—Sin
> Moses—Need
> Christ—Answer

Adam's sin infected us all. The law given to Moses showed us our need, made it clear that we couldn't fulfill God's perfect standards on our own. And Christ provides us with the answer. Through faith in him, in his finished work on the cross, in his resurrection, we can be declared righteous in God's sight. That is God's plan, in all its beautiful simplicity.

Once you do enter into a relationship with God through Jesus Christ, the law ends its domination in your life. Paul puts it this way in Galatians 3:19,24-25:

> Why the law then? It was added because of transgressions, having been ordained through angels by the agency of a mediator, until the seed should come to whom the promise had been made .... Therefore the Law has become our tutor to lead us to Christ, that we may be justified by faith. But now that faith has come, we are no longer under a tutor. (NASB)

FREE AT LAST!

When we come to Jesus Christ, the law's relationship to us is over, finished, kaput. We're freed from it. It has fulfilled its purpose in showing us our need of a savior, but now it has no legitimate place in our life. Our sins have been paid for; our broken laws have been dealt with. We're free, in Christ, to become all that God wants us to be as we grow in our relationship with him.

What a mistake it is to accept Christ, then turn around and become a performance-oriented Christian. We'll discuss later the fact that we shouldn't intentionally disobey God so that his forgiveness might increase (Rom. 6:1), but the fact is that we're not under obligation to strive legalistically to fulfill the minutiae of the law. We can't, anyway. What God wants is a relationship, not a performance!

The law multiplies sin, for the believer and the non-believer. Satan delights in getting us on a continuous guilt trip, torn up inside by our constant failure. But as the law increases sin, so also does God's grace increase, "in order that," as Paul ends Romans 5, "just as sin reigned in death, so also grace might reign through righteousness, resulting in eternal life through Jesus Christ our Lord" (5:21 DAV). The chapter thus begins and ends with reference to the Lord Jesus Christ. If we've responded properly to Christ's invitation, we should lift our eyes from the pages of Romans 5 and find a tremendous weight lifted. And here's one more thing to comfort us: the relationship that begins the moment we receive Christ as savior is absolutely permanent. It will never cease to be. We'll never lose our salvation. Christ's own words assure us of that in John 10:27-29:

> My sheep hear My voice, and I know them, and they follow Me; and I give eternal life to them; and they shall never perish, and no one shall snatch them out of My hand. My

> Father, who has given them to Me, is greater than all; and no one is able to snatch them out of the Father's hand. (NASB; see also Rom. 8:38-39, Phil. 1:6)

When our eyes are on the relationship, we realize that it cannot be broken. Only when we start playing around with performance do we begin thinking of God's giving up, withdrawing his approval, and crossing us off his list. It just won't happen. Salvation is not a joint venture. In the words of the hymnist, "Jesus paid it all,/ All to Him I owe;/ Sin had left a crimson stain,/ He washed it white as snow."

When you come to Christ, you're instantly free—free from the bondage of the law, free from the penalty of sin, potentially free from the compulsion to strive to follow every "thou shalt not," free to pursue the purpose for which God created you: relationship with him. There's more, so much more, to learn about the relationship God desires to have with us, and we'll discover bountiful treasure as we continue in Romans. I hope that, as we read on, we'll be freed from the hunger to perform to please the Lord, and convinced of the unutterable beauty of learning to know him better and better.

AT THE SUMMIT

During my seminary days, I served as a Young Life staff member in Dallas. Our ministry involved establishing contact with groups of young people, working on communicating to them our love and concern, with emphasis on life over lip, and eventually presenting the truth of Christ to them in club meetings.

There was a progression we'd follow when getting to know a certain group of kids in a club. For the first four or five weeks the club met, we'd talk about things of interest to get the kids coming. They knew it was some kind of "religious" organization, but we wouldn't talk about anything theological for a while. We'd try to show them our love and acceptance, but we'd hit nothing heavy for a month or so. Once the kids knew us and we knew them and a climate of trust and caring had been established, the night would come to talk about sin.

In the clubs I led, I'd generally approach the subject by using the Ten Commandments. We'd first go through the evening's skits and fun activities, then when the laughter had died down, I'd get up and say, "Okay kids, grab a pencil and paper. We're having a test tonight."

"Thanks a lot," they'd bellyache. "What do you think we go to school for? We ought to be able to get out of that stuff here."

"The test has ten questions," I continued, "and we don't grade on the curve. If you miss one, just one, of the questions, you flunk."

"Ooh, that's not fair! You've gotta be kidding!"

"Nope. It's real. Maybe you've heard of my questions before. They're called the Ten Commandments. If you've broken any of them, you've failed the whole test. The Bible says that 'whosoever shall keep the whole law, and yet offend in one point, he is guilty of all' (James 2:10 KJV). If you're guilty of one, you're guilty of all."

So we'd start down the list. "Thou shalt have no other gods before me. Thou shalt not take the name of the Lord, thy God, in vain." The kids would realize that they'd tuned into their radios more often than they'd read the Bible. Almost every one of them could recall a time when a curse word had slipped out—some of them had spouted a whole dictionary of them.

"Thou shalt not commit adultery."

"At least I haven't done that!" several would exclaim.

"Oh no?" I'd answer. "The Lord knew you'd figure that. That's why he said in the book of Matthew that to look on someone in lust was to have already committed adultery in your heart."

"Oh," they'd answer, and the fellows who had been flipping through girlie magazines in the locker room would sink several inches lower in their chairs.

"Thou shalt not kill."

"Well, I haven't done that!" would come a chorus in reply.

"God knew that too," I'd continue. "So Jesus said that whenever you get angry with your brother, you've already murdered him in your heart. Anybody still innocent?" (See Matt. 5:22.)

And thus we'd go on until the list was finished and the kids were, too. Everyone's score was F, and all were convinced that in God's sight they were lawbreakers. They'd been born in sin and had fulfilled their destiny of disobedience. It would give them something to think about for the next week, because I'd stop talking then. Maybe we'd go for a hike or do another activity, but I wanted to let the reality of their guilt before God soak in. In the mind and heart of many present, the law had indeed fulfilled its purpose.

The next week we'd talk about the solution to the problem of sin: Jesus Christ. The kids had been convinced they were sinners; now they were relieved to learn there was a savior. The law had done what it was designed to do. Once those young people came to Jesus Christ and were convinced of his claims, they were finished with the law. I'd tell them how to go about marking their decision of faith as follows:

1. Acknowledge the fact that you have sinned and fallen short of God's standards. In Romans 3:23, Paul states that "all sinned and are falling short of the glory of God" (DAV).

2. Realize that the penalty for your sin is death, but the gift of God is eternal life through faith in Christ. John 3:16 says, "For God so loved the world, that He gave His only begotten Son, that whoever believes in Him should not perish, but have eternal life" (NASB). Romans 6:23 states, "For the wages of sin is death, but the free gift of God is life eternal in Christ Jesus our Lord" (DAV).

3. By faith, appropriate the gift of God's salvation. Make it your own. Believe that Christ died for your sins, and that there is nothing you can do apart from faith in him to earn your way into heaven. "For by grace you have been saved through faith; and that not of yourselves, it is the gift of God; not as a result of works, that no one should boast," writes Paul in Ephesians 2:8-9 (NASB).

4. In prayer, which is nothing more than talking to God, thank him for coming into your life and saving you.

5. Welcome to the family of God! For future reference, record the date, time, and place of your new birth. And rest assured, now that you are born again, you'll never be "unborn." You're in God's fold for good! (See John 10:27-29.)

What about you? Have you made that choice to leave the family of Adam and join the family of Christ through faith? If so, are you seeing the results of your relationship with Christ in your life? Are you growing closer to him, or are you stuck just trying to do more for him out of a sense of obligation?

Now is the moment that matters. I beg you to consider the promises of Jesus Christ, and leave you with food for thought from cartoonist Bob Thaves. Either we do things God's way, or like Frank and Ernest, we find we've flunked the biggest final exam of all.

1

FRANK & ERNEST reprinted by permission of Newspaper Enterprise Association, Inc.

Questions to Consider

1. In your own words, what does it mean to be "in Adam"? How does one leave the family of Adam and join the family of Jesus Christ?

2. According to Romans 5:20, what is one purpose of the law? Give an instance from your personal, family, or professional life in which you've noticed that the law (or a law) actually multiplies sin.

3. By yourself, quiz yourself on the Ten Commandments. Is there even one that you have not broken, at least in your heart? What does this tell you about your status before God? Are you a lawbreaker, a sinner, in his sight or not? Remember, the Lord doesn't grade on a curve.

CHAPTER 4

"Let us behave decently, as in the daytime, not in orgies and drunkenness, not in sexual immorality and debauchery, not in dissension and jealousy. Rather, clothe yourselves with the Lord Jesus Christ, and do not think about how to gratify the desires of the sinful nature" (Rom. 13:13-14 NIV).

Our Choice: Answering the Call of the New

Romans 6:1-10

"God Is Dead," blared newspaper headlines in the 1960s, chronicling in print a controversy raging across college campuses. As a seminary graduate involved in my first ministry in Washington state, I was invited to address the issue at a local university. My insistence that God was very much alive and well wasn't fashionable then. Today, however, I believe the pendulum has swung in our country to the awareness that God—or some divine presence—is there. "In God We Trust" has become popular again in our post 9-11 world. We are witnessing an increasing acknowledgment in our fast-paced culture that there must be a creator, a driving entity or force, a God.

On September 11, 2001, I was in Fort Worth on the first week of a Bible teaching tour: destination Starbucks and a non-fat vanilla latte before my noon class at State National. The news wires broke in with the report that one of the twin towers in New York City had been struck. Life in America changed forever as a result of that September morning.

Some weeks later country singer Alan Jackson couldn't sleep, and so he got up and began writing the words to a song asking "where were you when the world stopped turning that September day"? Jackson's lyrics end with:

> I'm just a singer of simple songs
> I'm not a real political man,
> I watch CNN but I'm not sure
> I can tell you the difference in Iraq and Iran,
> But I know Jesus and I talk to God,
> And I remember this from when I was young,
> Faith, hope and love are some good things He gave us,
> And the greatest is love.[1]

America may have changed, but God remains the same, and so does his word.

If the unspeakable happened and every book of the Bible were destroyed except one, I'd hope that the single remaining book would be Paul's letter to the Romans. The apostle's message is that vital. The book is a highly polished looking glass revealing to us our shortcomings and our utter inability to go it alone without God.

As we saw in Romans 5:12-21, each of us must make a decision concerning the claims of Christ. We're born into the family of Adam; we can choose to stay there or we can choose, by faith, to enter into the family of Jesus Christ.

Adam or Christ—these are the only two choices. We're either in Adam, dead in our trespasses and sins, or we're in Christ, prepared for our eternal destiny. Lightness or darkness? These are our only two travel options for eternity.

CHANGING SUBJECTS

In Romans 6, Paul turns from dealing with the salvation of the sinner and begins to talk about the struggles of Christian living. Romans 5 speaks chiefly to the unsaved; Romans 6, 7, and 8 are addressed to believers. Salvation isn't the question in the text any more; instead Paul tells how Christians, possessors of the righteousness of God, may begin to appropriate and reflect that righteousness in daily life.

If you're like the average Christian, you're probably much like the man Ronald Dunn describes in his book *Victory*. Writes Dunn:

> Many Christians are like a man who comes home and finds his house flooded because he forgot to turn off the bathtub faucet. Frantically he grabs a mop and begins sweeping out the water—*but the bathtub faucet is still running wide open.* After a few frenzied swipes, he sees he's making no headway against the water, so he gets a bigger mop. Still no success. Determined to live in a victoriously dry house, he enrolls in a seminar on Effective Mopping Techniques, receives a diploma with a gold seal, and once again wades into the battle. But still the water pours out faster than he can mop it up. He invites a professional mopper to come for a week of intensive mopping. At the end of the week, success is measured by the number of gallons swept out—but more have rushed

> in to take their place. As the situation worsens, he rededicates himself to better mopping, vows he'll never again leave the faucet on, and once more takes up the mop. The bathtub faucet is still running.
>
> Weary and waterlogged, he finally concludes that God never intended him to live in a dry house, so he buys a pair of galoshes and a waterbed and settles down to live the rest of his life in a flooded house.[2]

Is your Christian life too much like that flooded house? Have you contemplated, consecrated, dedicated, and committed yourself to Christ, and then within days, sometimes hours, of that decision, turned around and committed an act of sin that nearly scared you to death? All feelings of victory vanished in the aftermath of the lie you told, the angry outburst you vented. Trying frantically to keep God's commandments, you find your efforts a total washout, and the guilt you feel over your failure is overwhelming.

The answer? Typically the Christian who is experiencing lack of victory in his or her life puts up a good front. Oh, he may pore over a few self-help books, even religious ones, but as his house continues to flood, he mainly tries to keep up appearances. He slaps on paint, puffs up the pillows, plasters on a smile, and acts as if the creek isn't rising at all. Inside, he knows that he's failing miserably. His behavior is far below par and it seems being a Christian hasn't changed him a bit. What he is falls so short of what he ought to be that the hypocrisy of his existence gets to him, causing him to want to shuck the whole idea of living for Christ. He doesn't realize that the faucet is running and the bucket is overflowing *because* he is striving to perform in the flesh—under his own efforts—to please God, and it just cannot be done.

How do we then genuinely begin to reflect the righteousness of God in our day-to-day living? How do we experience authentic victory over sin? How do we Christians break the bondage of performance and learn to develop a relationship with God that will change us into his image? These are some of the questions the apostle Paul deals with in Romans 6. Let's read on and discover how to begin to enjoy the new life we have in Christ Jesus.

THE NEW ORDER—ROMANS 6:1-2

MOTIVATED FOR CHANGE

Let's recall Romans 5, which reveals that God's law given to Moses has no dominion over us once we become Christians. The law shows us our sin; it puts that sin to our account (5:13), but it is not a standard God expects or instructs us to strive to attain. Remember, the presence of the law actually increases our sin (5:20), resulting in the expansion of God's grace, his unmerited favor. Paul explains what this means as Romans 6 opens.

Where sin is, God's grace abounds all the more. Christians are forgiven for the sins that were, that are, and that are to come. But this principle, if misunderstood, can also cause problems. For instance, such questions as these may arise. If God's grace increases in proportion to sin, why don't believers increase their sinning? That way there will be more grace! And since the law has no authority over us as believers, why not sin? God will forgive us! We're free to disobey! There are honest-to-goodness Christians who actually live—or think about living—by that philosophy. This mind-set creates a lackadaisical attitude toward the holiness of God. It becomes easy to rationalize a divorce, an affair, an abusive outburst, a dishonest action. It's okay—believers aren't perfect, just forgiven—why not sin up a storm? When you get into trouble, just dial 1 John 1:9!

The Bible says otherwise. Paul begins Romans 6 with

this question, "What then shall we say? Are we to continue in sin in order that grace might increase?"(6:1 DAV). In verse 2 the apostle gives his reply, "May it never be!" The mind which assumes that it is okay to intentionally persist in verbal, physical, sexual, or psychological disobedience, or anything contrary to God's principles, is sick indeed. When we enter into a relationship with Jesus Christ, we come to know someone who cared enough for us to die on a cross. Our sins nailed him there. Can we legitimately figure it's all right to choose consciously to disobey him? No way! When we have the option of intentionally increasing our sin, we must exclaim with Paul, "May it never be!" Paul might as well have said, "Perish the thought!" or "Not a chance!" or "God forbid!" He is repulsed by the idea. A recovering alcoholic would call it "stinkin' thinkin'"!

Think of it this way. As Christians, we're in a relationship with Christ, and our acts of sin harm that relationship. They displease the Lord. They grieve and quench the Spirit who indwells us. The Bible promises that Jesus will never leave or forsake us (Matt. 28:20), but our friendship, our sweet fellowship with him, will be broken if we consistently allow patterns of sin to characterize our life. We're called to develop an increasing awareness of those things that offend the Father and bring him displeasure. These are to be cut from our life, *not because the law says we must, but because we've been brought into a vital, living union with Jesus Christ and we love him.* He died for us, and we, over a period of time of Christian growth, should gradually become so sensitized to him and to sin itself that we stop certain wrong practices. It's a process, often a slow-moving process, and God's Spirit himself will empower the effort, as we'll note in Romans 8.

Marilyn's story is a classic illustration of how victory over sin comes, in time, as the result of a growing relationship with the heavenly Father. When Marilyn first accepted the Lord as a college student, she drank in biblical knowledge as if it were cool water and she a hot, dusty, desert straggler finding an oasis. Shortly after her conversion, God's word and Spirit convinced Marilyn that she was interested in a young man at school for all the wrong reasons, so she broke off their relationship. Time passed. She married someone else, had a little boy, quit her teaching job to stay home with the tot and the baby sister who soon followed. Her husband, Bob, made more than enough money to support the family. On the surface, things looked wonderful.

In the midst of setting up marriage and starting a family, though, something happened to Marilyn. Her spiritual life began to seem dry and dusty. Oh, she and Bob and the kids attended church, but the word held no excitement for her. Realizing something had to be done, Marilyn became involved with a local women's Bible study ministry. Slowly she found her love of God's word returning. She realized her absence had displeased the Lord, and she began joyfully to reestablish communications with him. Once this happened, another area of her life rose up to confront her with its ugliness: her temper. Her quick retorts often sliced into her kids, husband, and friends. The Holy Spirit worked in her heart to show Marilyn that her temper needed taming. She realized how much her anger offended the Lord and hurt their relationship. Daily, sometimes hourly, sometimes minute by minute, she commits herself afresh to the power source, the Spirit of God, to control her temper and it is working! Marilyn's angry outbursts are fewer and farther between. Her temper is being tamed, not because she has to quiet it in order to fulfill the mandates of the law, but because she wants to, because she is responding to a growing relationship with the God she loves, and she is willing to rely on his Spirit to work in her.

Think of any close human relationship you enjoy. Many times you'll change things about yourself in response to the one you care for; you'll do things for him or her that you'll do for no one else. If you've got teenagers around the house, watch them to see this principle in action. Now, they won't change for their parents. But when Junior's interest in a certain young lady is aroused, that boy who never wore socks suddenly spends hours in hot showers. When the steam dissipates, a new sound is heard from the bathroom: the hum of a blow dryer. The kid who favored dingy tee shirts now begs Mom to iron his shirts. He splashes on cologne, and Saturday mornings find him vacuuming out his truck in preparation for the evening's date. Girls are just as bad—maybe worse. The daughter who months before was a gawky adolescent reaches puberty and starts to spend more time in front of the mirror than she does in front of the TV—unless, of course, she's on the phone or the internet. Crimping irons blow fuses and cosmetics dress up a face that suddenly looks too mature. Eyebrows beg to be waxed, nails to be manicured. The changes arrive not because our teens have been told to clean up their acts, but because they want to please their peers.

The principle is the same in the Christian life. We begin to give up our sinful ways because we respond to the relationship we have with Christ, not because a list of do's and don'ts imprints itself on our heart. We aren't likely to want to change for a stranger, either. The more we know of the Lord, the closer we grow to him, and the more we want to please him. It's a cycle, one behavior feeding on the other, as we're enabled by the Holy Spirit to, in the words of the writer of the book of Hebrews, "run with perseverance the race marked out for us" (12:1 NIV).

DEAD TO SIN

In Romans, Paul is thoroughly appalled at the thought that anyone who has received the Lord Jesus Christ as savior would even consider consciously sinning so that God's grace might abound. He continues in Romans 6:2, "How shall we who died to sin still live in it?" (DAV).

As Paul tells us, Christians are dead to sin. What this means is when Jesus Christ died on the cross nearly two thousand years ago, believers died with him. We died to the penalty of sin. We'll suffer earthly consequences—traffic tickets, jail sentences, illnesses, and even death—because of our sins, but a heavenly reward is ours for eternity. We escape the permanent spiritual death we would deserve were we judged solely on our own merit.

But there is more. As Christians, we are not only dead to the penalty of sin, we are also dead to the rule of sin in our life. Sin's domination over us is technically ended the moment we come to faith in Christ. We were all, remember, born in Adam. With the sin nature, the old nature, which we inherited from Adam, it was inevitable that we would sin. We lived under a dictatorship, without choice, controlled by the nature we received from Adam. Everything we did, even seemingly good things, was tainted by that adamic nature.

The difference between then and now is that once we accept Christ, we die to the power of the dictatorship of sin and enter into the freedom of the democracy of God. We suddenly have a choice as Christians, because at the moment of our salvation, not only does the Holy Spirit indwell us, but we also receive a new, divine nature, a new disposition. Paul speaks of the old and new natures in his letter to the Colossians, where he writes: "Do not lie to one another, since you laid aside the old self with its evil practices, and have put on the new self who is being renewed to a true knowledge according to the image of the One who created him (Col. 3:9-10 NASB; see also Eph. 4:22-24).

When confronted with the opportunity to sin, we now have a decision to make: will we respond to the old nature or will we respond to the new? The new nature or disposition hasn't replaced the old. The old is still there, ready to rise up the second we allow it. Every time a Christian commits an act of sin, he is responding to his old nature, that "dictator" who has been deposed positionally but is still a threat practically. The new nature is incapable of sin, and the divine life that came to dwell within us in the person of the Holy Spirit can only act righteously. But we still have a choice to make. Will we respond to the old or new?

I said earlier that we were dead to sin as Christians. That is true, but what is also equally true is that *sin is not dead to us*. Sin is a very real power in the world today, as newspaper headlines of murder, mayhem, and manipulation scream to remind us. As we approach Romans 7, we'll see that the apostle Paul was far from free from sin himself! There are struggles in the Christian life. Although our position is that of people free from sin's power, it is almost reflex action sometimes to respond to the old nature, which lurks ever ready in the wings.

Picture the scene. You're driving along the interstate, humming "Let's just praise the Lord" to yourself. Everything is cool. Then some guy (okay, some jerk) in his little black sports car cuts in front of you and you have to swerve and brake. As the tires squeal, the old reflex kicks in—a tenth of a second later, if you're not hollering stuff that would make a pro wrestler blush, you're at least muttering it under your breath. It can happen that quickly; the split second you give the old nature an entrance, you're a goner. During my 60 years of being a Christian, there have been numerous times when my old nature has been in the saddle, fellowship with God broken, and Satan clapping his hands with glee. I'm grateful that the older I get, the sweeter the fellowship and the shorter the times of stubborn stress under the old nature's control. I am slowly learning what pleases the Lord.

Christians who are not experiencing victory over sin are answering the call of that old nature. Quite possibly doing this has become a habit pattern. They may try to "be good," but they go about it the wrong way. They struggle with keeping the law, never relying on the new nature through the power of the Holy Spirit to give them the victory. And yet apart from the Spirit, no one can be victorious over sin. His power is necessary to energize the new nature.

A fellow approached me after Bible class several years ago, sharing the following with a huge smile, "God is doing something incredible in my life. I am discovering the sheer and unutterable joy of responding to my new nature." Friends, that is authentic Christianity. That is letting the rubber meet the road. Remember, responding to the new is a process, but as we become sensitive to the desires of the new nature, we begin to experience the terrific joy felt by my friend.

It's like a marriage. The more sensitive we become to the needs of our mate, the better we are able to deal with the areas that hurt and help, and the happier we are in the relationship. The same can be said of our relationship with our children. The more we know them, the more we honestly listen to them, the more we are aware of what it is like to be eight, thirteen, or seventeen, the better our relationship with them will be. It won't be free of conflict, but endowed with understanding.

Sadly, we base many relationships on how others perform. We judge. We wound. We love conditionally instead of unconditionally. Horizontal relationships are often reflections of the vertical too. When we put ourselves on a performance basis with God, we ache because we fall so short. We wound him because we try so hard to do rather than to be. God's message to us is essentially this, "I wish you'd become sensitive to the new nature I put within you! By the power of the indwelling Spirit who energizes your new nature, you could begin to experience victory in your life! You could begin to know joy. You could quit trying to perform for me. You'd focus on deepening our relationship by becoming sensitive to things that hurt it." And then we'd be exclaiming with the apostle, "How shall we who died to sin still live in it?" (Rom. 6:2 DAV).

A CHANGE OF IDENTITY—ROMANS 6:3-7

When we recognize the ugliness of sin, and how terrible the old nature is when it responds to sin, we become aware of the fact that we as believers must avoid sin or deal with it out of love. We must choose to answer the call of the new because we love God; obedience is the supernatural outgrowth of our ever-deepening union with him.

Why we must not persist in sin is considered next by the apostle Paul. "Or do you not know," he continues in Romans 6:3, "that all of us who have been baptized into Christ Jesus have been baptized into His death?"(DAV). *Baptism*—that theological term has sparked much controversy, but the apostle is not referring here to the ordinance of water baptism. Water baptism is merely a picture of what is going on in Romans 6. The word for baptism that Paul uses is the Greek word *baptizo*, meaning "to change identification" or "to become identified with."

As Christians, we've changed our identity. We have left the family of Adam and become baptized into, or identified with, Christ. Imagine a yardstick that has been dipped in black paint and allowed to dry. The yardstick is black in color; it is identified with that black paint. Now imagine that this black yardstick is then dipped into a can of red paint. Its color changes. It is now identified with the red paint; it has been "baptized" into the red. When we came to know Christ as savior, we permanently changed our identification, too. No longer stained with the blackness of our sin, we are covered with the righteousness of Christ's death, of his shed blood! The Holy Spirit is the seal; he comes into our heart as a permanent resident to mark our *permanent* change of identification from unsaved to saved.

Paul speaks of our baptism, our change of identification,

in several other passages in the Bible, such as Galatians 3:26-27:

> For in Christ Jesus you are all sons of God through faith. For as many [of you] as were baptized into Christ [into a spiritual union and communion with Christ, the Anointed One, the Messiah] have put on (clothed yourselves with) Christ. (AMP)

And in 1 Corinthians 12:13, the apostle states the following, "For by one Spirit we were all baptized into one body, whether Jews or Greeks, whether slaves or free, and we were all made to drink of one Spirit" (NASB).

The Holy Spirit takes us out of Adam and places us in Christ when we trust Jesus as savior. Christ becomes our new leader. Paul gives an illustration of this idea in 1 Corinthians 10:1-2, where he tells of the exodus of the children of Israel from Egypt in the days of Moses: "For I do not want you to be unaware, brethren, that our fathers were all under the cloud, and all passed through the sea; and all were baptized into Moses in the cloud and in the sea" (NASB).

Pharaoh's armies pursued the Israelites after they left the land of Egypt in the time of the exodus. As the Israelites reached the edge of the Red Sea, with the Egyptian chariots thundering in the background, escape seemed impossible. "Do not be afraid. Stand firm and you will see the deliverance the Lord will bring you today," ordered Moses (Exod. 14:13 NIV). Miraculously, the corridors of the Red Sea parted and the Israelites stepped onto dry land and followed Moses across. As they followed Moses, they were baptized into him—they were identified with him. They were making a commitment to him. He was their leader. Using the same logic to understand Romans 6:3, we recognize that as Christians we become followers of Christ. We are baptized into him. He becomes our leader, and we commit ourselves to him.

Not only are we baptized into Christ, but we are baptized into, identified with, his death! Being identified with Christ's death is essential for us. Why? Think of it this way. When you die, you are freed from any obligation to the penalty of the law. Earthly jails are not filled with dead men. Even the condemned on death row are still breathing. Yet when we become alive in Christ, we also become eternally identified with his death.

A story Ronald Dunn includes in *Dead Reckoning* illustrates this well, and I'd like to paraphrase it here. Let's say that while you are sitting here reading this, a store down the street is robbed. Sirens wail. Police officers jump out of their patrol cars. Witnesses are interviewed.

"Did you see the guy who did it?" asks Officer Maloney of the shopkeeper.

"Sure did."

"Did he look familiar?"

"Yes," replies the victim. "It was George Washington."

"What? You mean the fellow who chopped down the cherry tree? Impossible! He died two hundred years ago!"

And of course, George Washington is reckoned not guilty of this crime, because he's already dead in the eyes of justice.[3]

What about you? If you've received Christ and you commit an act of sin, you too have already died in the eyes of the eternal chief justice, God. You died with Christ on the cross.

"See Don Anderson down there?" says the accuser to the Lord in the heavenlies. "Anderson just committed an act of sin. He's guilty. You've got to condemn him to hell."

The Lord Jesus reaches for a book on the shelf and opens it to section A. "Anderson, Don," he says, his eyes scanning the page. "I'm sorry, Lucifer, Don's name is listed here. He died two thousand years ago. He isn't guilty of what you've accused him."

It's that miraculously, wonderfully simple.

What inexpressible joy and peace are ours when we realize the implications of our baptism into Christ's death. We'll not be condemned for our sins because *we're already dead in the eyes of justice.*

THE POTENTIAL: A NEW LIFE

Positionally, as Christians, we are dead to the penalty of sin in the eyes of God. Positionally, we are free from sin. The problem is not our position. The problem is our practice.

"Therefore," continues Paul, "we have been buried with him through baptism into death, in order that in the same manner as Christ was raised up from the dead through the glory of the Father, so also we too might walk in a new life" (Rom. 6:4 DAV). Yes, we are identified with Christ's death. But we are also identified with his burial and his resurrection. When God the Father looks at us, he sees us as men and women who have died with Christ, been buried with him, and have experienced resurrection with him. The result? It's so that we "might walk in a new life," according to the apostle Paul.

Christians, dead to the old life, have the potential of enjoying a brand new one! Paul isn't just talking about the life we'll live with God in eternity, either. He's not just talking about the sweet by-and-by, but the sweltering, seamy, seedy here and now. The new nature provides the potential for us to live this new life, one in which we experience progressive victory over sin. As we'll see from Paul's experiences in Romans 7, our practice of sin doesn't immediately vanish as we accept Christ, but the possibility is there for us to steadily conquer our shortcomings. The old nature is always ready to rear its wretched head, but for the

Christian, victory is possible where it once was hopeless.

Paul's logic continues: "For if we have become united with Him (Christ) in the likeness of His death certainly we shall be also in the likeness of His resurrection" (Rom. 6:5 DAV). When we pass from Adam into Christ, we are united with the Lord. We are brought into a living union with him. It's like a marriage in which there can be no divorce. Remember your marriage vows? The preacher probably said something like this after you said, "I do": "And these two have become one flesh. What God hath joined together, let no man put asunder."

Our earthly marriage is a reflection of the union with Christ we have as believers. Think of your own wedding day. On the honeymoon, probably everything about your mate seemed perfect. It's only after—often soon after—that you both notice the snoring, scratchy feet, and irritating habits. Some couples let the differences drive a wedge between them; others adjust, becoming more sensitive to each other and changing accordingly.

In our "marriage" to the Lord Jesus Christ, we are called to become more sensitive to the things that keep us from becoming closer to him. He is perfect; the chasm exists because we are not. The gap closes as we respond to the new nature instead of the old. We must be willing to let God deal with areas of sin. The key to doing this lies in drawing closer to Christ. "I am the vine, you are the branches; he who abides in Me, and I in him, he bears much fruit; for apart from Me you can do nothing," says Jesus in John 15:5 (NASB).

Believers are branches connected to a living vine, grafted on a living trunk, a vital savior. His life flows through us; his nature dwells within us; his Spirit stands by to give us the victory. We do not have to answer the call of the old nature any longer. It's revolutionary!

Christians are even able to become free from the compulsion to sin! Paul echoes this in verses 6-7, where he says, "our old self was crucified with Him, in order that the sinful body may be done away with, that we should no longer be slaves to sin; for the one who died has been freed from sin" (Rom. 6:6-7 DAV; see also Gal. 2:19-20). The "old self" to which Paul refers is our old position in Adam, our old identification with him. Once we received Christ, that old position becomes completely null and void in the eyes of God. Our old self has been crucified with Christ. Our body is freed from the condemnation of having to be a vehicle of sin. We no longer must be slaves to sin, but are freed from its dominion. The potential to sin will always be present, but it'll also always involve a choice we make. We are, as I mentioned earlier, now living in a democracy, not under a dictatorship.

LIVING TO GOD—ROMANS 6:8-10

We've died with Christ. The wanted posters have been ripped from the wall and we've been reckoned dead and buried in the eyes of the law. "Now if we died with Christ, we are believing that we shall also live with Him, knowing that Christ, having been raised from the dead, no longer is dying. Death no longer is exercising lordship over Him" writes Paul in (Rom. 6:8-9 DAV). Here the apostle is talking in part about eternal life. Christ has been raised from the dead. Christ is alive. Someday we'll join him. But Paul is also talking about the abundant life here and now. The believer's everlasting life in fellowship with the Father begins at the moment of salvation. It's not just a death benefit—it's a life-changing reality!

Paul continues speaking of Christ, "For the death He died, He died to sin once for all; but the life He lives, He lives to God" (Rom. 6:10 DAV). Christ's physical death was a one-time-only occurrence, an isolated instance in which the sin of the world rested on his shoulders and the purchase price of every believer was paid for with his blood. Christ's death occurred but once; his life continues. He is alive today!

If we carefully consider Paul's words, we see that Jesus lived a life open to God the Father. He lived under the scrutiny of God the Father. In the 33 years he walked on the earth in human flesh, he committed not a single sin or a solitary transgression. If he had been less than perfect, his sacrifice would have been considered insufficient or blemished by God the Father.

A believer's life is open to God too. What is there certainly isn't spotless. Make no mistake about it; we cannot hide from him. "And there is no creature hidden from His sight, but all things are open and laid bare to the eyes of Him with whom we have to do," states the writer of the book of Hebrews (4:13 NASB). The Lord knows what we thought today. He knows what we did. He is aware of those acts of compromise, those areas of failure, those unnecessary words and regrettable actions. Still, he loves us unconditionally. Still he's committed to us for eternity. In our unending relationship united with him, we begin to discover that we have the potential for victory over sin. We've got to quit trying and start trusting, and as we'll see in the second half of Romans 6, there will be a marvelous result: we'll bear fruit for God.

STEPS TO DEEPENING THE RELATIONSHIP

In Philippians 3, Paul states that one of his main purposes in living is that he might know Christ fully and personally. "I count all things to be loss in view of the surpassing value of knowing Christ Jesus my Lord," he writes in Philippians 3:8 (NASB; see also 3:10). Paul knew that part of desiring to get to know Christ better and better involved learning what things in his life offended the Lord and kept their relationship from deepening (see 2 Tim. 2:3-4, Titus 3:8, 1 Thess. 4:1).

How do we go about doing as Paul did? To begin with, we've got to immerse ourselves in scripture, for in it we find the expression of the will of God. We must, like newborn babes, long for the milk of the word; from it we learn what helps and what hurts the relationship. The truths of the sacred page must not remain only in our mind, but must sink into our heart, causing us to cry to God for his power. As God's word works in us, we begin to live for only one purpose: pleasing Jesus Christ. And we do this not because he demands it but because we want it. Our willing obedience is, to him, high praise from us. The song of the psalmist becomes ours, "I delight to do thy will, O my God: yea, thy law is within my heart" (40:8 KJV).

THE FAMILY LABORATORY

As we've seen, Christians enjoy a union with Christ closer than any relationship possible on earth. But of all human relationships, perhaps none prepares us for relating to God more thoroughly than marriage and parenting. Marriage is a laboratory in which two individuals learn to live unselfishly for each other. A marriage is meant to be a progressively more harmonious and richer song for two in which problems are resolved and offenses dealt with properly. Nothing is more frustrating for a husband or wife than to think that his or her spouse misunderstands, and little is more gratifying than realizing the reverse is true.

As a marriage is designed to teach us about our union with God through Christ, being a parent can do much the same thing. Conflicts happen in all families. No couple consistently wins the *Newlywed Game*, and no parents ever escape disagreeing with their kids. Yet just because we disagree with, argue with, or even offend our spouse or children doesn't mean the marriage is over or the family shattered. Communication may be broken, but the sparring partners are still related. In the same way, when a Christian responds to his old nature and commits a sin, his relationship with God is not nullified. Communication—fellowship with

God—will be broken until things are straightened out, but the sinner is still a child of God. He just isn't on speaking terms with the Lord for the moment (Isa. 59:1-2; 1 Pet. 3:7).

With five kids, Pearl and I have had ample opportunities to test the principle that fellowship can be broken while relationship remains intact. I remember the weekend our youngest son turned 15. I'd been out of town that week on a teaching tour; and when Friday finally arrived, I anticipated spending some special time with Pearl and the two children still at home: Andy, the 15-year-old, and Julea, our daughter who was then 13.

If your children are small, let me warn you. There will come a time when they hit 13 or 14, and suddenly their ideas about schedules become quite definite. They have their own opinions about what weekends are made for, and their plans don't always include Mom and Dad. Incidentally, this phenomenon continues through college. Sometime later, when grandchildren come, there is a reversal and Mom and Dad—Grandma and Gramps, that is—begin to figure prominently in plans again, especially when babysitting is an issue!

On this particular weekend, Andy breezed in before dinner. "Let's go to the Lee game!" he said. Over a span of some ten years Anderson offspring attended Robert E. Lee High School in Tyler, Texas. Julea's graduation in 1982 marked the end of an era. At any rate, I was thrilled that Andy wanted us all to attend the football game that night. We'd get a couple of hours together as a family, which would be super!

We checked with Pearl. "Sure, let's go," she said immediately. It was all set. The only problem was I had forgotten about Julea. In she sauntered about ten minutes later. She'd been over at her friend Barbara's, just down the block.

"What's going on?" Julea asked.

"We're going to the Lee game," I told her.

"But I don't want to go to the Lee game," came the less than enthusiastic reply.

"C'mon, Julea, it'll be fun."

"I don't want to go!"

"Honey, it's already decided. We're going."

"Well, can Barbara come too?"

Barbara was a nice girl, but Julea and she couldn't have spent much more time together if they'd been Siamese twins. Still, if Barbara went, at least we'd get Julea too—and in a halfway decent mood.

"I guess so," I sighed.

Out Julea ran to Barbara's house. Five minutes went by, then ten. Fifteen passed, then twenty ... and still there was no sign of the two girls. It was ten after seven and kick-off was at seven-thirty. Was I in a stew!

"Pearl, Andy, let's get going!" I rounded them up and we all jumped in the car—everyone but Julea. I backed the car out of the driveway and headed for Barbara's. Julea and she were in the front yard.

"We've got to go!" I said loud enough for the whole street to hear.

"But, Dad," Julea answered, "Barbara's mom is out walking or jogging or something. We haven't been able to find her to ask if Barb can go."

"I'm sorry about that, but we're gonna miss the kick-off. Get in the car!"

"But, Dad!"

"Julea, get in this car NOW!"

And she came. Slam! She banged the door shut. The thick silence in the car was punctuated only by the sounds of sniffles and choked sobs. This certainly was not the fun-filled family event I had anticipated. Julea began crying more loudly. Pearl was fuming at me for my display in our neighborhood. Andy was looking out the window, sorry he had suggested the whole thing. And so in virtual silence, interrupted only by sobs from the back seat, we drove to the football game. It was 7:29, one minute to kick-off, when I pulled the car off the road and stopped.

"Look," I turned around to face my accusers, "I'm sorry. I really didn't mean for things to turn out this way, but they did. I was selfish and thoughtless. I was wrong. I know you kids are getting older. We've only got a few years left with you before you'll be out on your own. My schedule's so heavy that I just want to be with you when I'm home. Please forgive me." We prayed together, went on to the ball game, and although we missed the kick-off, we had a good time.

Let's think about what happened. Just because I offended in the relationship, was I no longer my children's father? Was I no longer Pearl's husband? No! I was still married; I was still their dad. But something had come into the relationship to hurt it. The problem needed to be dealt with, and it was.

The same thing can be true of your relationship with the Lord. How are you and God doing? You're his child if you've received Christ as savior—that's not going to change. But how is the relationship going? Maybe there is something in your life that's offending the Lord. Victory is absent. There's only coldness and distance between you. If that's true, guess who moved? Not God, but you.

What can you do about it? Swallow your pride, get down on your knees, and admit it to God. "The righteous cry out, and the Lord hears them; he delivers them from all their troubles. The Lord is close to the brokenhearted and saves those who are crushed in spirit" (Ps. 34:17-18 NIV). Tell him about the area in your life that you feel is a barrier between the two of you. Ask him, by his grace and his Spirit, to energize your new nature and give you the victory. And then, moment by moment, begin to rely on his strength, not your own, to help you overcome the problem. Wait patiently and watch him work. Watch him begin to transform your home, your marriage, yourself. Watch people begin to see someone different in you, because in the confines of that human body of yours, the potential is there for them to see the risen Christ. Christianity isn't just an insurance policy for the hereafter; it's a progressive life in which victory over sin can be steadily won by God's own Spirit.

Questions to Consider

1. What is Paul's response to those who consider intentionally increasing their sins so that God's grace might abound (see 6:1-2)? What happens to our fellowship with the Lord when we consistently allow patterns of sin to characterize our life? If we're Christians, can our relationship with God be terminated because of continual sin?

2. What does Paul mean when he says we are "baptized into Christ Jesus" (6:3)?

3. Paul tells us that as believers we are dead to sin (6:2). In your own words, explain what this means. What is meant by the observation that sin is not dead to us?

CHAPTER 5

"I delight greatly in the Lord; my soul rejoices in my God. For he has clothed me with garments of salvation and arrayed me in a robe of righteousness" (Isa. 61:10a NIV).

Dealing with a Deposed Dictator

Romans 6:11-23

Songwriter Jim Connor corralled some memories of Grandma's house that might ring a bell or two with some of you old duffers. The late John Denver made Connor's lyrics famous in a popular song. Picture in your mind that big four-poster with down pillows, patchwork quilt, and crocheted blankets piled high. To small eyes, it looked like a mountain ... but it was only Grandma's bed: nine feet tall, six feet wide, soft and spongy. No doubt it was sturdy around the ends and edges but surely sagged in the middle!

Firm on both ends and sagging in the middle—what a graphic description that is of the lives of many Christians, too. We look like we have it all together; but come pressure in the soft spots and we buckle and bend. We have assurance of our salvation. We look ahead expectantly to the joys of heaven. But in the here and now our spirits drag the ground, and as we try to influence the world for God, the most we seem to do is kick up a little dust.

The worst part of it is that it's always the same old thing tripping us up: sin. Paul teaches us in the first part of Romans 6 that Christians are in a living union with Christ Jesus (6:5). It is such a close relationship that we are the branches and Jesus the vine. His life flows through us. Because of the intensity of our relationship with him, our attitude toward sin should be changed once we receive Christ as savior. In daily life, believers can begin to reflect the righteousness that is ours in Jesus Christ.

The reflection of righteousness is a process. When we come to Christ, we receive a perfect standing before God that will never be changed. Despite this perfect standing, we still fail. We make mistakes. We sin. So we dedicate and consecrate, and still the picture of our life is too closely captured by the poster I have, which reads, "Now that I've finally got it all together, I can't remember where I put it!" We fall so short of what we think we ought to be that we throw up our hands in exasperation and wonder if that's all there is. Being a Christian hasn't done a thing for us (evidently) except to cause us to feel guilty! Slowly the realization dawns that living for Christ isn't what we thought it was cracked up to be. We may even wonder if we're really saved at all.

What is especially discouraging is that the old nature still lies within us, dormant but ever ready to spring into action the moment we give it the chance. As we discussed in the last chapter; we may live in the democracy of God and the sin nature may be a deposed dictator; but it's still a tangible threat. Sin is a problem for every Christian. The beautiful thing is that God knows all about our problems, and he has given us tools and power for winning the victory.

Oh, you might run across a fellow sometime who

figures he has it made. "I'm no sinner!" he'll exclaim. "I'm saved. I haven't sinned in 25 years!" I always ask such spiritual heavyweights if they're proud of themselves and of their accomplishments. "Sure am!" they smugly respond, and then the contradiction of it all slowly dawns as they realize that pride goeth before a fall. Their theology is inconsistent, because their pride is as great a sin as Hank's cheating on his income tax or Helen's endless stream of gossip. Sin by any other name, including pride, is still sin (Prov. 6:16-19, James 4:6).

What the Holy Spirit offers us through the words of the apostle Paul in the second half of Romans 6 is a formula for the process of winning the battle against sin. It's not an automatic cure-all. You won't rid yourself of sin instantaneously and completely by following the steps in chapter 6. Complete freedom from sin in your life won't come till Christ calls you home to glory. But in the meantime I heartily recommend the wisdom of Romans 6 as a practical guide for overcoming specific areas of disobedience in your life, one by one. The game plan is clear, and it will work.

Is a terrible temper your downfall? Do you struggle with integrity in your business? Is it easier for you to tell a white lie than to be completely candid with others? Is lust a problem? Unfaithfulness? Materialism? Selfishness? Let's turn to Romans 6, where Paul helps us learn how to deal practically with that deposed dictator, the old nature, who affects us all.

THE ATTITUDE—ROMANS 6:11

Step one in experiencing victory over sin involves a change in attitude. "So also you consider yourselves to be dead to sin, but alive to God in Christ Jesus," says Paul in Romans 6:11 (DAV). Victory begins with the deliberate adoption of the attitude that we are dead to sin but alive to God through Christ. In other words, from heaven's perspective we are free from the penalty and power of sin, so on earth we ought to begin living like it. We must think that way!

God's truth is first positional, then practical, as we appropriate it by faith. The great doctrines and principles of scripture must be squeezed into shoe leather and brought onto the pavement of everyday living. The position we enjoy as Christians is one of freedom from the domination of sin. Whatever happens, we're saved for eternity and will not suffer spiritual death or separation from God. But if we don't believe the truth that we've been freed both from sin's penalty and from its power, life down here won't be very pretty. We must clothe ourselves with the attitude that we are dead to sin. We must believe God! His truth is absolute, but it's our choice whether or not to take him at his word.

What does it mean to adopt the attitude that we are dead to sin but alive to Christ? In answering that, let's first talk about what it *doesn't* mean. It doesn't mean we suck in our stomach, grit our teeth, and grab our bootstraps to pull ourselves up to a level of perfection. We'll never make it. What it does mean is that *we put our faith in the fact that God is adequate to give us victory over sin.* It means we believe that we are free to be what we already are in Christ!

As a man "thinks within himself, so he is," says Proverbs 23:7a (NASB). It's crucial that we think right if we hope to be victorious over sin. In athletics, mental toughness is a mainspring to victory, and so it is in the Christian life. Peter was perhaps thinking along those lines when he wrote these instructions, "Therefore, gird your minds for action, keep sober in spirit, fix your hope completely on the grace to be brought to you at the revelation of Jesus Christ" (1 Pet. 1:13 NASB). Paul, too, addresses the topic often: "Have this attitude in yourselves which was also in Christ Jesus" (Phil. 2:5 NASB). "We are taking every thought captive to the obedience of Christ" (2 Cor. 10:5b NASB).

PART ONE: DEAD TO SIN

Satan loves it when we think wrongly. Once we accept Christ, Satan can't keep us out of the kingdom of heaven, so he settles for manipulating our minds. He sneaks subtly into our thoughts and affects our attitudes. If he can prevent us from believing that we're dead to sin, he won't have won the ball game, but he'll have surely robbed us of a few critical innings.

What were your first thoughts this morning? Did you start the day with any of these gripes: "Oh, good grief—it's morning! I don't want to get out of bed!"? If you did, Satan already won the first inning of the day. When he gets the first thought, you might as well sink into the pillows for another 30 minutes rather than face the cold, clear light of day. With a rude awakening like that, by the time your snooze alarm sounds for the fourth time and your feet finally hit the floor, your outlook is probably so negative that it's a miracle if God has a chance to speak to you at all that morning. You're probably running too late to have some quiet, quality prayer and study time with him. You don't feel like it anyway. The outcome of the A.M. is already decided. You've surrendered a key period of the day. Satan has snagged you. The psalmist knew how to start off right: "The Lord has done this, and it is marvelous in our eyes. This is the day the Lord has made; let us rejoice and be glad in it" (Ps. 118:23-24 NIV).

Satan can chisel away at our mind, so the apostle Paul's prescription for dealing practically with sin in our life starts with an attitude: *we've got to reckon ourselves dead to sin!* God's word says it; we believe it; that settles it.

Think of Abraham. When the Lord first promised him he would be the father of many nations, he was 75 years old and childless (Gen. 12:2). His wife was 65 and barren. Yet, as Paul writes in Romans 4:18, "Who being beyond hope upon the basis of hope (Abraham) believed" God's promises

(DAV). Twenty-five years later; as Abraham approached the century mark and Sarah closed in on 90, God gave them the amazing news flash that within a year they would have a son (Gen. 17:21; 18:10ff). Despite two and a half decades of waiting, Paul tells us that Abraham "staggered not at the promise of God through unbelief; but was strong in faith, giving glory to God" (Rom. 4:20 KJV). Throughout his life, despite heavy doses of delay, Abraham's attitude stayed, for the most part, right on target: he believed in the Lord's adequacy and ability to fulfill his promises. So must we. While we've not been called to be patriarchs of nations, we have been told that we are dead to sin. The logical thing for us to do, based on the veracity of God's word, is to recognize that as a fact and reckon ourselves dead to sin. We must believe God!

PART TWO: ALIVE TO CHRIST

And let's remember the rest of verse 11. We are also to reckon ourselves alive to God through Jesus Christ. In Christ we have everything we need. He is alive in us, providing the base for victory and for righteousness. In the words of Charles Wesley:

> He breaks the power of canceled sin,
> He sets the prisoner free;
> His blood can make the foulest clean;
> His blood availed for me.

Our proper response is echoed by another hymnist:

> Jesus, I am resting, resting
> In the joy of what Thou art;
> I am finding out the greatness
> Of Thy loving heart.

Victory begins with a mind-set. What a man is thinking will eventually be displayed in his actions. Solomon agrees: "Above all else, guard your heart, for it is the wellspring of life" (Prov. 4:23 NIV; see also Phil. 4:8, 2 Cor. 10:5). Satan knows that the mind is the citadel of action, so there is where he lobs his shots. Wrong thoughts about God, ourselves, our fellow man, and our circumstances stifle growth and stop victory. A misdirected human will provides a perfect setup for Satan to lead us into sin.

THE WILL—ROMANS 6:12

Step one in conquering sin involves an attitude. Step two involves the will. "Therefore," continues Paul in verse 12, "do not let sin reign in your mortal body so that you are obeying its desires" (DAV). In other words, take your stand. If gossip is your problem, determine right now—before the phone rings and you're tempted to talk too much—that you'll not gossip. You've already adopted the attitude that you are dead to the penalty and power of gossip. Now willfully choose not to let gossip reign in you. The same goes for whatever area of disobedience the Holy Spirit and God's word show you in your life. Paul gives us a command to take our stand! "Be on the alert, stand firm in the faith, act like men, be strong" (1 Cor. 16:13 NASB).

Why? When you and I as Christians willfully continue in a pattern of sin, we stand in the way of the purpose of God in our life, which is to daily make us more and more like Christ. "But we all, with unveiled face beholding as in a mirror the glory of the Lord, are being transformed into the same image from glory to glory, just as from the Lord, the Spirit" (2 Cor. 3:18 NASB). 1 Peter 1:15 says, "But like the Holy One who called you, be holy yourselves also in all your behavior" (NASB). 1Thessalonians 4:3a states, "For this is the will of God, your sanctification" (NASB). We are dead to sin, remember, *but sin is not dead to us.* Sin is powerful, and we have the option of choosing to respond to the old nature and answering its call. God doesn't want us to respond to the old. "May it never be!" exclaims Paul earlier in Romans 6:2 (DAV). Yet God gives us free will in the matter.

It is crucial for the Christian to take the advice of the apostle Paul in Romans 6:12. If we fail to reckon with that twelfth verse, if we allow sin to reign in us, if we refuse to let God deal with a specific sin area and we continually obey the desire of the old nature in that area, we're asking for trouble. As Christians we are in a relationship with a loving God. His very life is flowing through us! If we consciously continue in a pattern of sin, we're desecrating our body, the temple that belongs to him. "Or do you not know," writes Paul, "that your body is a temple of the Holy Spirit who is in you, whom you have from God, and that you are not your own?" (1 Cor. 6:19 NASB). There will be consequences to our actions. God can easily stir up our circumstances so that we suffer because of our disobedience. As we'll see in Romans 6:23, he may even call us home in physical death (see also 1 Cor. 11:30-31). His heavy hand of discipline is often applied to his sinning child (Heb. 12:5-11).

"I can't do it!" you cry. "I just don't have the strength to stop what I'm doing! Desire always seems to pin me down!" Friends, God never intended for us to resist sin all by ourselves. As we've discussed earlier; he's given us the Holy Spirit as our guide, comforter, and helper. As Paul shows us at greater length in Romans 8, the indwelling Holy Spirit is there to energize our new nature and to give us the victory as we learn to be dependent on him. In Galatians 5:16 Paul tells us, "But I say, walk by the Spirit, and you will not carry out the desire of the flesh" (NASB). The verse is a picture of a polio victim who is unable to walk without braces. We are the victims of our own crippled humanity, unable to be what God would have us to be, to live as God would have us to live, to walk as God would have us to walk, without the assistance of the braces of the Spirit. With—and only with—the Spirit's strength and power are we able to deal appropriately with the desires of the old nature, or the flesh, as it is sometimes called.

There is a conflict in the life of every Christian, a war between the old and the new. The closer we grow to the Lord, the more sharp and vivid that conflict becomes. We become increasingly sensitive to the sins we commit. We become more and more aware of the things in our life that hurt the closeness of our relationship with God. And along the way we should come to recognize two essential ingredients in willfully choosing not to let sin reign in us.

First, there is trust. That means reliance on the Holy Spirit. It means dependence. It means realizing we're not able to cleanse ourselves of sin by ourselves. We cannot say no alone! Instead, we're moving under the power of God's Spirit.

Second, dependence on the power of the Spirit involves discipline. Self-control is a fruit of the Spirit mentioned in Galatians 5:23. As our old nature is controlled by the Spirit, the Spirit is free to make us more like Christ! Paul writes in 1 Corinthians 9:27 that he treats his body roughly so that it might serve him. He recommends the development of discipline. Do you want to be able to say no to sin? Do you desire to submit to the control of the Spirit? A principle to follow is to begin to develop the habits of discipline in your life. Physically, determine to start eating right and exercising. Spiritually, set aside a portion of time to read and study God's word and to regularly pray. Don't become self-absorbed, but do get into a routine of taking care of things spiritually and physically. The closer you get to the Lord, the more evident the qualities of discipline in your life should become, and you'll be a man or woman of determined direction. It will be easier and easier to stop specific sins from raging out of control! The more you say yes to the

Spirit and no to the flesh, the easier it becomes to do what Paul tells the Thessalonians: "possess his own vessel in sanctification and honor" (1 Thess. 4:4 NASB).

Victory over sin starts with an attitude. It continues with a decision of the will to stop, by the strength of the Holy Spirit, a sinful behavior. It involves incorporating discipline into your life. And finally, as Romans 6:13 shows us, it calls for the involvement of the emotions in submission to the process.

THE EMOTIONS—ROMANS 6:13

We are called to make a presentation to the Lord of the members of our body for his service. "Moreover, stop presenting the members of your body to sin ... but present yourselves to God as those who are alive from the dead, and your members as tools of righteousness to God," writes Paul in verse 13 (DAV, see also Rom. 12:1-2). Victory involves an emotional response in addition to a change of attitude and a willful decision.

How do we present ourselves to God for his use? Paul is talking about a presentation of ourselves that has ongoing results. He uses the Greek *aorist* tense for the verb *present* to communicate the idea that the presentation should be a once for all action with *continuing results*. Remember, the phrase in Galatians 5:16 is "walk by the Spirit." Every single step of that walk, the Christian life, is either a potential fall or a potential point of progress. And every single day brings with it the opportunity for us to start anew. The fact that daily we may experience afresh the results of presenting ourselves to God is one of the most exciting things about being a believer! It is essential for us to focus each morning on the new chance God is giving us that day to act on the fact that we've yielded ourselves to him.

How do we achieve that focus? Here is a prayer that I believe captures the heart of Paul's meaning in verse 13. Perhaps with the dawning of each new day we could communicate thoughts such as these to the Lord:

> Heavenly Father, I am dead to sin. I know it's true, but I also realize that I cannot completely control my body. I place myself at your disposal so you can do your thinking and your acting through me. Whatever it is you want, Lord, I am willing to be used by you. In other words, Lord, I'm freely making a presentation of my arms, legs, mind, and entire self to you for you to use today. Think through my mind; walk with my legs; reach out with my arms; grasp with my hands; see with my eyes; listen with my ears; speak with my tongue.

Every morning I begin my prayer time with the psalmist: "Morning by morning, O Lord, you hear my voice; morning by morning I lay my requests before you and wait in expectation" (Ps. 5:3 NIV). "But how can I know what sins are lurking in my heart? Cleanse me from these hidden faults. And keep me from deliberate wrongs! Don't let them control me. Then I will be free of guilt and innocent of great sin. May the words of my mouth and the thoughts of my heart be pleasing to you, O Lord, my rock and my redeemer" (Ps. 19:12-14 NIV). "Test me, O Lord, and try me, examine my heart and my mind; for your love is ever before me, and I walk continually in your truth" (Ps. 26:2, 3 NIV).

"Search me, O God, and know my heart; test me and know my anxious thoughts. See if there is any offensive way in me, and lead me in the way everlasting" (Ps. 139:23, 24 NIV).

> "I want my heart His throne to be
> So that a watching world may see

His likeness shining forth in me;
I want to be like Jesus. —Chisholm[1]

Ian Thomas compared the Christian life to an empty glove. When the glove, or life, is given to the Lord, and the master's hand fills it and begins to activate it and empower it, great things happen to an empty glove. And great things happen through a yielded life. Being in the power of the master's hand is the source of Christ-likeness in our life. That's what Paul means in Galatians 2:20, where he tells us, "I have been crucified with Christ; and it is no longer I who live, but Christ lives in me; and the life which I now live in the flesh I live by faith in the Son of God, who loved me, and delivered Himself up for me" (NASB).

How ironic that we who have entered the kingdom of God through faith in Christ have done so because we have realized that we cannot save ourselves. We recognize our helplessness, and so we call on Jesus to rescue us. Then, for some reason, once we've received Christ, we figure we can live the Christian life on our own. We place God on a distant throne; we forget that he is vitally involved in our lives, and we try to deal with sin and temptation on our own. We try to perform rather than realizing that victory comes from our union with the living Christ and the power of the indwelling Holy Spirit!

"Present yourselves to God as those who are alive from the dead, and your members as tools of righteousness to God," urges Paul in Romans 6:13 (DAV). Recall that he also implores his readers, earlier in that same verse, to "stop presenting the members of your body to sin as tools of wickedness" (DAV). We've seen how we may present ourselves for righteousness. But how do we avoid presenting our members for wickedness?

That's easy. We refuse to fraternize with the enemy. I'm not suggesting we only associate with Christians. But when we run across a situation that becomes too hot to handle, we must run. There is no shame in that. It's the only sure way to avoid sin. When the going gets tempting, the smart steer clear.

Think of Joseph. When Potiphar's wife attempted to seduce him, Joseph refused. "How then could I do such a wicked thing and sin against God?' he exclaimed in answer to her advances (Gen. 39:9 NIV). Later, when she seductively grabbed his cloak with all the subtlety of a heat-seeking missile, Joseph took off like a bolt of greased lightning. He ran! He read the situation for what it was, a sin against God, and he fled (Gen. 39:llff).

Paul writes the Corinthians:

> Therefore let him who thinks he stands take heed lest he fall. No temptation has overtaken you but such as is common to man; and God is faithful, who will not allow you to be tempted beyond what you are able, but with the temptation will provide the way of escape also, that you may be able to endure it. (1 Cor. 10:12-13 NASB)

The apostle's words should encourage us. Temptation for the Christian always comes with a God-given escape hatch; we need to be ready to read the signs and run.

In the office mail the other day we received a card with a penny taped on it, offering us a penny for our thoughts about some trivial matter. The tone of the message was sarcastic and cynical. Now, the fact that the writer expressed his opinion didn't bother me. What bothered me was that he mailed his opinion to us in one of our own postage-paid envelopes! It cost us cash for that fellow to air his feelings. Believe me, the thoughts I was thinking and was ready to write him in return were not originating with the Spirit! I thanked God that he brought to my mind Romans 12:17, "Do not pay back evil for evil to anyone" (12:17a DAV; see also 17b-21). Restrained by the Spirit and God's word, I did not respond. In this case, fleeing temptation meant tossing the annoying note into the trash.

King David had reached his fiftieth birthday and to celebrate he decided to stay out of harm's way and skip his annual spring military jaunt. Time on his hands and no accountability structure led him into a set of satanically designed circumstances, resulting in illicit sex and the illegitimate pregnancy of a military wife. How much heartache would have been avoided if David had fled temptation? Listen to Paul's words to young Timothy: "But flee from these things, you man of God; and pursue after righteousness, godliness, faith, love, perseverance and gentleness. Fight the good fight of faith; take hold of the eternal life to which you were called, and you made the good confession in the presence of many witnesses" (1 Tim. 6:11, 12 NASB).

We must not, as Christians, willingly place ourselves in positions where we'll be enticed to sin. It's too easy to give in. We must not allow our energy, appetite, speech, mind, imagination, or emotions to serve sin! We've got to surrender these to the Lord daily, hourly, even minute by minute.

The word Paul uses for "present" in verse 13 is the same used in Romans 12:1, "I beseech you therefore, brethren, by the mercies of God, that ye *present* your bodies a living sacrifice, holy, acceptable unto God, which is your reasonable service" (KJV). It is the word used of a bride who presents herself to her bridegroom as a gift. It's the same word that is used in Ephesians 5, where Paul tells us the Lord Jesus is going to present us to the Father as his perfect bride in glory. We, without spot or blemish, transformed into perfect Christ-likeness, will be presented to the Lord ultimately one day (Eph. 5:27). In the meantime, we have the responsibility not to present ourselves as tools of wickedness, but to present ourselves to the Lord so that righteousness through the power of the Spirit begins to manifest itself in our life. That's the essence of Luke 9:23, where the Lord says, "If anyone wishes to come after Me, let him deny himself, and take up his cross daily, and follow Me" (NASB). It's not something we do ourselves; it's something we allow God to do through us!

To sum things up, victory over sin comes as we:

- With our mind, adopt the attitude that we are dead to sin.
- With our will, energized by the power of the Holy Spirit, refuse to choose to let sin reign in us.
- With our emotions, present ourselves to the Lord and act on that presentation daily.

These three essential concepts are the foundation of triumphant Christian living. The rest of Romans 6 builds on them.

OF LORDSHIP, LEGALISM, AND LICENSE—ROMANS 6:14-18

Victory is a tough assignment. It is difficult to maintain the right attitude by consistently considering ourselves dead to sin. It's often easier to give in to sin than it is to allow the Spirit to energize our will and enable us to say no. It can be hard to remember every day that we have made a presentation, by our emotions, of our members to the Lord for his use. When we start to confront problems like lust, envy, anger, vindictiveness, or some other sin, it may seem that victory is impossible. Like the ten spies sent to reconnoiter in the promised land who saw the giants there and returned to Moses only to say, "We are not able" (Num. 13:31 NASB), we may feel our chances of successfully overcoming sin are sparse. In the words of the old cowboy: our chances seem "slim and none and slim is saddled up and leaving town." At the gateway to the promised land, only Joshua and Caleb saw the God-given opportunities for victory there. Like them, we must recognize that we've been given the miraculous capacity for triumph in our Christian life too. The giants can be slain!

Romans 6:14 contains a truth to encourage us in the thick of things. "For sin shall not exercise lordship over you," says Paul, "for you are not under law, but under grace" (DAV). Sin's power over believers has been broken, and that is an irrefutable truth we can cling to. We are not under law, but grace.

Before we became Christians, we were under the authority of the law. We were in bondage to it. The Father's only alternative, had we died as unbelievers, would have been to judge us according to that law. Since we'd broken part of it, we would be considered guilty of all. The law can only bring death! But now we're under a new relationship; we're under grace. We've been given God's special, undeserved favor. Someone has said that grace is God's riches at Christ's expense. It is God himself making provision for the sin problem. It is God catching us raiding the refrigerator without permission, guilty, yet forgiving us, cleansing us, making every provision necessary for our eternal destiny and our earthly victory over specific sins.

What also ought to encourage us is that just because we have faced defeat in certain areas doesn't mean that we'll never taste victory. The potential exists for us to be winners, through God's power and for his sake, not because he tells us to but because we love him. The defeats in our life are not God's fault, but ours, and yet he is faithful to love, forgive, and facilitate a fresh start.

So many evenings I have looked back on the day and found myself depressed about some things I have thought, said, and done. Downcast and defeated, I have had the urge to throw in the towel. Instead I have learned to throw it all at God's feet. I can't undo what's been done or unsay what's been said. There's no way to erase the tape. The only viable option is to learn and get on with it. I am discovering that I must live life just one day at a time. When the day is done and I haven't done too well, I just give it all to the Lord and ask him to take care of it. He's going to be up anyway, watching while I sleep. I awaken with Lamentations 3:22-24 in my thoughts. It's a new day and another opportunity to deepen the relationship by depending more fully on him.

What a sense of freedom there is in realizing that God can enable us to be victorious. What a joy there is in recognizing that the sin which remains doesn't indicate that we're not really Christians, but is a normal by-product of the old nature, which is still there. What a thrill to discover that we can overcome the old nature, through God's grace! When we give up on human performance and focus on our relationship with the Lord, the giants in the land are doomed to fall. With the faithful throughout history, this battle cry can be ours: if God is for us, who can be against us? Just read over the following words from Old Testament history if you'd like a little object lesson to remind you of God's power:

> Moses, to the Israelites before God parted the Red Sea: "The Lord will fight for you; you need only to be still" (Exod. 14:14 NIV).
>
> God, speaking to Joshua on the eve of a battle that never took place because God first destroyed the enemy with hailstones: The Lord said to Joshua, "Do not be afraid of them; I have given them into your hand. Not one of them will be able to withstand you" (Josh. 10:8 NIV).

> David, speaking to Goliath before slinging it to him: "All those gathered here will know that it is not by sword or spear that the Lord saves; for the battle is the Lord's, and he will give all of you into our hands" (1 Sam. 17:47 NIV).

God proved himself faithful in each of these humanly impossible situations. Surely he'll prove no less dependable in enabling us to overcome the spiritual struggles we encounter. "Sin shall not exercise lordship over you," claims the apostle Paul (Rom. 6:14 DAV). Friends, if God hadn't meant it, he wouldn't have included it within the canon of scripture. He never makes a statement in the Bible without providing the enabling power and the grace for its accomplishment. He is faithful to whatever he says. The prayer of Jehoshaphat in 2 Chronicles 20:12 must be often the expression of our lips: "O our God, will you not judge them? For we have no power to face this vast army that is attacking us. We do not know what to do, but our eyes are upon you" (NIV).

Paul continues, in verse 15, to reiterate a point made earlier in Romans 6:1-2. "What then?" he asks. "Shall we sin because we are not under law but under grace? May it never be!" (6:15 DAV). As stated before, just because we're in an incredibly liberating relationship with the Lord doesn't mean we're free to sin intentionally. Not at all. The person living with God on a performance basis may well fall into one of two camps. Either he will tend to be legalistic, striving to stick strictly to the minutiae of the law and condemning all who fall short, or he'll realize his inability to perform well enough to please God and he'll take license. He'll do what he wants to because he can't be perfect anyway. He'll decide to continue in disobedience—not so grace might abound, but *because* it does! The godly life thrives on a living relationship with Christ, and is neither bound by legalism nor saturated with license.

"Are you not knowing that when you present yourselves to someone as slaves resulting in obedience, you are slaves of the one whom you are obeying, whether of sin resulting in death, or of obedience resulting in righteousness?" continues Paul in verse 16 (DAV). The verse is a promise. We can present ourselves for wicked purposes or we can present ourselves for obedience. And what is that obedience resulting in righteousness? It's the obedience of verses 11, 12, and 13. It's the obedience of the attitude, will, and emotions. It is a turning to the new nature and a turning from the old.

Victory is possible! The apostle is so excited by the prospect of God's provision that he breaks into the doxology in verse 17: "But thanks be to God that though you were slaves to sin, you obeyed from the heart to that form of teaching, for the learning of which you were given over" (DAV). As Christians we *were* (note the past tense) slaves of sin. Why are we no longer slaves of sin? It's not because we had an experience of some sort—not because we walked down an aisle, raised a hand, or fell on our knees. It's because we obeyed from the heart the form of teaching to which we were given over. In other words, we first received Christ as savior. Then we obeyed biblical truth and followed the New Testament pattern for victory over sin. Out of our relationship with God we find delight in doing his will. Genuine obedience is that which originates from the heart and is not the result of subjecting ourselves to any external requirement or performance quota. Paul calls himself (and every Christian) a bond slave of the Lord (6:22), meaning that he has willingly presented himself to Jesus Christ.

As I find myself standing on the brink of celebrating the gold (fifty years of marriage to the same woman) I feel both joy and sadness. The joys are obvious: we've made it! Changes have produced closeness. We are treasuring every day we have together. We are in the dessert stage of marriage: lots of sweetness.

The sadness comes from knowing all the mistakes I have made over the years. I wish we could do some things over again. Praise the Lord for forgiveness and the freedom of victory.

Each morning as I pray for Pearl, I ask the Lord to help me be an encouragement to her: to speak of things positively, to praise her person and her good deeds.

My stubborn critical spirit did a lot of damage in our earlier years, but I'm here to tell you, there is nothing that you can't have victory over in your life. Confessing sin on a daily basis and asking the Spirit to fill you causes great things to happen. I will treasure to the grave Pearl's note on my 49th anniversary card: "I'm so happy for this time in our lives. It makes up for the not so good times we have gone through. I enjoy being with you and just hanging out, doing our routine activities. God is so good and wise. He lets us experience things so we will understand why he blocks us sometimes. My true love to you, Pearl."

There is hope for victory over sin. "And having been set free from sin," Paul goes on, "you were made slaves to righteousness" (6:18 DAV). From freedom we enter a slavery of a different sort: a joyous captivity in which we are able to cooperate with the Spirit to make us more Christ-like. It is *transformation by contemplation.* As we behold the living word within the written word, we begin to be transformed into the Lord's likeness. That is the crux of Paul's message in Romans 12:2: "And stop being fashioned to this age, but let yourselves be transformed by the renewing of your mind, resulting in your putting to the test what the will of God is, that which is good and well-pleasing and perfect" (DAV).

One of the Ministries' friends, Sara, comes to mind here. With a religious background which stressed performance to earn God's favor, Sara was frustrated by the nagging feeling that she was never doing enough. For years she plugged along trying desperately to perform to please the Lord. In recent years she has found such joy in finally finding a relationship with Christ, and in realizing that what she does or doesn't do will never toll the death knell of that relationship. Oh, Sara is still busy. She writes letters of encouragement; she is always the first to volunteer to teach vacation Bible school or Sunday school. But Sara is no longer busy *for* the Lord, she is busy *because* of the Lord—because of what he has done, because of what he means to her, because of the opportunities he provides. Her service flows from a heart filled with love for God. What she does, she does out of compassion, not necessity. The freedom she feels is incredible, and her personal ministry flourishes as a result. Others see Christ's love in her, and they respond.

OF FREEDOM AND FRUIT—ROMANS 6:19-23

Paul continues, his words building on the key concepts of verses 11, 12, and 13. "I am speaking in human terms because of the weakness of your flesh," he tells the Romans. "For just as you presented your members as slaves to uncleanness and lawlessness, resulting in lawlessness, so now present your members as slaves to righteousness, resulting in holiness" (6:19 DAV). Paul knew his audience well. The Romans thoroughly understood the concept of slavery; over half of the 120 million residing within the boundaries of the empire were slaves, including many, many Christians. Paul calls for them—and us—willingly to place ourselves in subjugation to righteousness. He is echoing verse 13, reiterating that the emotional response of presenting our members to God will result in righteousness. In the past, the Romans presented their members as slaves to unclean thoughts, actions, habits, and behavior patterns. Now the admonition is for them to present themselves to Christ. In the process, they'll become his slaves—ironically, slaves with far more freedom than even Caesar. They'll learn the joy of serving and being spent in his service. "And He died for all, that they who live should no longer live for themselves, but for Him who died and rose again on their behalf" (2 Cor. 5:15 NASB).

"For when you were slaves of sin, you were free with respect to righteousness," the apostle goes on in verse 20 (DAV). No obligation to act righteously exists for the one enslaved to sin. The non-believer serves the taskmaster of disobedience. He doesn't worry about whether or not he is righteous in God's sight. Because he has no relationship with Christ, he has no responsibility toward righteousness. He is free to do his own thing and follow the desires of the flesh. With the relationship comes the responsibility to be concerned about reflecting Christ.

The fruit we bore as unbelievers, as slaves of sin, was foul and putrid. Our "good deeds" were always tainted by our sin nature. They were done to enhance our reputation, to create a good impression, or to make us appear humane or religious. Their outcome, as Paul states in verse 21, was "death." How different that is from the fruit that can be produced in the life of a child of God!

When Paul speaks of the results of the relationship with God in the life of a Christian, he often uses the term *fruit*. Verse 22 tells us that since we've been set free from sin and have been made bondslaves of God, we are actually able to bear fruit resulting in holiness and eternal life. Our faith ensures that we are holy in the sight of the Father, and that we'll dwell in his presence forever. Since that is so, if we incorporate the attitude that we're dead to sin but alive to God, if we willfully determine in the power of the Spirit not to let sin reign in us, if we present ourselves to God for his use, then the fruit that is manifested in our life will be rich indeed. "My true disciples produce much fruit. This brings great glory to my Father. You didn't choose me, I chose you.

I appointed you to go and produce fruit that will last" (John 15:8, 16 NLV).

The hymnist writes, "And they'll know we are Christians by our love." People should know we are Christians by that, certainly, and also by some other qualities. Fruit should be manifested in our life. The fruit of the Holy Spirit listed in Galatians 5 is as follows: "love, joy, peace, patience, kindness, goodness, faithfulness, gentleness, self- control" (5:22-23 NASB).

How is this fruit produced in us? Think about it. Branches don't struggle to form fruit, do they? The branch abides in the vine; the life of the vine flows through the branch, and fruit results. It takes time, too. First the blade appears, then the blossom, then finally the fruit. We cannot take the nine manifestations of the fruit of the Spirit listed in Galatians 5 and decide we'll produce them in our life just like that, either. We can't say to ourselves, "I'm going to love! I'm going to be patient! I'm going to be joyful!" We're tempted to do that. We hear a sermon on loving our brothers as ourselves, and we decide we're going to do that. Pretty soon we're whaling on the brother we're supposed to be loving! We've failed again. We're frustrated and miserable. We want to perform. We want to produce our own fruit so we can present it to God, and he simply says no, my son, my daughter, it doesn't work like that.

Instead of saying, "I'm going to be patient. I'm going to have self-control. I'm going to love," we need to say something like this:

> Dear Father, the fruit of the Spirit is not manifesting itself in my life. I need to deepen my relationship with you so that the Spirit can manifest that fruit in my life. Help! Spirit of the living God, if I am grieving you by sin or quenching you in my resistance, please

> purify my heart. Spirit of God, fill me to overflowing and may your fruit ripen in my life.

That's the only way. Trying to produce fruit on our own and gain victory over sin ourselves is much like trying to run up a down escalator with our shoelaces tied together. We fall on our face before we take the first step.

To remind us that bearing fruit is important but is not the means by which we gain access to heaven, Paul concludes chapter 6 with these words: "For the wages of sin is death, but the free gift of God is life eternal in Christ Jesus our Lord" (6:23 DAV). Eternal life is not earned; it is freely given as we come to faith.

Verse 23 provides meat for many a salvation sermon. It's used as a call to Christ and repeated with rote intensity at the conclusion of Sunday services galore. While the wages, salary, or just desserts of unbelief is death, or spiritual separation from God, it's important to realize that Paul was not talking to unsaved people in Romans 6. He was talking to Christians! The death he is talking about in verse 23 is not spiritual death, but physical death. The wages of sin, he warns his readers, will be physical death. If believers consciously continue in patterns of sin, it is quite possible that the Lord will call them home prematurely in physical death (1 Cor. 5:5, 11:30). The gift of God is eternal life. That can't be taken away from the Christian, but it may start a little sooner than he expects! Jack was a tragic example of such a believer.

Jack was a very dear friend whose lifestyle literally killed him. He had a personal relationship with Jesus Christ, and he loved doing things for the Ministries. Yet the power of the bottle was so strong that he found himself mastered by it. Though warned by scores of doctors and friends who cared, his addiction continued while he made little attempt to control it, and his health deteriorated as a result. Confined to a hospital bed, Jack was called home by the Lord. He was only in his early forties when he died. He left behind a wife and family. What a tragic loss! What a waste!

GOD GETS IT DONE BIG TIME

We can perhaps sum up Romans 6 with these words: *lordship* and *life*. They are the lifeblood of Paul's message to us in the chapter. The apostle reminds us that Christ is Lord in our relationship with him; sin no longer exercises lordship over us. Because of Christ's lordship, we are given eternal life, abundant life, the chance of earthly life in which we experience gradual, progressive victory over sin. Our attitude, will, and emotions play integral roles in the process, but the Holy Spirit is the power behind it all. He energizes the new nature. He empowers the effort. It's a revolution all right, a life-changing turning from the old to the new.

In the book *I Am with You Always: Experiencing God in Times of Need,* Chip Ingram tells of Jerry and Lori, a couple from his church, whom he calls: "Two stories of amazing grace":

> At age eighteen, Jerry was a college football star. One night, Jerry saw two guys fighting and tried to break it up. One of the men pulled a gun and shot Jerry at point-blank range. Jerry was paralyzed, his football career over, and his future shattered. Jerry has had to endure thirty major surgeries to deal with complications and has nearly died many times.
>
> He described it for me, "When I first got hurt, I didn't know the Lord. I was an athlete, so I tried to get through everything by being physically and mentally tough. But

the challenges became increasingly more difficult as time went on. I couldn't win on my own. Then I met Christ, and it was like the Lord jumped on the team. That made it a little bit easier. I started trusting the Lord. He got me through the times when it was hard for me to get through."

Jerry is a very tough-minded, mentally intense athlete. He is very strong-willed. His struggle, he told me, is to resist trying to do it himself and to really trust God, believing that God will turn a situation around to bring about good. When I asked Jerry to tell me exactly what good has come out of this, he said, "There's been a lot of good things. I guess the premier one is my relationship with the Lord. The second biggest is God bringing my wife, Lori, to me. She is just an incredible woman. I used to pray, 'God, if you want me to be married, bring the woman into my life you want me to be with.' When he didn't, I said, 'Okay, I guess you don't want me to have a wife.' Well, one day God did, when I met Lori here at church."

"...When I got shot, I thought, 'I can't walk, but there must be something I can do.' I just didn't know what it was going to be. With God's help, I eventually found many things I can do."

Jerry played on the U.S. Olympic wheelchair basketball team and won a gold medal. He's a world-class wheelchair marathoner and has traveled all over the world, both in competition and as a missionary. He teamed up with Joni Eareckson Tada and shared how

Christ took his bad situation and turned it around for good.

He recounted one moment when he was on the starting line in the Olympic Games in the fifteen hundred meters. "The final event in the pentathlon (a competition that combines five events) was about to begin when I looked up and saw myself on the big screen with my name there to show that I was representing the United States. I thought, "Wow. This is really cool. Thank you, Lord. It doesn't get much better than this!"

I asked Jerry how he keeps going, even with all the physical challenges he faces every day. He gave me this example. "Let's say I had a really hard marathon, which is twenty-six miles, but I knew at the beginning of the race that no matter what happened, I was guaranteed to win. So no matter how bad the hills were, or whether there was a crash, or how tired I got, I would win. Would I enter the race? Of course. So would you. It's the same idea in my relationship with the Lord. I have an advantage. I read the end of the book and I know the end of the story. We win. I know there will be an eternity where I will not be hampered like I am here. So it doesn't matter what I have to go through here. I'm looking forward to the finish line and the medal ceremony."

The story of Jerry's wife, Lori, is just as inspiring. Lori was raped and beaten while serving in the military as a young woman. ... She's had twenty-three major surgeries in the last few years to deal with her physical problems, but she too lives with a positive outlook and an eternal perspective.

Lori says she couldn't have survived without God's presence in her life. She says of Jerry, "God has blessed me with somebody who understands the kinds of challenges I face. God has given me support through Jerry and through friends who are there for me and who don't hesitate to stop and talk." When I asked Lori what she does when it's one of those days and she has thoughts like, "I can't go through one more surgery. There are too many hassles. There's too much pain," she said she turns to God in prayer and to her friends.

... Even though she has endured terrible injustice and pain inflicted on her wrongfully, Lori knows there is a God who has good plans for her. As she calls on him and seeks him, she is confident that God will be there for her and lead her to the fulfillment of the good plans he has for her.

She goes on to say, "If I had to do it over again, I don't think I would change it because I wouldn't be the person I am today without the trials and the struggles—and I do mean struggles—I had to go through and still do. God took two people who had a really rough time and put us together as a team. Now we can go out and speak to just about anybody. Because of all we've been through, we have some inkling of what has happened to others. We can let them know that God can turn it all around. Whether you have been attacked or you've been abused or you were a victim of

> violence, God is faithful. He will carry you through it. He will take your hand. He will walk with you there. But there is a process you have to go through and you have to trust him. Don't just look at the circumstances. Circumstances are like quicksand; I'd drown in them in a heartbeat. But if you look at God and keep that eternal perspective, keep your eyes on him, not on yourself or what anybody else thinks, he will lift you up."[2]

Wow! What a story. Yes! God is still alive and active on planet earth! To God be the glory! Great things he has done!

Questions to Consider

1. According to Romans 6:11-13, what are the three steps we may follow in seeking victory over sin? Explain each of these in your own words. Consider how you might apply the scriptural steps to a specific sin area in your life.

2. As Christians, we are supposed to bear fruit for God as the Holy Spirit works in our life to make us more like Jesus. Is any of the fruit of the Spirit listed in Galatians 5:22-23 being manifested in your life?

3. Romans 6:23 says that "the wages of sin is death." What does this verse mean for the believer in Christ? Can a Christian ever experience spiritual death, or separation from God for eternity? What may happen to the Christian whose lifestyle is extremely sinful?

CHAPTER 6

"When he sees all that is accomplished by his anguish, he will be satisfied. And because of what he has experienced, my righteous servant will make it possible for many to be counted righteous, for he will bear all their sins" (Isa. 53:11 NLV).

The Picture and the Problem

Romans 7:1-13

"A tumor with a main section the size of a small grapefruit is lodged against your rib cage," said the physician. "It isn't a completely solid mass, either. Its edges are ragged and touch most of the major internal organs. For lack of a better word, 'fingers' from the tumor have stretched out to attach themselves to your heart, lungs, kidney, liver, and spleen. We cannot hope to remove the entire mass through an operation, and unfortunately a biopsy has shown it to be cancerous. The most we can do is treat the area with radiation, and of course you can pray."

Ominous news, isn't it? Surprisingly, the patient

described above won't die from his cancer for years and years to come. He will, however, live with the malignancy the rest of his life.

The picture of that cancer patient is a picture of every Christian. We too live with a cancer within—a spiritual malignancy. It's called, as we've discussed earlier, the old nature. It will never go away completely. We'll live with the old nature and the new nature coexisting within us for the rest of our life. Someday we will probably suffer a physical disease and physical death, the result of living in a fallen world. Until then we are victims of an inoperable, aggressive spiritual tumor. The sin nature may go into remission periodically, but it'll never be eradicated until we reach glory, and thus much of the Christian life is learning to live with a cancer that won't quit.

CATCHING UP

In Romans 5 we looked at the results of having a relationship with Christ, and also how to go about beginning that relationship. In Romans 6 we saw that as believers we've been brought into a living union with Jesus Christ and that his life flows through us. We saw that victory over sin starts with an attitude, continues with a decision of the will, and also involves presenting ourselves daily to God for his use and service. We've spoken about the seriousness of sin in the life of a Christian, the potential consequences of consciously continuing in a pattern of sin. Now we come to Romans 7.

THF PICTURE—ROMANS 7:1-6

In the first six verses of Romans 7, Paul uses that most intimate of human relationships, marriage, as an illustration of what it is like to come into relationship with the Lord Jesus Christ. We remember that in Romans 6:14, Paul writes, "For sin shall not exercise lordship over you, for you are not under law, but under grace" (DAV). In Adam, we were in sin. God through Moses brought the law to show us our need of righteousness. In Jesus Christ we find the solution.

The headship of our life changes when we enter the family of God. When I perform a marriage, I include in the ceremony what I call the transfer of headship, which also illustrates our change of position as a believer. Looking the wide-eyed, tuxedo-clad groom squarely in the eye, I tell him:

> Son, God says in his word in Genesis 2:24 that a man shall leave his father and his mother and shall cleave to his wife, and they shall become one flesh. Just a few short years ago, Judy was a gift of the Lord and a fruit of her parents' union. Children are a gift from God, but they are also a stewardship and a responsibility. It has been the purpose of Judy's parents to follow the scriptural admonition to train up a child in the way she should go, so that when she is old, she will not depart from it. Her parents have prepared her for this moment, when she steps out of their life and into yours. Her security, peace, and well-being have resided under their headship and authority. But now that headship and that authority are transferred to you.

It's a heavy responsibility ... and I silently pray that the young man in front of me will commit his leadership of the family to the control of the Lord.

Much the same transfer of headship occurs in our life when we accept Christ. No longer bound to the law, under its authority, Christ becomes our new head. He is our authority. Our security, peace, and well-being rest in his hands. We'll not be made holy by adhering to the law but by clinging to the savior.

Still, so many Christians mistakenly take the law from their old life and bring it over into their new life in Christ. Paul was especially vulnerable to this kind of legalism. In Acts 26:5 he says of his own background, "I lived as a Pharisee according to the strictest sect of our religion" (NASB). As a Pharisee, a Jewish religious leader whose mission it was to adhere as strictly as possible to the Mosaic law, Paul had lived much of his life trying to be made righteous by the law. He struggled with performance practically from day one. The natural mind assumes that it is possible to legislate righteousness, that man can become holy and good and just by keeping the sections and subsections of the law. The truth is that there will never be a law which will legislate righteousness. Trying to foist the law onto our Christian life is taking a principle of scripture given for an express purpose and using it incorrectly (see also Phil. 3:4-9).

It is serious business when Christians use God-given tools in the wrong way. Today the practice of using spiritual gifts improperly, for self-edification instead of as a ministry to others, runs rampant throughout the Christian community. Gifts are given to make each of us a more effective witness for Christ, not for us to use to build ourselves up (see 1 Cor. 12:7; 14:12). The law was given by God as a tool for a specific purpose: to show us our sin (Rom. 5:13). It also, as we've discussed, actually stimulates our sin (Rom. 5:20). For every "thou shalt not," the natural response is "I will, too!' And the law has its intended result.

But the law is not, and never has been, meant as a measure we Christians should strive to attain. We'll never become righteous through the keeping of the law. When we apply the law to our life in Christ, we're asking for a miserable Christian experience. We're using the law improperly. We're quenching the possibility for the abundant life because we're limiting God to what *we* can perform on our own. For a loaded example, consider the tithe.

The Bible teaches that God loves a cheerful giver. One of the fruits of the Spirit listed in Galatians 5 is joy. When we slap the law of the tithe onto our checkbooks and we give because we think we *have* to, we may become reluctant ten-percenters. We resent giving. God gets no glory from grudging givers! In our new relationship with Christ, we're dead to the *have to* and alive to the privilege of freely giving out of love. We are not bound to the limits of the law. When we insist on living legalistically, we doom ourselves to be guilt-ridden and unfulfilled. It is perhaps because of this truth that Paul begins chapter 7 with a clear-cut illustration of our relationship with Christ. The apostle graphically shows us that the influence of the law upon us should be shattered when we become Christians.

THE PRINCIPLE

"Or do you not know, brethren," begins Paul in verse 1, "for I am speaking to those who are knowing the law, that the law is ruling over the individual as long as he lives?" (Rom. 7:1 DAV). Many times in scripture Paul first states a principle, then follows with an illustration of the principle as he does here. The principle in verse 1 is simply this: as Christians we are dead to the law. The law rules over an individual as long as he lives. When a death takes place, he is freed from the law to which he was bound. Remember in Romans 6, the apostle taught us that when we came to faith in Jesus Christ, we were identified with, or baptized into, his death, burial, and resurrection (6:3). This process of "dying" was necessary so that a new relationship in Christ Jesus could be established. Before we entered into that relationship, we were bound by the law of sin and death. We were bound to the dictatorship of an old nature that could only respond to sin. When we came to faith, we were freed from that and identified with Jesus Christ.

The law has nothing to do with our justification, or our

salvation, except to convince us that we need a savior. The law also has nothing to do with our sanctification. It does not make us more like Christ, although it is human nature to think that it does, and so even the evangelical church is saturated with men and women who are performance oriented. We question the salvation of folks who don't appear up to snuff in their spiritual lives. We assume that someone isn't growing if he isn't, to our way of thinking, doing great and mighty things for God. And we're often wrong. There's a balance. We are to bear fruit, but the fruit must be the result of God's work, not our own.

"For through the Law, I died to the Law, that I might live to God," says Paul in Galatians 2:19 (NASB). And then he goes on to write those familiar words, which we've previously quoted, "I have been crucified with Christ; and it is no longer I who live, but Christ lives in me; and the life which I now live in the flesh I live by faith in the Son of God, who loved me, and delivered Himself up for me" (Gal. 2:20 NASB). When the law pinned Jesus Christ to the cross, it did all that it could do. Christ died to abolish the authority of the law over those who believe in him. By faith, we die to the law because we're identified with the death of our savior. Now comes the illustration of the principle.

THE ILLUSTRATION

The picture Paul paints in verses 2-6 is one of a marriage relationship. Many people assume the passage contains teaching on marriage, but the verses actually expound on the principle stated in verse 1. The subject matter is the believer's relationship with Christ.

"For the married woman has been bound by law to her living husband," writes Paul. "But if her husband dies, she has been released from the law of her husband" (7:2 DAV). The wife is bound to her living husband by the law of the marriage relationship. A death occurs. When her husband dies, the wife no longer is bound to him. She no longer is a wife; her "wifedom" is abolished by the death of her husband. She's set free from the law of marriage and discharged from the authority of her first husband, and she can now be joined to another. The spiritual application of this is clear. In Galatians 4:4-5 we read, "But when the fulness of the time came, God sent forth His Son, born of a woman, born under the Law, in order that He might redeem those who were under the Law, that we might receive the adoption as sons" (NASB). Galatians 3:13 states, "Christ redeemed us from the curse of the Law, having become a curse for us" (NASB). Only *before* receiving Jesus Christ, were we bound or "married" to the law. God had no alternative except to judge us on the basis of that law (Rev. 20:15). When we come to faith in Christ, like the wife whose husband has died, we are no longer under the authority of the law. We've been discharged, just as surely as a widow is set free from the obligations of marriage.

Paul continues the illustration in verse 3, saying of the wife, "So then, if while her husband is living, she is joined to another man she shall be called an adulteress; but if her husband dies, she is free from the law, so that she is not an adulteress, though she is joined to another man" (DAV). The first marriage relationship must be terminated before the second one can become a moral reality. When a woman's first husband still lives, and she is joined to another, she becomes an adulteress. Bringing the old over into the new relationship desecrates the new. When applied to the Christian life, the principle is this: we cannot give our total loyalty and devotion to both Christ and the law at the same time. We must die to one so that we can live for the other in a new relationship. To desecrate the new by bringing the old over into it is to commit spiritual adultery! If we are to be "married" to the Lord Jesus Christ, which is what essentially happens in a relationship with him, then marriage to the law must be terminated by death. It is vital to the new that the bindings of the old be broken.

Jesus, speaking to an audience into which some Greeks had been brought by Philip and Andrew, said this, "Truly, truly, I say to you, unless a grain of wheat falls into the earth and dies, it remains by itself alone; but if it dies, it bears much fruit" (John 12:24 NASB). Just as the grain of wheat must fall to the ground and die before it bears fruit, so you and I must, in Jesus Christ, die to performance once and for all. We must die to the law and accept the grace offered by Christ. He loves us unconditionally, accepts us totally, and, by the power of his indwelling Spirit, he'll begin to produce fruit out of the union. The fruit, which is genuine and lasting, is not—and can never be—the result of our own work.

The twelve disciples illustrated that truth dramatically. Some may put "saint" before their names and fashion each into a hero in the mind's eye, but the twelve only became what they became as a result of their vital, dynamic relationship with Christ. We can identify with every single one of them, for each had some area of weakness in his life. Peter denied Christ; Judas betrayed him; James and John had quick tempers; Thomas was a pessimist. Each longed to exercise power in the kingdom. They were plaster saints at best! Thanks to God, the disciples (except Judas) became men who accomplished much because they grew in the knowledge and understanding of Christ, and they learned to depend on the Spirit. The Lord is still in the business of changing lives today, but the authentication of New Testament Christianity is often absent because we live bound to the law of performance rather than to a commitment to deepen our relationship with God. In Romans 7, Paul says we must do away with that sort of thinking! Our relationship with Christ must grow so that the fruit might follow. The law says, "Do!" but grace says, "Done!"

"Therefore, my brethren," the apostle goes on, "you also

were put to death to the Law through the body of Christ, resulting in your being joined to another, to the One who was raised from the dead, in order that we might bear fruit to God" (7:4 DAV). The apostle reiterates that we are dead to the law. The reality of the cross and the empty tomb joins us to Christ, to the one who was raised from the dead. What is the purpose of this new relationship? It is given in the last part of the verse: "In order that we might bear fruit to God."

It's interesting that the only thing which permanently terminates a relationship is death. The only thing that could terminate our relationship, our marriage, to the law was the death of Christ. What about our relationship with Christ, once we've received him by faith? It's forever. Consider it. We have a living Christ who has already passed through the veil of tears. Death no longer has lordship over him. He's never going to die, and spiritually, neither will we who are believers, so our relationship with him will never end! As Jesus tells Martha, "I am the resurrection, and the life; he who believes in Me shall live even if he dies, and everyone who lives and believes in Me shall never die" (John 11:25-26 NASB). We're eternally secure in the relationship, a fact that Paul further explains in Romans 8.

We die, yet we bear fruit. We are freed from the law, yet we choose to serve. Before we became Christians, our motivation was a feeling that we somehow ought to do good. Now we delight in serving God because we love him. We're free, in love, to give ourselves to the savior as we could never do under the law. And the fruit we bear, as we discussed in the last chapter, is a holiness of life, the quality of character that Jesus Christ produces in us. It's Galatians 5:22-23, the fruit of the Spirit's work in our life. It's also 1 Corinthians 13:4-7, where Paul lists fifteen characteristics of love:

> Love is patient, love is kind, and is not jealous; love does not brag and is not arrogant,

> does not act unbecomingly; it does not seek its own, is not provoked, does not take into account a wrong suffered, does not rejoice in unrighteousness, but rejoices with the truth; bears all things, believes all things, hopes all things, endures all things. (NASB)

Watchman Nee said, "It's our responsibility to be, and it's God's responsibility to do." As we make ourselves available to God, he produces the genuine Christian character, the qualities to which others respond, the things that make the difference between one who knows Christ and one who does not.

Lisa Beamer's book *Let's Roll* tells the story of her husband, Todd, who died September 11, 2002, while trying with other passengers to wrest control of the highjacked United flight 93 from terrorists. Lisa describes what it was like to go to the crash site:

> Following September 11, I saw firsthand many dear people who were trying their best to cope with loss, hurt, anger, fear, and a host of other feelings. Some had lost a husband, father, daughter, mother, or friend. They wanted to soar like eagles; they deeply desired to get on with life. They wanted to look on the bright side and do the things the clichés recommend, but they didn't have the strength. Worse yet, they had no *hope*. My family and I mourned the loss of Todd deeply that day ... and we still do. But because we hope in the Lord, we know beyond a doubt that one day we will see Todd again. I hurt for the people who don't have that same hope, and I pray that somehow the events of September 11 will encour-

> age them to investigate the possibility that faith in Jesus really is the answer to all of their questions."[1]

Truly, Lisa Beamer's life reflects her deep knowledge of Jesus Christ. Yet as we consider Romans 7:4, it should be pointed out that there are Christians whose lives seem to change little following their conversion. I frequently meet professing believers who tell me, "I haven't changed very much," as though God had somehow failed them. Christians whose lives give no evidence of fruit ought to be deeply concerned. The fact that there's no fruit could indicate several things. First, it could mean that there is no relationship, that there's never been a commitment to Christ through faith in the first place. Second, it could mean that the Spirit is being grieved and quenched in their life. God is not producing a Christ-like character in them because they are unaware of his desire to do so, or are blocking his efforts in some way. Their lives are not manifesting what God intends. We mustn't forget that one of the last statements Jesus made before he walked down the path toward the garden of Gethsemane was, "You did not choose Me, but I chose you, and appointed you, that you should go and bear fruit, and that your fruit should remain" (John 15:16 NASB). It is the overwhelming desire of the Father to produce fruit in us as a direct result of our relationship with the Son!

TIGER FISH IN THE TANK

In the opening verses of Romans 7, Paul has made it clear that the law's authority has been terminated as far as Christians are concerned. The final two verses of the passage deal with issues tying it all together. "For when we were in the flesh, the sinful passions were at work in our members through the Law to bear fruit for death," states Paul in verse 5 (DAV). What does this mean? Paul is reminding us that before we became Christians we were in the flesh. We were in Adam. The old nature was fully at work, desiring things that were not pleasing to the Lord. The law showed us our disobedience and convinced us of our need of righteousness. Functioning properly, the law stirred up our old nature and prompted us to sin. When the law was introduced to our old nature, it was tantamount to throwing raw meat into a pool of piranhas.

I remember when our son Andy was a young teenager, our house was cluttered with his gerbil cages and glass containers of snakes. Why shouldn't he have a few fish, too, we thought. The rest of the house was pet-packed. So we bought an aquarium at a garage sale and stocked it with goldfish and tropicals. Then one day at the pet store, a sale sign in front of a tank filled with tiny little fish—pretty ones with black and white stripes and a streak of fluorescence underneath—caught my eye.

"Can we put those fish in the aquarium with our others?" I asked the sales clerk. His reply should have made me suspicious.

"Well, probably ... how big are your goldfish?" he asked. I indicated the length with my thumb and forefinger. "Oh sure, they'll be okay," the expert assured us.

So we bought the fish. They were tiger fish, and did they live up to their name. As soon as Andy and I dumped the fish into their new accommodations, they began zipping around the tank, nibbling at the fins of the goldfish and angelfish. If we'd left them in there we'd have had finless fish, and maybe even a few fish fatalities! It's the nature of tiger fish to eat the fins of other fish. When you put them in the tank, they'll behave as their nature dictates. It's unavoidable.

When we introduce the law into our Christian life, it's the same as throwing tiger fish into the tank. Our old nature will respond to the law. The evil one delights in removing us from dependence on God's Spirit and reliance on our new nature. He knows our old nature erupts when confronted with the law, and he knows that we'll constantly fail. Jesus came to take care of all of that. He lived the law perfectly and died to free us from the pressure to perform in our new relationship. That's what verse 6 says.

"But now we have been released from the Law, having died to that by which we were being bound, so that we are serving in newness of the Spirit and not in oldness of the letter," concludes Paul in the passage (7:6 DAV). Let me give you two verses to go along with that. 2 Corinthians 3:5-6 states:

> Not that we are adequate in ourselves to consider anything as coming from ourselves, but our adequacy is from God, who also made us adequate as servants of a new covenant, not of the letter, but of the Spirit; for the letter kills, but the Spirit gives life." (NASB)

And 2 Corinthians 3:17-18 tells us:

> Now the Lord is the Spirit; and where the Spirit of the Lord is, there is liberty. But we all, with unveiled face beholding as in a mirror the glory of the Lord, are being transformed into the same image from glory to glory, just as from the Lord, the Spirit. (NASB)

Progressive change comes with relationship. Christlikeness comes with time. "'For I am confident of this very thing," says the apostle in Philippians 1:6, "that He who began a good work in you will perfect it until the day of Christ Jesus" (NASB). As we cooperate with the indwelling Holy

Spirit, the process is accelerated, but that's the only way. As God finds us submissive, obedient, and sensitive to the things that deepen our relationship with him and the things that hurt it, the work goes on toward Christlikeness.

To sum this section up, we've learned three principles concerning the law, Christ, and the believer:

- As Christians, we're reminded that our living union with Jesus is much like a marriage relationship.
- When we came into this union, we died to the law and also to performance. Our lives are not to be oriented toward living by legalistic standards.
- Our purpose in being joined to Jesus Christ is to bear fruit to God.

With those three in mind, let's take to heart the benediction of Jude 24-25:

> Now to Him who is able to keep you from stumbling, and to make you stand in the presence of His glory blameless with great joy, to the only God our Savior, through Jesus Christ our Lord, be glory, majesty, dominion and authority, before all time and now and forever. Amen. (NASB)

God alone has the strength and the grace, the power and the adequacy, to make us like Christ. The time is now to begin to allow him to start the quiet work of making us like the Son. "Search me, O God, and know my heart; test me and know my anxious thoughts. See if there is any offensive way in me, and lead me in the way everlasting," we might exclaim with the psalmist (Ps. 139:23-24 NIV).

"Lord," we might ask him, "where am I offending you in this relationship?" Then we can let him work. And as he puts his finger on any given area of our life, let's confess it, admit it, saying, "Lord, I'm sorry. I've done that for years. I didn't realize it was offending you. I'm willing to let you deal with that area." And we'll be amazed at the joy and the sense of freedom and the liberty we'll experience. The fragrance of Christ-likeness will come as we meticulously, one by one, confront the things to which we've been oblivious that have hurt our relationship with him. When you ask God to work in your life, get ready for the rubber to meet the road, sometimes with a screech, squeal, and the smoke of a seared conscience.

Trust me—when you're willing, God will let you know the areas he's ready to remodel. One day, a close friend phoned with some comments about my pulpit demeanor. "Don, lately when you preach, you've got a frown on your face and you're angry. It's hurting your effectiveness." I acknowledged the criticism and hung up the phone, unconvinced of its truth. Later that day, another good friend called with much the same message, and my wife gently confirmed his opinion.

I've observed that when one person calls you a donkey, you should pay no attention. When a second person calls you a donkey, maybe you'd better start checking for hoofprints. When a third person follows suit, it's time to change or else buy a cart to pull, especially when number three is your wife! "Okay, Lord," I sighed, humbled. "I'm wrong. Thank you for showing me this area you need to clean up." It was necessary for me to, in humility, bring matters before the Father. If I had resisted, rebelled, or rationalized the wrong, an opportunity for growth and the deepening of my relationship with Christ would have passed me by.

THE PROBLEM—ROMANS 7:7-13

As Paul has shown us in the first part of Romans 7, our

relationship to Christ is something like a marriage—a second marriage, actually. We were bound to the law, and we died to that old relationship, that old "marriage" partner, when we came to know Christ and he became our new partner. God designed the law to create a need in our heart. When we look at the law, we ought to be frustrated; we ought to feel guilty. We ought to recognize our shortcomings. That's normal! But we do not, cannot, must not, bring the law over into our new relationship with Christ. With every restriction comes the desire to exceed it. We're tempted to blame it all on the law, to think of the law as bad. But the problem is not the law. Let's continue with Romans 7:7-13 and discover more about the real culprit that prevents us from living a victorious Christian life.

Paul begins verse 7 with a question: "What therefore shall we say? Is the Law sin?" Then he gives the answer: "May it never be! On the contrary, I would not have known sin except through the Law; for I would not have known evil desire except that the Law was saying: 'You shall not desire evil'" (7:7 DAV). Since the law is responsible for pointing out sin, it's natural to assume that the law itself is sin. But Paul says no, the law is not sin. The real culprit is something else: that old nature we received from Adam. As we saw in Romans 6, it's still within us, and it will still respond to the law the same way it did before we became Christians. The law cannot make us righteous, saintly, or holy—either before or after we accept Christ!

It's been said that the law is like an X-ray machine, seeing directly through us, showing us the problem areas. Another has said that the law is a detective, probing us, revealing clues and giving indications about areas where we need to let God work in us. The New Testament writer James probably describes it best when he says the law is like a mirror (James 1:22-25). If you look into a mirror and see that your hair isn't combed or your face is dirty, do you become angry at the mirror? Is it the mirror's fault that you have uncombed hair and an unwashed face? Of course not. The mirror is simply fulfilling its function by giving you a reflection of yourself. Can you use the mirror to wash your face? Not a chance. The fact is you need a brand new relationship with a washcloth, some water, and a bar of soap in order to deal with the dirt.

In the same way, we must not become angry at the law because it shows us our defilement, our dirty face. That is its function. And we surely can't clean ourselves up with the law! This is accomplished by the cleansing of the Spirit of God, the "washing of regeneration and renewing by the Holy Spirit" which Paul writes of in his letter to Titus (Titus 3:5 NASB). In Romans 8, we'll see that the Spirit is capable of giving us victory over certain sin areas, but regardless, we'll never be completely rid of the sin nature that lies within. Nothing in scripture suggests that we're ever to be freed from the old nature until we join the Father in eternity.

For now, let's admit that the old nature is not going to go away. Paul prayed earnestly that the Lord would remove a thorn from his flesh. God said no with these words of assurance, "My grace is sufficient for you, for my power is made perfect in weakness" (2 Cor. 12:9 NIV). It is doubtful that Paul was referring to his sin nature, but rather some physical infirmity. Yet the principle is the same. God will never totally deliver us from the old nature in this lifetime. He doesn't want us to be robots, but responders who willingly choose to answer the new and obey him. Saying no to the old and yes to the Spirit, who will energize the new nature, is the key. Then comes the abundant joy of a fulfilled life in Christ. The remaining verses of Romans 7 show us that Paul is on a journey of his own, trying to understand fully how he himself might gain victory and begin to reflect righteousness in his life.

"But sin," continues Paul, "grasping an opportunity

through the commandment, called forth within me every kind of evil desire; for without law, sin is dead" (7:8 DAV). Let's consider this verse. Substitute the term "sin nature" for "sin," and you'll have the picture. Paul is saying that his old nature, when confronted with a commandment of the law, responded to that commandment in the natural way. With prohibition came the determination to do it anyway. After a slip, perhaps Paul promised himself, "I'll never do that again." But even then the old nature simply responded, "Oh, yes you will! Just wait! I'll get you yet!" And, as Paul puts it, "every kind of evil desire" was called forth from him. Things must have seemed hopeless. But they really weren't.

"For without Law," continues Paul, "sin is dead." The sin nature doesn't leave, but if the law is not used to activate it, then the sin nature is effectively dead, helpless, powerless. The question then arises that if the law is going to aggravate the old nature, why don't we leave it at the cross? That's where it belongs! The law brought us to Christ ... now we must not make the mistake of dumping it onto our Christian life. Doing just that is a major cause of guilt among Christians. When we determine that we have to act in a certain way because we have to, not because we want to because we love God and are allowing his Spirit to work in us, then we're asking for guilt, failure, and emptiness in our spiritual life. We've got to learn to live without the law!

INHERENT INCOMPATIBILITY

I shared with you earlier in this chapter the saga of the tiger fish at the Anderson aquatic arena. Now I'd like you to meet Sasha and the senior citizen. The senior citizen was our cat, a Heinz 57 variety who looked like Felix the cartoon cat and who'd been hit by a car once or twice. His name was Toodles. At age seven—49 in human years—Toodles was easing into mid-life pampered, purring, and mostly motionless for much of each day. Then came Sasha.

Sasha was a little Lhasa Apso puppy given to us by some friends. When I brought playful Sasha home to the domain of the senior citizen, I witnessed a predictable response: the playful puppy chased Toodles all over the place. The cat was never the same. Instead of leisurely lounging around the house, he started sitting nervously on a perch, jumping down periodically to run for his food, eating, jumping up again to the perch—all with amazing speed so that he didn't have to deal with a pesky pup. Often Toodles retreated underneath the couch. Pug-nosed Sasha would come walking by and all of a sudden Toodles's black and white arm would come flipping out. Whop! The feline would strike Sasha across the face, just to tell him he was getting too close to cat territory. The dog would duck, bark, and dive. Out then zipped Toodles, arching his back, hissing. The two simply never got along! My kids even prayed about the problem. Desperately they wished the two would learn to love each other. But it was never to be so. It was in Toodles's nature to respond negatively to Sasha, and the cat was incapable of change.

Introducing the law to the old nature is like placing Sasha and Toodles into a windowless, locked, five-by-five room. When it happens, the claws appear, the back arches, and the old, dormant nature springs forth with devastating surprise. It's capable of everything it did before you became a Christian. It's capable of infidelity, dishonesty, ingratitude, lack of love. Christianity is not an instant cure-all and Christians who respond to the old nature will surely fall.

When a person continually answers the call of the old and practices illicit behavior, it's true that we might question his salvation. But the man or woman who slips up in his life, or even has a major crash, has merely done what we are all capable of doing: answering the call of the old. The old nature will hungrily devour us every opportunity it gets to bare its teeth. As Paul tells us in verse 8, our inclination is toward forbidden fruit. Proverbs 9:17 reinforces the idea: "Stolen waters are sweet, and bread eaten in secret is pleasant" (KJV). Proverbs 5:3-6 says, "For the lips of an adulteress drip honey, and her speech is smoother than oil; but in the end she is bitter as gall, sharp as a double-edged sword. Her feet go down to death; her steps lead straight to the grave" (NIV). There is a certain attractiveness and a definite danger about sin. There is a power to it, and when we try to resist it by ourselves, we lose. The old nature grabs us the moment we allow it.

A PHARISEE OF PHARISEES

"And I was once alive without Law; but when the commandment came, sin became alive, and I died," Paul goes on to say in verse 9 (DAV). The verse is puzzling at first glance. When was Paul alive without the law? He may be talking about the time before he was 13 years of age. In Jewish society, a child assumed the responsibilities of the law in the Hebrew home at the age of 13. Before then, he was free from the law, not accountable to it, alive apart from it. It was taught that God dealt with Jewish children in grace until they were old enough to comprehend his teachings.

Paul tells us that he was alive without the law until the commandment came—whenever he reached an age of moral awareness—and he assumed the responsibility for the law at that time. Then sin became alive to him and, as he writes, he died. He suffered spiritual separation from God because of his sin. He was, as he puts it in Ephesians 2:1, dead in his "trespasses and sins," and in desperate need of spiritual life (NASB).

Paul lived like every other Jewish boy of his day, with the hope that if he did the best he could in keeping the commandments and living by the law, he would have spiritual life as a result of the keeping of the law. But ironically, all he found was what we've discussed before, that the law both revealed and stimulated his sin and that, in his words, "this commandment, which was to result in life, I discovered to result in death for me" (Rom. 7:10 DAV).

Oh yes, to the best of his ability, Paul adhered to the law. As he tells us in Philippians 3:5-6, he was "circumcised the eighth day, of the nation of Israel, of the tribe of Benjamin, a Hebrew of Hebrews [in other words, born of Jewish parents]; as to the Law, a Pharisee; as to zeal, a persecutor of the church; as to the righteousness which is in the Law, found blameless" (NASB). But immediately after he lists his attempts at keeping the law, Paul says this, "But whatever things were gain to me, those things I have counted as loss for the sake of Christ" (Phil. 3:7 NASB).

As a Pharisee, Paul committed himself, along with 5,999 other Pharisees, to the most rigid adherence to the law imaginable. He was zealous in the keeping of the law, a superachiever outstripping the pack in the marathon of striving for sanctity. In Philippians 3:4-7 he tells us that his efforts at keeping the law far exceeded those of others. He blazed a trail of attempted righteousness, and it was all performance. It was also hopeless, for the law said "Thou shalt not covet," and one day Paul coveted, as he told us in Romans 7:7-8. Remember, scripture says, "For whosoever shall keep the whole law, and yet offend in one point, he is guilty of all" (James 2:10 KJV). The moment Paul coveted, he died spiritually. The game was lost. The party was over. Life for him would have to come from some other source than the law. He found it in Christ Jesus, and came to count all performance loss except for the surpassing riches of the Lord! (see Phil. 3:8.)

"For sin, grasping an opportunity through the commandment, deceived me, and through it killed me," further explains Paul in Romans 7:11 (DAV). The word *deceived* used here is the same word used to describe what happened when Satan beguiled Eve in the garden (see also

2 Cor. 11:3). The devil is the great deceiver, and the only entrance he has into our life as a Christian is through the sin nature. The devil doesn't directly make us do bad things, but he definitely stirs up the old nature to sin when he's given the chance. Man is led into temptation by Satan, the old nature responds, and sin results.

The problem is not with the law. "So then," continues Paul in Romans 7:12, "the Law is holy, and the commandment is holy and righteous, and good" (DAV). God's law was "ordained through angels" (Gal. 3:19 NASB). God's standards expressed in the law are holy and just. The law is holy because it expresses the will of a holy God. It is righteous because it condemns sin. It is good because it directs us toward the redeemer. It points us toward our need of Jesus Christ and is beautiful precisely because it does convince us that goodness is impossible without the savior.

"Therefore, did that which is good become death for me?" concludes Paul in Romans 7:13 (DAV). "May it never be!" he answers his own question, returning to the fact, as in verse 7, that the law is not the problem. The sin nature is. Paul puts it this way in the rest of verse 13, "It was sin, in order that it might be shown to be sin by accomplishing my death through that which is good, in order that through the commandment sin might become sinful in the extreme" (DAV). The purpose of the law is to show us that sin is there. It will show sin to the extreme when it's functioning properly. It reveals sin, provokes sin, condemns sin. The old nature is the culprit that responds.

Paul has told us of a time in his life when he was self-righteous, self-satisfied, self-confident. He thought he had it all together. Then in came the law and he broke it and died spiritually. Later, he was pointed toward Jesus Christ.

We believers can think of ourselves as individuals hung by a strand over the burning fires of eternity, facing eternal death, and then snatched from judgment by the great lifesaver, Jesus Christ, who plunged into human history. By his death on the cross, Christ takes care of the judgment, pays the penalty of broken law. Having assumed that responsibility by his death, he reaches out and offers us the gift of eternal life if we but believe. "Who gave Himself for our sins, that He might deliver us out of this present evil age, according to the will of our God and Father" (Gal. 1:4 NASB). Once we've accepted him, we need never doubt our salvation. Doubting that we're saved is the same as doubting the adequacy of Christ. In Jesus we have a righteousness that can never be tarnished, never be changed, is totally acceptable to the Father. If it were not so, the Father would have left the Son in the grave on that Easter morn, but instead he raised him triumphantly from the dead!

IN THE WOLF PACK

A national magazine carried the account some years ago of a group of scientists who went to Alaska with the intent of photographing and researching the caribou. It was necessary for them to be there for a number of seasons. One day, while out taking photographs, the researchers happened on an abandoned wolf den. Assuming the mother and father had been killed, the researchers removed the two cute, roly-poly wolf pups they found within the den. The two creatures acted like dog puppies in the house; they were playful and docile. And they were loved and treated with gentleness and care. But they grew, and one day, despite the tender loving care, both of them turned on their human masters and the men barely escaped alive. The once-playful cubs, now full-grown wolves, ran off to join a wild wolf pack. They inevitably, inescapably, responded to the nature with which they'd been born.

Let's admit it. No matter how hard we try to educate the sin nature, no matter how we try to psychoanalyze it or explain it away, it's there. It will continue the same old habits it did before we became Christians. It will raise its ugly head when we give it the chance. That much is undeniable, and the apostle will convince us of that as we approach the remainder of Romans 7. Please read on, for the rest of the story!

Questions to Consider

1. How does Paul's marriage example in Romans 7:2-3 illustrate the relationship of the Christian to the law of Moses? Is it possible to be "married" both to the law and to Jesus Christ? Explain why or why not.

2. Is the law itself sinful or evil? Why or why not? What good things does the law accomplish in the lives of people before they receive Christ as savior?

3. Can you think of an area of sin in your life that the law revealed to you before you became a Christian? Share your answer, if you wish.

CHAPTER 7

"But I say, walk by the Spirit, and you will not carry out the desire of flesh. For the flesh sets its desire against the Spirit, and the Spirit against the flesh; for these are in opposition to one another, so that you may not do the things that you please. But if you are led by the Spirit, you are not under the Law" (Gal. 5:16-18 NASB).

The Conflict

Romans 7:14-25

Take a moment and imagine yourself ready for bed. You lie down, propping your head on the pillow in order to read through a favorite magazine before drifting off. Just as you're nearing the end of an article and are about to turn out the light, you hear it. Buzzzzz. A fly swoops in for a better look at you. You wave the magazine to shoo him away. No sooner is he gone than he comes back again. Buzzzz. You try to ignore the noise. Buzzzz. No good. You wait as long as you can, then when the irritation level reaches the intolerable, you roll up the magazine and wait some more. The fly makes a low pass and you strike. You miss. Now he knows you're after him, and the warfare has begun in earnest. You jump up from bed and scan the room for a sign of the enemy. Meanwhile, the fly hides in the drapes, catching his breath, planning his next attack. Buzzzz. There he is again. Swing! Another miss ... and your wife puts on her glasses in order to see the show. Twenty minutes later a loud smash of the magazine against the bathroom counter signals victory at last. Two stubbed toes, one broken lampshade, and debris strewn in your wake indicate the price of winning the battle. I *have* been there, done that, and got the scars. Pearl's response at the moment of victory: "This was more entertaining than television."

As Paul has already indicated, the old nature is a fly that will never be destroyed. It will be a constant irritant in our Christian life, catching its breath in the curtains, ready to seize control each time we give it a chance. At the conclusion of his account of the temptation of Jesus, Luke records these words: "And when the devil had finished every temptation, he departed from Him until an opportune time" (Luke 4:13 NASB). We lived totally under the old nature's dominion before we came to Christ ... but even after our conversion the old is a lingering presence, a constant source of conflict. People promise that you'll never sin again once you become a Christian, that everything will come up roses. But these folks are either blatantly dishonest or else they are in denial of the fact that their lives are still tainted by sin. The truth is that the beginning of our life in Christ also signals the inception of a lifelong struggle between the old and the new. Sometimes it will seem that the old is gaining ground and the new is surrendering territory at an alarming rate.

THE MARINES HAVE LANDED

Lane Adams's *How Come It's Taking Me So Long?* is reading I highly recommend. Adams, who has been a minister for many years and who has honestly struggled with some of the concepts about sin and victory that we're discussing here, considers the reasons why our spiritual progress sometimes seems at a standstill, why our victories often are few and far between. He uses an unforgettable illustration to depict the Christian life, and I'd like to borrow his example here.

Adams served as a navy pilot during World War II. In the Pacific theater, the United States implemented a war plan to regain possession of each strategically important island that had been lost to the Japanese. After photographs taken from reconnaissance planes were analyzed to determine the locations of fortifications, an aerial assault was begun on the targeted island in order to weaken enemy resistance and enable an invasion of the beachhead to begin. When enemy fortifications were sufficiently weakened, troop ships carrying platoons of Marines would move into the area. Soon the Marines would find themselves aboard a landing craft, then rendezvousing at a prearranged section of the beach. They'd dig in, secure that beachhead, and radio back these confident words, "The Marines have landed, and the situation is well in hand."

Actually, the situation was not at all well in hand. The Marines were on the beach, but there was a whole lot more of the island left to conquer! The radio transmission, "The Marines have landed," merely signified that the battle had begun in full. Bit by bit the Marines would have to push ahead, securing the rest of the island section by section, aided by continued aerial bombardment and the barrage from the heavy artillery and tanks that had followed them onto the beachhead.

Lane Adams argues that the picture of the Marines landing and conducting a systematic onslaught against an enemy-held island is an apt illustration of what happens to us following conversion to Christ. Writes Adams:

> We are all islands of self in the hands of the

> enemy. Conversion is like an invasion, and the Christian life is like a war. When we respond to the invitation of Jesus ... then the Holy Spirit of Christ invades us and establishes a beachhead in our lives. An enemy-held island now has inside it the invading force of our friendly God. He is beginning a conquest by love, not by tyranny, but we must always remember it is just a beginning.
>
> There is a sincere but mistaken form of evangelism which gives the impression that the total conquest of the island is accomplished by the mere invasion. Both the Bible and human experience deny that this is the case, yet such notions persist, and when they are believed by the new Christian he is being set up for an agonizing experience in the not too distant future. The realities of life with the continual sin problem still staring him in the face will finally lead him to deny that reality, or he must assume there is something faulty with his conversion. Some begin to wonder if they are converted at all.[1]

Figuratively speaking, when you became a Christian, the Marines landed on the beachhead of your life. The Spirit of God came into enemy territory. He secured a beachhead, and the life of Jesus Christ began flowing through you. But Christian growth is war, a continuing conflict between the new divine nature and the old sinful one. There's a bit of gain here, and a bit more there, and, throughout the remaining years of your life, the warfare of your becoming Christ-like continues. Progress seems terribly slow at times—almost like taking three steps forward and two steps back ... again and again and again. You hasten the Christ-likeness by manifesting a willing, teachable spirit of obedience, but the battle isn't over till God calls you physically home. As we've discussed in previous chapters, when we try to conquer sin ourselves by attempting to follow the rules and regulations of the law, we find that our old nature is stirred up all the more. It responds to our desire to perform, and we find we sin despite ourselves. The law points up our sin, it stimulates our sin, but it can never erase the presence or power of sin in our life.

The question we might consider as we continue to look at Romans 7 is this: *How can I experientially find deliverance from the control of the sin nature that still dwells within me?* When beginning to answer this question, Paul is very honest. We'll see in the second half of Romans 7 that it is possible to be a mature Christian and still fail. We can know the Lord, realize that he desires to bear fruit in us, and yet still answer the call of the old nature. In fact, Paul tells us that even he was prone to respond to the old, and that even the spiritual life of an apostle could be one of dryness, drudgery, deadness, and defeat.

THE NATURE OF THE BATTLE—ROMANS 7:14-25

"For we are knowing that the law is spiritual," says Paul in verse 14, reiterating his earlier message that the law is holy (DAV, see 7:12). The problem is not the law itself. Instead Paul finds that the problem is with him. He is the reason he is not experiencing the victory he would like in his Christian life. "But I am fleshly," he tells us, "having been sold under sin" (DAV 7:14b). The old sin nature is an undeniable reality in Paul's life. He is its unwilling victim. The law, though holy because it expresses God's standards, could not help him become better before he encountered Christ, and it cannot help him become a better person after receiving Jesus as savior.

Paul's admission that he is still a victim of the old nature shows us that he has taken a major step toward spiritual maturity. It's rare that a carnal Christian, one living under the consistent control of his old nature, will admit that he is sinful. Generally, such folks have trouble spotting their own sin. They're often too self-righteous to recognize their own shortcomings; they look for splinters in the eyes of others and ignore the logs in their own. Men and women who tout their own sinlessness are talking about a ball game that, frankly, I'm not playing. Within the confines of the institutional church, we've created an ugly monster which roars the message that everything is okay. We're not tempted. We don't fail. We are spiritual giants easily swatting the flies that spiritually assail us. We bury ourselves in the Bible and deny that there are personal battles and horrible failures. Yet you and I know that even the godly Christian life contains its share of the agony of defeat.

Paul's honest admission that sin lingers in his life is the statement of a spiritual man. A person who is walking with the Lord is sensitive to the sin that remains in his life, and he doesn't mind saying so. He knows he fails. Like Paul, he knows he is fleshly, that he is prone to sin. Indeed, the truth is that we'll never cry for deliverance until we become aware of our own wretchedness. We'll never yield ourselves to the Lord's strength until we are able to admit that nothing good will ever come from us or out of us apart from God's grace.

Why can't we just get rid of the sin nature? Why doesn't God remove it at the moment of our salvation? Why must we continue to be "fleshly" after coming to Christ? God prefers that we always have a choice in matters. He longs for us to obey him by choosing to respond to our new nature because we love him, but he will never violate our free will. He doesn't operate that way.

Instead, we have two natures and we have the opportunity to present our members to the Father for righteousness and daily to act on that presentation (6:13). Daily we have the opportunity to delight him by responding to the new.

The old nature doubts. The old nature fears and is filled with depression. The old nature demands its rights. The old nature curses and struggles and lies. It envies and covets and steals. The old nature shows indifference and loses its temper. It becomes arrogant, bitter, and abusive. The coexistence of the old and the new within us enables us to have mountaintop moments of victory, which are rapidly followed by freefalls into the valley of despair.

As a result of recognizing that two natures co-exist within us, we learn tremendous lessons of dependence on God the Father. If a man like the apostle Paul cannot experience victory by going it alone, then certainly you and I cannot either. The power of sin is greater than we are, with our natural human resources. There must be a more effective way to victory, and so we learn dependence. We learn to trust that God will provide the means of overcoming sin. And we learn to realize that whichever nature we fuel is the one that will predominate.

"UNDOING" IT YOURSELF

As Paul continues in Romans 7, he gives us the graphic picture of his own confusion and frustration. "For that which I am doing, I am not understanding; for I am not practicing that which I am desiring to do, but I am doing that which I am hating," he writes in verse 15 (DAV). There it is in a nutshell: the conflict between the old and the new. Paul admits that his conduct is not what he would like it to be. He is doing that which he hates. He is responding to the old. Why?

Remember, responding to the old can almost be a reflex action for us. When we approach a red light at an intersection, we don't have to send a conscious message to our brain in order for our foot to step on the brake. It's reflex action to respond. In the same way, when we are confronted with the temptation to sin, we often don't have to consciously send a message of "go ahead" to our brain. It's reflex to respond wrongly. We may not understand it, but the reality is that it's awfully easy to answer the old instead of the new. And if the apostle Paul finds it frustrating, why shouldn't we?

We'll notice as we read through the rest of Romans 7 that there is no mention of the power of the Spirit of God in the conflict between the old and new in Paul's life. That doesn't come until chapter 8. Instead the picture in Romans 7 is of Paul responding by himself to the problem of sin. It's a portrait of the apostle trying to perform in the flesh to produce righteousness in his life—a depiction of a man responding to the old despite his own knowledge of the new. If we don't learn to appreciate the power of the new nature, energized by the Spirit, and if we don't learn to give up on our human resources in favor of God's heavenly ones, we'll be stuck in the same rut.

"Now if I am doing that which I am not desiring, I am agreeing with the Law that it is good," Paul continues in verse 16 (DAV). In other words, my deeds are evil because they are contrary to God's law, which I admit is good. The law shows us that what the old nature does is not good. Like the thief hanging on the cross beside Christ, when confronted with the law, we can only conclude that we deserve condemnation for our crimes (Luke 23:41).

AN HONEST ADMISSION

"So now, no longer am I the one doing it, but sin which indwells me," Paul goes on (7:17 DAV). The "I" to which he refers is his new nature in Christ; the "sin" is his old nature. The old nature is the villain; Paul is the respondent, and because he responds to the old, he experiences defeat. The verse should convince us of the power of sin. We desperately need help to control our old nature.

"For I am knowing that nothing good is dwelling in me, that is, in my flesh; for the being desirous is present in me, but the doing of the good is not," states Paul in verse 18

(DAV). We want to do good. We want to become free of sin. But the power to do so lies not in our flesh. We are incapable of performing victoriously in the flesh. The "doing of good" is simply not naturally in us. How much we can learn from Paul's willingness to be vulnerable and open.

I think again of how easy it is for Christians to hide behind a facade of pseudo-righteousness. We like to give the impression that we have it completely together when the reality is that the wheels have already come off and the wagon has flipped. In the process, we forget that feigned holiness only makes others feel worse because they aren't on the same apparent spiritual level. Owning up to the fact that we struggle is often more encouraging than proclaiming our victories!

I think of a letter printed in the alumni edition of *Kindred Spirit*, the magazine published by Dallas Theological Seminary. This letter, penned by a former student, pierced my heart. The writer voiced his discouragement about the fact that all the other graduates seemed to write glowing letters describing the successes of their ministries. Just once, the writer admitted, he would like to read about someone who was struggling. He wanted to hear that someone else was having a tough time, that another heart was breaking, that somebody else's life was coming loose at the seams. Instead of numbers of baptisms, converts, and sizes of building programs, he desperately yearned to know that other people's gardens also had thorns.

So many times we fail to minister to others because we are afraid to admit the truth, which is that we all struggle with the old nature. And even more tragically, when someone does tell us about the thorns, we often feel compelled to share his or her burden over the phone with a select number of others who will pray for the poor guy! So we become afraid to share, encasing ourselves in the armor-plated cocoon of cool reserve while our hearts cry for warm fellowship and the comfort of knowing we're not alone in the war.

THE PRINCIPLE

Paul knows that life is tough, and he is finding that victory cannot be achieved alone. "For the good which I am desiring, I am not doing, but I am practicing the very evil that I am not desiring," he states in verse 19 (DAV), repeating what he has already said in verse 15. "Now if I am doing the very thing I am not desiring, I am no longer the one doing it, but sin which dwells in me" (7:20 DAV), he says next, this time reiterating the major point of verse 17. There is a fly in his house, and Paul is finding that he responds to the pesky old nature every time he turns around, despite his desire to do good.

"I am finding then the law, that evil is present in me, the one who is desiring to do good," continues Paul in verse 21 (DAV). The "law" to which he refers here is not the Mosaic law. He is using the term *law* in the same way that we might use the term *principle*. Paul reveals that he has discovered a principle about his attempts at living the Christian life. He realizes that evil is present in him. The sin nature is there, even though he is an individual who "is desiring to do good."

Have you ever watched a little baby discover the law or principle of gravity? Little Chad sits in a high chair, and one day reaches for his silver spoon. He knocks it to the floor. Mother picks it up. When she turns her back, Chad decides to see if the law of gravity also applies to bowls of cereal, and so the breakfast dish is knocked off. Mother whirls around with a loud, "No, no, darling!" and the game is set for months. Toys, spoons, shoes or everything not strapped down gets dropped by the inquisitive tot. Chad has learned the law of gravity. Unfortunately, one day he falls out of the high chair and finds out for himself that the law of gravity can be painful.

Paul simply tells us in verse 21 that he has discovered a

principle in his life as consistent as the law of gravity: evil is present in him in the form of the old nature, although he has the burning desire to do good. It's human nature to want to perform well; it's also human nature to respond to the old. When we try to perform in the flesh to please God, when we try to live a good life apart from his strength and Spirit, when we place ourselves on a performance basis with him, we doom ourselves to defeat.

There is an unavoidable conflict in the Christian life, Paul tells us. "For I joyfully agree with the law of God concerning the inner man," he writes in verse 22 (DAV). "But I am seeing a different kind of law in my members warring against the law of my mind, making me a prisoner of war to the law of sin which is in my members," he says further in verse 23 (DAV). In other words, Paul joyfully acknowledges the presence of the new nature, "the law (or principle) of God concerning the inner man." But the cold, hard fact is that the law of sin, the old nature, is still there and the clash between the old and new is inevitable. Galatians 5:17 puts it this way: "For the flesh sets its desire against the Spirit, and the Spirit against the flesh; for these are in opposition to one another, so that you may not do the things that you please" (NASB). When we respond to the old, we move out of fellowship with God; when we respond to the new, we resume fellowship with him. Our relationship with him cannot be ended, but the quality of our friendship with him can be positively or negatively affected by the choices we make. We're forgiven no matter what, but the richness of the relationship hangs in the balance.

HELP! WE NEED SOMEBODY!

From the midst of his frustration, Paul cries out for assistance. "Wretched man that I am!" he exclaims in verse 24. "Who shall set me free from out of the body of this death?" (7:24 DAV). A spiritual man recognizes his own shortcomings and sin, and Paul is a spiritual man. He is also an exhausted one. His cry for help speaks of his weariness, his struggle, his brokenness, his defeat. He has tried to do the good that his heart desires, yet he has encountered only his sheer inability to succeed alone. Try as he might, he simply cannot live up to the law. The more he labors and works, the more he is defeated and the more the old nature gets the mastery and ugly qualities emerge.

Notice that Paul calls himself a "wretched man." He does not label himself a "guilty man." He is wretched, not guilty, and there is an important distinction. His sins are forgiven; his salvation is irrevocable because he has trusted Christ once for all time. God will never reckon him guilty. But Paul is, in his own eyes, wretched.

The word for "wretched" which Paul uses is also found in Revelation 3. There the Lord addresses the church at Laodicea, a bunch of believers grown wealthy, comfortable, and complacent. Despite their creature comforts, the Lord tells the Christians at Laodicea, "You do not know that you are wretched and miserable and poor and blind and naked" (3:17 NASB). The Laodiceans did not have an accurate picture of themselves; they were unwilling to see themselves as they really were. They thought everything was great, when really the picture of their spiritual life was pathetic. They were shipwrecked in the midst of their sanctimony.

The Pharisees too thought they had it all together spiritually, when really their life was drenched in insincerity and wretched in the sight of God. "Woe to you, scribes and Pharisees, hypocrites!" exclaims Christ in Matthew 23:27, "For you are like whitewashed tombs which on the outside appear beautiful, but inside they are full of dead men's bones and all uncleanness" (NASB, see also 23:1ff). The Jewish religious leaders, blind to their hypocrisy and confused morality, had no idea that their appearance before God was that of foulness and decay. Their spiritual deadness was coated by a thin layer of phony righteousness, which may have fooled man but was easily penetrated by the piercing eyes of the Lord.

That same sort of self-deception can go on in our own Christian life also. The farther we get from the day of salvation, the more content we become with mediocrity, the more we rationalize away the manifestations of the old nature, the more we settle for experiencing defeat, the more wretched we become in the eyes of God. Oh, we may appear spiritual to the world. We may know the proper Christian buzz words. In groups we may rattle off sentence prayers with glibness and ease. But the Lord knows our heart. And remember what he tells the church at Laodicea: "I know your deeds, that you are neither cold nor hot; I would that you were cold or hot. So because you are lukewarm, and neither hot nor cold, I will spit you out of My mouth" (Rev. 3:15-16 NASB). Their spiritual mediocrity made him sick. Oh that God would give us a clear picture of what he sees in us rather than what we see in ourselves! Instead of making excuses and concocting rationalizations, we should see ourselves as we really are, and that recognition of our own wretchedness will serve as the prelude to victory.

"Wretched man that I am!" exclaims Paul. His appraisal of himself indicates that he is a spiritual man. Remember, the closer such folks get to the Lord, the more they become aware of the sin in their life. Paul isn't the only one in scripture whose statements about himself illustrate this principle. Look at the words of three other giants of the faith:

> Abraham: "... though I am nothing but dust and ashes" (Gen. 18:27b NIV).
>
> Job: "Behold, I am vile" (Job 40:4a KJV). "Therefore I despise myself and repent in dust and ashes" (42:6 NIV).

> Isaiah: "Woe to me! ... For I am a man of unclean lips" (Isa. 6:5 NIV).

The closer we walk with God, the more vividly we recognize our own wretchedness. "Who shall set me free from out of the body of this death?" asks Paul with desperate hope (Rom. 7:24b DAV). The answer will be given in part in the next verse, and continued in the next chapter. For now, let's think about the graphic terminology Paul uses in the preceding verse. He paints a verbal portrait of a man accused of murder. The Romans made a practice of chaining the corpses of their victims to jailed murderers. The accused was forced to drag around the decomposing body of the one he had slain as a constant reminder of what he had done. Paul calls his own body that—a foul corpse with the old nature within it—a constant source of temptation and reminder of the sins of the past. He wants to be set free! He thirsts for righteousness and hungers for victory!

Who can deliver Paul out of the body of this death? "Thanks be to God through Jesus Christ our Lord!" he exclaims in the next verse (7:25 DAV), and gives part of the answer. The Lord Jesus is the key to victory over his problem.

"So then, on the one hand I myself with my mind am serving the law of God, but on the other, with my flesh the law of sin," continues Paul (7:25 DAV). Basically, Paul tells us that he is thinking right, but he is not acting right. Mentally, he desires to serve the law of God, to answer the new nature, but practically, his actions are something else. Despite his own best efforts, he is still serving with his flesh the law of sin, or the old nature.

The crux of the dilemma is this: Paul is trying to go it alone. He has trusted Christ as savior, now he must trust him as the means of victorious Christian living. Mixing the law and relationship will only aggravate the old nature and result in sin. It's impossible, by human performance, to answer the call of the new nature, no matter how much we desire it. We must come to the point in our Christian life where we cry to God for deliverance from the continued power of sin, much as we once cried to him for deliverance from the penalty of sin. We must reach the point of human helplessness in order to experience holiness. From our own brokenness and contrite spirit can emerge something beautiful.

THE BEAUTY OF A BROKEN AND CONTRITE HEART

The theme of Romans 7:14-25 might be Paul's contrition. He is desperately sorrowful about his shortcomings, his bitter lack of victory, the searing evidences of sin that remain. When we become tangibly aware of our own sin as Christians, we become repentant, and that is what we see happening to Paul in Romans 7.

Webster defines repentance as "a feeling of sorrow ... especially for wrongdoing; compunction; contrition; remorse." Repentant is how we might describe David following his adultery with Bathsheba. "Surely I was sinful at birth, sinful from the time my mother conceived me. ... Create in me a pure heart, O God, and renew a steadfast spirit within me" he cries to God (Ps. 51:5,10 NIV). With a contrite heart such as David's or Paul's, the door is open for the Lord to work. It's a question of surrender to him. Successful, victorious living comes as we surrender to his lordship and allow his Spirit to begin to energize the new nature within us. Then we become increasingly sensitive to the things in our life that hurt our relationship with God. With hearts beautiful to him because of their brokenness, we might even ask him the following:

> Lord, what is it that is hurting you? What is it that I'm justifying? What is it that I'm failing to recognize as a product of the old nature?

> What is it that's making my spiritual life an arid desert experience? I feel like a dried up well, and I am grieved because there is such an absence of fruit in my life.

When we do that, God begins to work through his word—he convicts us. Through our times of prayer we start to know the joy of his presence. We begin to experience the incredible joy of the new nature beginning to manifest itself in our lives. It's fantastic!

And yet, let's never forget that the Marines have landed. The situation really is well in hand, because the Spirit of God is unconquerable, as we'll see in Romans 8. But the battle merely begins when we receive Christ into our life, and it continues until the day we joyously enter directly into his presence. Then the enemy-held island will be completely conquered by the king—the king of kings!

Questions to Consider

1. In verse 15, Paul admits that he is not practicing the good which he desires to do, but is doing that which he hates. What does this honest admission tell you about his level of maturity in the Lord? Do you agree that a spiritual man or woman is sensitive to the sin in his or her life, and doesn't mind saying so? Why or why not?

2. Read Romans 7:17-18. What should these verses convince us of concerning our own ability to control our old nature?

3. Paul is very candid in revealing that he struggles spiritually. Have you ever found yourself hiding behind the appearance that everything is going well for you spiritually, when really things are not? What are some dangers of "phony" holiness?

CHAPTER 8

"So now I will show them my power and might," says the Lord. "At last they will know that I am the Lord" (Jer. 16:21 NLV).

The Spirit in the Relationship

Romans 8:1-11

Office machines were created for frustration and the fracturing of confidence, I've decided. Recently I saw the following cartoon tacked above an office computer, depicting a man with goggles in place, a fiendish smile on his face, and a mallet raised above his head. "Strike any key when ready," the caption read!

A friend ran across this sign posted above the office copier one day. Whoever wrote it knew worlds about the exasperations of photocopying.

> WARNING! This machine is subject to breakdowns during periods of critical need. A special circuit in the machine called a "critical

> detector" senses the operator's emotional state in terms of how desperate he or she is to use the machine. The "critical detector" then creates a malfunction proportional to the desperation of the operator. Threatening the machine with violence only aggravates the situation. Likewise, attempts to use another machine may cause it to also malfunction. They belong to the same union. Keep cool and say nice things to the machine. Nothing else seems to work. *Never let anything mechanical know you're in a hurry.*

Our old nature operates very much like that "critical detector." Whenever we are desperate to do the right thing and we attempt on our own to perform the requirements of the law, the old nature reacts to create a malfunction in our spiritual life. Romans 7 is a portrait of the apostle Paul frantically trying to become righteous by adhering to the law, and finding that his "critical detector" sets off a chain reaction of misbehavior every time he turns around. "I am not practicing that which I am desiring to do, but I am doing that which I am hating," he admits in Romans 7:15 (DAV). He is a Christian, without doubt, but he is always doing the wrong things. Finally Paul comes to a great moment of futility and exhaustion, where he cries in desperation, "Wretched man that I am! Who shall set me free from out of the body of this death?" (7:24 DAV). Who, indeed? The answer is the Spirit of God, and the method is given in Romans 8.

So far in the book of Romans, we've seen Paul's arguments follow a logical progression to this great chapter of victory. Romans 5, remember, gave us eight evidences of knowing Christ as savior. The latter part of the chapter showed us what it meant to be born in Adam and challenged us with our need to be reborn in Jesus Christ.

Romans 6 explained more about the relationship with Christ which comes with that rebirth. It is a vital, living union in which we are permanently identified with the Lord. So closely linked are we with him that we should become increasingly sensitive toward sin. We should desire not to let sin reign in us. We should be careful to present our members as tools of God's righteousness and act on this presentation daily. It's essential that we draw on the power of God's Spirit to energize our new nature; otherwise, failure is certain. Such failure is seen in Romans 7, where Paul struggles under his own steam to be made righteous by the law. His efforts end in the frustration we've already discussed. His works are all sound and fury, signifying nothing, because the Lord wants him *to be*, not *to do*. The law has served its purpose in convicting him of his sin; now it holds no practical dominion over Paul's life.

There's always a conflict. The old nature and the new nature war within; the old kicks in with extra horsepower whenever a Christian tries to perform solo rather than to respond to the Spirit. Many believers settle for spiritual mediocrity. They accept consistent lack of victory as the norm. They don't realize that the Lord deeply desires to produce righteousness in them. More importantly, they don't realize that the production has got to be his and his alone. The only part we have in the process is to be willing to let him work. In Paul's words in Philippians 4:13, "I am ready for anything through the strength of him who indwells me" (DAV).

All this brings us to Romans 8, the fabulous chapter of victory. Here we learn more about the Holy Spirit, the energizing person to whom we have been briefly introduced in Romans 5 (see 5:5). The Spirit has been mentioned once in the previous three chapters; in Romans 8, he is mentioned over 20 times. He is the key to overcoming the work of the "critical detector" that remains within us after our salvation.

Chapter 8 is the comforting account of life in him.

In Romans 8, Paul begins by speaking of the Spirit in the first eleven verses. He next discusses our status in Christ as adopted sons of God. As in Romans 6:3, he deals with the reality of suffering that inevitably characterizes the Christian life. And he closes with a burst of praise and thanksgiving for our eternal security as believers. If I were to outline Romans 8, it would be something like this:

I. The Spirit (verses 1-11)
II. Our Sonship (verses 12-17)
III. The Place of Suffering (verses 18-28)
IV. Our Security (verses 29-39)

As we turn to Romans 8, we leave behind the self of Romans 7. By now we should be thoroughly convinced that it is possible to be a Christian, to have the new, divine nature dwelling within us, and yet still experience little victory. We've seen that to be true of a spiritual giant like the apostle Paul. In honesty, we must admit that at least some of the time it is true of us as well. If lack of victory is a constant thing with us, it may be because we do not know how to allow the Spirit of God to control and energize our new nature, but it is never too late to learn. A good way to start is to recognize that we've already been given *everything* we need in order to be victorious!

STANDARD SPIRITUAL EQUIPMENT

When a baby is born, one of the first things the new mother and dad do is to check the little one to make sure everything is there. Grandparents are notorious for doing this, also. We count the fingers and toes, look at the eyes, ears, and nose. The pediatrician listens to the heart and examines the rest of the precious bundle. And, as it usually turns out, everything needed for growth and development is there at birth. It's all standard equipment.

After we're reborn through Christ into the family of God, we receive all the standard equipment we'll ever need for spiritual growth too! We receive the new nature. We receive the indwelling Spirit (Romans 8:14-16). Just as physical growth involves learning to use the developing limbs, organs, and appendages with which we were born, so Christian growth involves learning to appropriate what God has already given us at the time of rebirth.

This isn't meant to sound flippant, but in some ways navigating through the Christian life reminds me of maneuvering an automobile. I generally log around 36,000 miles per year driving to and from various Bible classes and camps, not to mention airports. Often my schedule demands that I travel by plane, so I regularly drive to DFW International in order to catch flights. When I hop in the car and head out for the interstate, I have options. I can choose to leave my foot on the accelerator for the entire two-hour trip from my home in Tyler to Dallas, or I can take the car up to the speed limit, push a button, and let the cruise control take over. Cruise control is standard equipment on my vehicle, and I've found that using it sure beats conventional driving any day. And yet the choice is mine. I can disregard the cruise control if I so desire. It's not stretching things too far to compare using cruise control to allowing the Holy Spirit to work in us. The Spirit is standard equipment for every Christian. He comes on every model. The question is, do we make use of him or not? Do we allow him to energize and control us, or do we refuse to yield to his direction?

There are many ways in which we may refuse to switch on our "Christian cruise control" and make use of the Spirit's power in our life. We can grieve him by consciously, remorselessly, continuing in a pattern of sin. We can refuse to ask him for help. We can resist his obvious overtures and attempts to lead us. We can insist on doing things our way, instead of God's way. The challenge for us is to learn to let the Spirit function like he is supposed to! Then comes the victory. Romans 8 is the instruction manual to teach us how.

If we were to place the labels "Self" over Romans 7 and "Spirit" over Romans 8, we'd hit the mark. Paul has shown us that what he can do by himself is woefully inadequate. The focus shifts from the pitiable efforts of man to the sheer sufficiency of God the Father, Son, and Holy Spirit—the three-in-one godhead who loves us totally and unconditionally. Let's turn to chapter 8 and discover more about submitting to the Spirit's leading.

NOW, NO DOOM—ROMANS 8:1

As Romans 8 opens, Paul's eyes are definitely fixed on Jesus. "Therefore now there is no doom for those who are in Christ Jesus," he states in verse 1 (DAV). There is no doom, no condemnation, nothing to fear as far as eternal judgment is concerned for all who know Christ as savior. "Truly, truly, I say to you, he who hears My word, and believes Him who sent Me, has eternal life, and does not come into judgment, but has passed out of death into life," says Jesus himself in John 5:24 (NASB). Christians needn't be concerned with matters of condemnation. We won't stand before the great white throne and be judged according to our deeds. That future scene is graphically described by the apostle John in Revelation 20:11-15:

> And I saw a great white throne and Him who sat upon it, from whose presence earth and heaven fled away, and no place was found for them. And I saw the dead, the great and the small, standing before the throne, and books were opened; and another book was opened, which is the book of life; and the dead were judged from the things which

> were written in the books, according to their deeds. And the sea gave up the dead which were in it, and death and Hades gave up the dead which were in them; and they were judged, every one of them according to their deeds. And death and Hades were thrown into the lake of fire. This is the second death, the lake of fire. And if anyone's name was not found written in the book of life, he was thrown into the lake of fire. (NASB)

The instant we receive the salvation of Christ, our name is written in that book of life. It will never be erased. We're free, forgiven, exonerated for eternity. God will never tell us that he's changed his mind about us. Our security is based solely on what Christ did on the cross.

We've been liberated from the torrid reality of the judgment that will be rendered unbelievers, just as we'll also escape the coming day of the Lord, the tribulation time of Jacob's trouble so graphically described in the book of the Revelation. We won't fight in the battle of Armageddon either (a fact that grieves to no end a certain Christian general I know!). Armageddon is a judgment against a sinful, unbelieving world, and we'll be eyewitnesses clad in white following in Christ's train, looking on with the loved ones in Christ who have preceded us in death (Rev. 19:11-21). Following this worldwide conflict will come the promised millennial kingdom. Truly, there is no possibility of doom for those who are in Christ Jesus! From the very minute of rebirth, we're safe in the arms of the one who has saved us.

In the meantime, we have the option of living in defeat or victory. We can choose to live in the power of God's Spirit, or in unhappy ignorance of his presence and power. We know that, in Romans 7, Paul's old nature kept answering the law the only way it could, and that the result was sin. Now the apostle turns to speak of the new nature, which can operate given the energizing power of the Spirit.

STORAGE OR CONSTANT CONTACT?

How does that new nature operate with the power of the Spirit? A popular misconception is that the new nature is operated by the Spirit on a sort of storage principle. The thinking goes something like this: as a car needs a tankful of gasoline at least once a week in order to get us where we're going, so we Christians need to be filled at least once weekly with a heavy dose of the Holy Spirit. Many believers live accordingly. They come to church on Sunday and get "filled up" by the power of the Spirit. Then they proceed to live out the week, never "refueling" until the next Sunday worship hour. Perhaps if their spiritual gas tank starts running dry, they might attend a midweek service or Bible study, but in the meantime there's little contact with the Spirit.

The storage principle is not what Paul is teaching us in Romans 8. Instead, Paul instructs us in the principle of *constant contact*. It's best illustrated by thinking of the old streetcar. Streetcars hold fond memories for me; they were a regular means of conveyance to see Pearl when she was my girlfriend and I was a college student in Minneapolis. What a racket those trolleys made as they rattled and rumbled along! I remember that extending from the back of the streetcar was a rod with a small wheel at the top connecting the car to the electrical cable above it. We could count on making steady, if bumpy, progress along the route as long as that little wheel rotated on the cable. Sometimes, though, there would be a screech ... and the whole trolley would jerk to an unexpected halt. Out would hop the conductor; with a rope in hand he'd again place the trolley wheel on the cable. Back into the car he'd spring, and as soon as he flipped a switch, we'd be off again. You see, the cable strung above the tracks on which the streetcar ran was the actual power source. The car had to be constantly connected to the cable in order for any progress to be made.

That picture of the old-fashioned streetcar is a representation of the spiritual life. Christians desiring to live under the power of the Holy Spirit must become very much like that trolley. We must be in constant contact with the Spirit, the power source who is able to energize our new nature to live the godly life. It's a matter of our willingness to allow God to work his will in us! The minute we grieve the Spirit by committing overt sin or we quench him by saying no to his leading, we experience a power failure as complete and certain as that of a streetcar disconnected from its electrical cable. God is still there; the Spirit still dwells within; but we have chosen to bring our spiritual life to a rumbling halt because we've not stayed in constant contact with our source of power.

The writer of the book of Hebrews tells his readers that through the process of time they have become dull to hearing God's truth; they've become slow to learn and must return to the basics of their Christian life again if they are to experience victory (Heb. 5:11ff). He continues with this warning, "For though by this time you ought to be teachers, you have need again for someone to teach you the elementary principles of the oracles of God, and you have come to need milk and not solid food" (Heb. 5:12 NASB). It's safe to say that there's been no recent progress spiritually for the Christians addressed in Hebrews 5 because they haven't remained in constant contact with the Spirit. They haven't longed consistently for the nourishment of the meat of the word. They haven't concerned themselves with staying vitally connected to the source.

Jesus promised his disciples, in the last statements he made recorded in scripture, "you shall receive power when the Holy Spirit has come upon you" (Acts 1:8a NASB). The

Holy Spirit had been present among the early believers, but would become resident within them on the day of Pentecost. Why did the disciples need to "receive power"? It was for the purpose of energizing the new nature to victory! God chose to allow us the privilege, the free will, of choosing to respond to him in obedience and love. He'll never violate that free will. We can choose not to accept Christ and therefore go to hell if we want. And after we receive Christ, we can choose to live a defeated Christian life if we want. What God desires is to receive the glory from that free will which chooses to receive his love and to experience the power of the Spirit energizing the new nature unto victory. Make no mistake about it, that Spirit is fully capable of defeating sin (see Zech. 4:6; 2 Tim. 1:7).

Every moment, Christians have the privilege of delighting the heavenly Father by, under the power of the Spirit, answering the new nature: embracing the principle of constant contact.

I think of my first pastorate. Excited about all I'd learned at seminary, overflowing with ideas and insights into scripture to share, I came into the church position like a house afire. It wasn't too long before the streetcar separated from the cable, however. My lack of personal discipline in my own walk with the Lord resulted in superficiality. Shallowness in my teaching, preaching, and counseling permeated my ministry. The only way out of the lukewarmness was to focus again on Christ, poring over his word, sinking to my knees in prayer, depending on his Spirit. I had to center my thoughts on his nature, his attributes, his character. It's been a lifelong process of slipping from the source and again plugging into the power. But revitalized starts are always possible. Now I make a practice of spending some moments with the Spirit of God each morning, asking him to purify my heart, to show me where I am grieving or quenching him, and then to fill me to overflowing as I begin the new day.

SUPERCEDING THF LAW OF SIN—ROMANS 8:2-8

Paul continues by repeating a principle he has already essentially stated in Romans 5 and 6. "For the law of the Spirit of life in Christ Jesus freed you from the law of sin and death" (Rom. 8:2 DAV). With our acceptance of Christ as savior, we're freed from the penalty and power of sin. The old nature remains, yet we do not have to answer its call. The reason? The Holy Spirit, "the Spirit of life," is able to give us the victory by energizing our new nature. Thus the law of the Spirit supercedes the law of sin and death.

You remember baby Chad from the last chapter and his high chair discovery of the law of gravity? The law of gravity is a constant. What goes up must come down. Yet physicists have discovered another law which supercedes the law of gravity, and if you've ever ridden on an airplane, you know what it is: the law of aerodynamics. The fact that a jetliner is able to take off, climb, maintain a cruising altitude thousands of feet above the earth, and achieve a controlled descent, proves that the law of aerodynamics supercedes the law of gravity. Notice the word is *supercede*. The law of aerodynamics does not nullify the law of gravity; open the hatch on an airplane in mid-flight and step outside if you don't believe me. You'll discover immediately that the law of gravity is still intact.

The apostle Peter could tell us volumes about the law of gravity (Matt. 14:22ff). According to the law of gravity, when a man steps off a boat onto water with nothing to buoy him up, he's going to sink. Peter stepped off a boat and walked across the water toward the Lord Jesus Christ. As long as he kept his mind and heart on the Lord, Peter was okay. The moment his attention was diverted, he began to sink. "Lord, save me!" he cried, praying one of the shortest prayers on record (Matt. 14:30 NASB). He didn't have time for more! When his gaze again focused only on Jesus Christ, and his hand was cradled in the master's, Peter once more walked atop the waves. Peter's faith in and focus on Christ superceded the law of gravity.

Just as the law of gravity remains intact, and yet can be superceded by other laws, the law of sin and death remains intact in the life of the Christian. The old nature hangs on. But the law of the Spirit is able to supercede that law of sin and death. It's a moment-by-moment thing. Constantly, consistently, we must walk in dependence on the Spirit. We have to say to ourselves, "Oh wretched creature that I am! I cannot do it alone. There is no way by myself that I will ever know the sweet taste of victory. It'll only come as the Spirit of God is allowed to empower my new nature and supercede the old." The moment we take our eyes off Christ and grieve or quench the Spirit, the law of the old nature takes over. Like Peter, we sink in the waves instead of riding the crest of victory.

Can it be done? Can focus on Christ be a constant, consistent thing? Can contact with the Spirit be unhindered? If the example of Dr. Jack Mitchell is to be believed, the answer is yes. For years Dr. Mitchell, a pastor and professor from Multnomah School of the Bible in Portland, Oregon, who had a radio ministry, taught a two-week Bible class at Dallas Seminary. Memories of these sessions burn brightly in my mind even 40 years down the pike. I've never seen a man exude the love and knowledge of the savior and the scriptures as Dr. Mitchell. From his innermost being flowed rivers of living water. He radiated the written word, spoke it, lived it. Questions of him evoked verses upon verses in reply. Such simple, practical truths! Such amazing insights! "Whatever you do, young man, preach the word!" he said when he served on my ordination council. Preaching the word is what Dr. Mitchell did, not just from the pulpit or in the classroom, but with every utterance, every step, every breath. The Spirit of God through the word of God molded him into that kind of man. He paid the price of poring over scripture, not to please God by his performance, but to experience the unsearchable riches of a thriving relationship with Christ. Dr. Mitchell has been home with the Lord now for some years. What joy must be his in the presence of the one he loved and served. Surely he heard: "Well done good and faithful servant, enter into the joy I have prepared for you."

STUFFED WITH CONTENT, YET CARNAL

The other day a friend made the statement that the church is populated by many knowledgeable Christians, but very few mature ones. The more I've thought about his words, the more I believe he is right on target. We seem to be stuffed with content, but still quite carnal.

Knowing God's word is an essential part of the growth process of becoming Christ-like, but just as crucial is learning to daily, hourly, minute-by-minute, walk in the power of God's Spirit. That's how we prove ourselves to be "doers of the word, and not merely hearers who delude themselves" (James 1:22 NASB). As Paul told us in Romans 6, the Spirit-filled life involves an attitude, a willful choice, a presentation of the members of our body and our emotions to God for his service. It means allowing the mind and heart to focus chiefly on Christ, on what he has done, on what his Spirit can do in us. It means poring through scripture for indications of his will, principles by which to live and relate to others. The knowledge we gain must penetrate our heart, convicting us of the areas in which we grieve the Spirit, convincing us of God's will.

Many individuals who have been Christians for 30, 40, even 50 years, are not necessarily mature Christians. They may be knowledgeable, but when it comes to walking in the power of the Holy Spirit, they just don't. Like the Corinthian believers whom Paul addresses in 1 Corinthians

3:1-3, they're still babes in Christ, preferring the burp, the bottle, and the spiritual diapers to genuine maturity in the Lord. They soak up knowledge like sponges, but when it comes to giving of themselves, they're dry and empty. Each day they have the option of presenting themselves to God for his glory, and each day they stay stuck instead in a spiritual rut. Oh they may work at Christian things. They may teach vacation Bible school and Sunday school and serve on the church building committee. They may witness to prisoners and campaign for the rights of the unborn. They may attend two Sunday services and a mid-week one to boot. But in the reality of life, all the Christian work, while good to do, hasn't enabled them to tame their tongues, forego their bitterness, quench their lusts, or experience victory over other stumbling blocks.

Spiritual maturity is a choice. It involves knowledge of the scriptures. It involves regular communication with God in prayer. And, at least as important as these, it involves a moment-by-moment decision to focus on the things of the Spirit and not the things of the world. Individual rights, prerogatives, and opinions diminish in importance when fellowship with and focus on God are constant! May God help us be increasingly more sensitive to the Spirit's presence and involvement.

And why shouldn't we focus on the Lord? Righteousness was an impossible goal for us before we knew him! As Paul says in verse 3, "For what was impossible for the Law, because it was weak through the flesh, God, having sent His own Son in the likeness of sinful flesh and concerning sin, He condemned sin in the flesh" (DAV). Christ, God's own Son, came to earth "in the *likeness* of sinful flesh." It is critical to realize that Jesus' flesh was *not* sinful, however, for he did what no one else has ever done before or since: he lived a perfect life. Jesus had no old, adamic nature. And, as Paul writes, Christ "condemned sin in the flesh." In other words,

Jesus did something about sin! His perfect life and sacrificial death passed judgment on sin, so that Christians are not condemned by sin.

Why did Christ fulfill every requirement of the law of Moses and die for us? One reason of course is that we might have eternal life in his presence. Another reason is "in order that the requirement of the law might be fulfilled in us, who are not walking according to the flesh but according to the Spirit," writes Paul in Romans 8:4 (DAV). Through Jesus Christ, God has made the provision for our victory over the power of sin. In spite of the fact that we will never be perfect and we will never be able to successfully, completely keep the law of Moses, there is a tangible way in which we are able as Christians to keep the requirement of the law.

Let me explain. Romans 8:4 does not teach that the Christian is able, through the Holy Spirit, to keep all the commandments which he was unable to keep before he became a believer. But, because of Christ's death and the presence of the Holy Spirit in his life, the believer is able to have an obedient heart motivated by love. This is what God asks of us. From the starting point of willing obedience, he is able to bear fruit in us. Yes, we'll still fail, but despite us, he'll work in us and through us because our heart is willing to cooperate with the Spirit. What a liberating concept!

Having an obedient heart motivated by love is the key to allowing the Spirit to work. That's what it means to set our mind on the things of the Spirit, as Paul states in verse 5. That's the core of becoming sensitive to the Spirit's leading. That's how we stop walking according to the flesh, and start walking according to the Spirit. The struggle for each Christian is not to perform the law himself, but to be willing, out of love, to let the Spirit work.

The results can be astonishing. "For the way of thinking of the flesh is death, but the way of thinking of the Spirit is life and peace," writes Paul in Romans 8:6 (DAV). We know that depending on the flesh brings spiritual defeat. Yet how does "the way of thinking of the Spirit" bring "life and peace"? The life brought is eternal life, as we've discussed earlier (John 3:16, 10:10; 1 John 5). But what about the peace?

The peace that comes with possessing an obedient heart, motivated by love, receptive to the Spirit, is truly that which passes understanding. Paul isn't talking here about our positional peace with God, as in Romans 5:1. He is referring to the peace of God. Christians consistently walking in the Spirit have the potential to have the peace of God—that quiet, sustaining rest in him which comes when we're willing to trust him to handle our circumstances. "And the peace of God, which surpasses all comprehension, shall guard your hearts and your minds in Christ Jesus" (Phil. 4:7 NASB). "The fruit of righteousness will be peace; the effect of righteousness will be quietness and confidence forever" (Isa. 32:17 NIV). We realize that someone greater than ourselves is in control. It's refreshment, surrender, contentment. And it comes as we keep our mind and heart focused on the Lord. In the words of Isaiah, "Thou wilt keep him in perfect peace, whose mind is stayed on thee: because he trusteth in thee" (Isa. 26:3 KJV).

A SPIRIT OF POWER—ROMANS 8:7-11

There is no hope for us if we depend on ourselves to live a victorious Christian life. Paul says in Romans 8:7, "the way of thinking of the flesh is hostile toward God; for it is not subjecting itself to the Law of God, for it is not even able to do so" (DAV). The flesh lives above authority. It will never respond in submission to a command. The law only aggravates the problem, for it provokes the flesh to rebel. Time and time again the apostle hammers home these points.

"And those who are in the flesh are not able to please God," he states in Romans 8:8 (DAV). It can't get much clearer than that, can it? If we live under the control of the flesh, there is no way that we can hope to please God. Victory is not in the energy of the flesh but only comes by the power of the Spirit! "It is the Spirit who gives life; the flesh profits nothing," remarks Jesus to his disciples (John 6:63a NASB).

In Romans 5:5, Paul writes that one of the evidences of our relationship with Christ is that we have the Spirit indwelling us. Paul reiterates that truth in 8:9 where we read that, as believers, the Spirit of God does indwell us, and that if anyone lacks the Spirit it is because he or she is not a Christian! This great truth sets the stage for the next verse.

"Now if Christ is in you," reasons, Paul, "on the one hand the body is dead because of sin, but on the other hand the Spirit is alive because of righteousness" (Rom. 8:10 DAV). Our bodies are decaying, some a little faster than others, and we'll all answer the call of the grave some day, unless the Lord Jesus comes to take us to himself. Yet the Spirit continues to be alive within us. "Therefore we do not lose heart," Paul writes to the Corinthians, "but though our outer man is decaying, yet our inner man is being renewed day by day'" (2 Cor. 4:16 NASB). Within the temporal shell, the Spirit resides as a living seal of our salvation, and a renewing, regenerating presence to invigorate us spiritually, no matter how old we are.

According to Paul in Romans 8:11, "And if the Spirit of the One who raised Jesus from the dead is dwelling in you, He who raised Christ Jesus from the dead will also give life to your mortal bodies through His Spirit who is dwelling in you" (DAV). It is the Spirit of the God who raised Christ from the dead. That same God promises to raise us from the bonds of physical death someday also. The mortal will put on immortality. In the meantime, the Spirit within us is capable of incredible power for victorious living—the power of the resurrection!

FALSE PROPHETS OR CHILDREN OF THE KING?

The theme of the first eleven verses of Romans 8 can perhaps be summarized by this: as Christians we have within us the power of God's own Spirit. We are given all the standard equipment for spiritual growth and victory, including that Spirit, the moment we by faith enter God's eternal family. By ourselves we cannot energize our new nature to victory. The key lies in coming to the end of ourselves and allowing the indwelling Holy Spirit to energize the new nature. That is the source of holy living. That is the basis for victory in the Christian life.

Remember Elijah's confrontation with the 450 prophets of Baal on Mount Carmel? As the people of Israel looked on, God provided an object lesson to remind them of his power and to turn sinful hearts back to him and away from the seduction of Baal worship. Two bulls were slaughtered and set atop altars piled high with stacks of wood. The wood was not set aflame, because the fire for the sacrifice was to be God's department. "Then you call on the name of your god," Elijah told the priests of Baal, "and I will call on the name of the Lord. The god who answers by fire—he is God" (1 Kings 18:24 NIV). The prophets agreed to the challenge.

For hours the priests called on the name of Baal. They shouted and danced and slashed themselves with swords and spears until blood spurted forth and freely flowed. Evening, the time for the sacrifice came, and as scripture tells us, "There was no response, no one answered, no one paid attention" (1 Kings 18:29b NIV). The frantic, frenetic attempt to win the favor of a false god was an abysmal failure. The star performance of the prophets evoked no response.

Elijah then simply stepped forward; with quiet dignity he prepared the altar. The sacrifice was set in place, and the wood and animal even soaked liberally with water, for Elijah knew God could handle the most difficult of challenges. Then Elijah addressed his Lord. The prophet didn't rant or rave, shout or slash himself. He just prayed:

> O Lord, God of Abraham, Isaac and Israel, let it be known today that you are God in Israel and that I am your servant and have done all these things at your command. Answer me, O Lord, answer me, so these people will know that you, O Lord, are God, and that you are turning their hearts back again. (1 Kings 18:36-37 NIV)

Next, the fire of the Lord fell, consuming the sacrifice, the altar, and the soil around it. All Elijah had to do was quietly, in faith, depend on the incredible power of the God he served.

The account of Elijah and the prophets of Baal is a good illustration of victorious Christian living. We don't need to rant and rave as the priests of Baal. God works wondrously in our circumstances when we trust him and seek to be obedient. He is almighty. It probably isn't in his plan for us to summon fire from heaven. But it is in his plan for us to depend on his Spirit to energize our new nature to victory over areas of sin. Surely the God who supercedes natural law and incinerates a soaked sacrifice can enable us to overcome our problems with sin!

So think about that, and ask yourself if God is working in your life today. Is there a problem area you need to prayerfully turn over to him? If you're willing to allow his Spirit to work, he is ready, and you can experience progressive victory over the manifestations of your old nature. It is possible, because the Spirit of an omnipotent God can handle it all! Still, let's not forget that the victories won't all be won overnight. That we'll see as we read on in Romans 8.

Questions to Consider

1. What does Romans 8:1 tell you about your eternal destiny as a Christian? Read Revelation 20:11-15 and describe in your own words what is going to happen at the great white throne judgment depicted there.

2. Does life in the control of the Spirit run on the storage principle or on the principle of constant contact? Do you feel that your spiritual life is more closely linked with the principle of storage or that of constant contact? If so, how so?

3. Paraphrase Romans 8:3. What has God done for us through Christ? What is the requirement of the law mentioned in verse 4 that God desires from us?

CHAPTER 9

"He has made everything beautiful in its time. He has also set eternity in the hearts of men; yet they cannot fathom what God has done from beginning to end" (Eccles. 3:11 NIV).

Our Sonship

Romans 8:12-17

Our society is saturated with instant solutions. We don't want it today; we want it yesterday. Think about TV. Television plots progress from crisis to resolution in 30 or 60-minute time slots. Week after week, father knows best; boy gets girl; problem gets solved. One evening I viewed a made-for-television movie in which, during the space of two hours, two marriages were healed, the relationship between an estranged father and son was restored, two characters made life-changing career decisions, another came to terms with a tragic episode from her past. To top it off, half a million dollars in investment capital was raised by middle-class family members who pawned heirlooms and liquidated assets overnight. Perhaps most amazing of all, scriptwriters would have us believe that all these events occurred during a family reunion which lasted only a few short days!

In between portions of the plot, we get to view commercials for fast foods, instant gelatin, quick pain relief, and rapid weight loss. Turn on the TV, especially during the daytime soap opera hours, and you'll see a plethora of ads for psychiatric hospitals promising immediate help and nearly immediate cures for alcoholics and drug addicts. A two-week stay at institution X is guaranteed to dry you out, sober you up (not to mention clean out your bank account too). Something that took months to do, like developing a substance addiction, we expect to see undone in weeks, even days.

Pearl and I have become involved in an awful lot of marriage counseling and conferences. I guess when you are pushing 50 years together, you have the right to say something. Most of the couples we counsel come with their marriage broken, and they want us to fix it right now. It doesn't work that way. Walls of separation and neglect are built brick by brick, and guess what? The way they must come down is brick by brick!

I remember when Don Anderson Ministries was incorporated in 1972. Our staff and board of directors fully expected to purchase a Christian camping facility within several months—maybe a few years, at the outside. Thirty years later, after viewing dozens of camps and coming close many times, we're still waiting. We conduct conferences and camps at facilities owned by other groups, but we don't own any property. God obviously has a better plan in mind and our responsibility is to submit to the one who truly knows what is best and to trust him who does all things well.

I'm not sure of all the reasons why humans expect instant solutions to problems. A tragedy of Christian life is that we also anticipate having immediate victory over areas of sin, too. We become frustrated when the bad habits and disobedience continue, even after we've implored the Lord to remove them and to change us. It is true that in certain cases, instantaneous divine deliverance from specific addictions, compulsions, and habits does occur, but the Bible does not promise us that this will always happen. While some evangelists and preachers contend otherwise, nowhere in scripture are we promised that Christ-likeness is an immediate thing. Instead, the Bible teaches that godliness comes with time, that progress is gradual, that the Christian walk is just that—a *walk*, with every single step a potential point of progress toward holiness or a potential stumble backward (Gal. 5:16-17).

As we continue to look at the words of the apostle Paul in Romans 8, we'll become more convinced than ever that growth in godliness takes time. The Christian life does not consist of instant cures, but, even more valuable than those, it is composed of the richest relationship imaginable. As we'll see in Romans 8:12-17, it is a relationship of sonship, with all its rights and privileges.

IN THE POWER OF THE SPIRIT OR FLESH?—ROMANS 8:12-13

"So then, brethren," Paul tells the Roman believers in 8:12, "we are those under moral obligation, not to the flesh, to live according to the flesh"(DAV). In other words, as Christians, we are no longer obligated to that old nature which resides within us. We no longer have to fulfill its desires. We are given the opportunity for victory over specific sin areas of our life.

Notice Paul says that we are no longer under moral obligation to live according to the flesh, or the old nature. He does not say that the old nature no longer exists. Some modern Christian teaching tells us that we can miraculously rid ourselves of the old nature in this lifetime, that we can become completely free of sin. An honest appraisal of every self-proclaimed sinless person, however, will show up a few cracks, dents, and chips in his or her character. The truth is we'll never be totally sinless till we get to glory, yet in the meantime the possibility of a life of increasing holiness is there for us, in Christ.

Paul tells us in Philippians 3:14: "I press on toward the goal" (NASB) John says in 1 John 3:2: "Beloved, now we are children of God, and it has not appeared as yet *what we shall be*. We know that, if He should appear, we shall be like Him, because we shall see Him just as He is"(NASB italics mine).

As we've discussed before, the old nature doesn't go away, and throughout the years the Lord gives us, it will remain the only entrance Satan has into our life. It's ready to respond with any small amount of fuel we may feed it. In fact, right now, if you're a Christian, one of two descriptions is true of you. At this very minute, you are either living under the control of the Holy Spirit energizing your new nature, or you are living under the control of your flesh, your old nature. You can't have it both ways in a single moment—you can't live under the control of the Spirit and under the control of the flesh simultaneously. You are either reading these words under the power of the Spirit, or you are reading these words under the control of the old nature. The same is true of me as I write. Living by the Spirit is a moment-by-moment thing. Only you know in your heart what is true of you right now.

We long for Christian maturity to arrive with the speed in which we microwave water to make it boil. Our high-tech, high-speed computer age tells us in our mind that Christianity should be instantly transforming, something akin to removing old software from a disk drive and replacing it with totally new, high-powered stuff. Make an emotional decision or a dramatic dedication, and when the lights come on, you'll be experiencing the abundant life. God didn't design us that way. Christian growth is neither that quick nor easy. It is even potentially painful, and like physical growth, it takes time.

They say you are over the hill when they start replacing

parts. I am now just about bionic. I have had a total hip replacement and just recently, a total knee replacement. The therapist made it quite clear that for the new knee to function with maximum efficiency, daily exercise would be necessary. It's painful, but he was right.

The fact remains that, as Paul says, we are not under obligation to the old nature, even though it still resides within us. Every day, therefore, is a brand new opportunity for us to walk by means of the Spirit. There aren't just second or third chances, but practically limitless possibilities for us to become more and more like Christ. Our victories will be more the moment-by-moment variety than the once-and-for-all-time type. As we discussed in the last chapter, the spiritual equipment is there already. The braces of the Spirit are in place; our call is to walk by his power.

A MATTER OF LIFE OR DEATH

Indeed, we must as Christians endeavor to submit to the Spirit's leading and control. We have no reasonable option, if we desire fulfillment. It is downright dangerous to do otherwise. "For if you are living according to the flesh," admonishes Paul in verse Romans 8:13, "you are about to die; but if by the Spirit you are putting to death the deeds of the body, you will live" (DAV). With these words, Paul delivers a frightening warning to us, echoing what he has already told us in Romans 6:23. When a scriptural principle is repeated, we can be sure God wants us to sit up and take notice!

Briefly, the apostle's meaning is this. Far from denying the continued existence of the old nature, he is telling us that if we consistently live under the power of that old nature, we are actually about to die. In Galatians 5:19-21 Paul lists the works of the flesh: a rap sheet of crimes against God and his standards, beginning with adultery and continuing with "immorality, impurity, sensuality, idolatry, sorcery, enmities, strife, jealousy, outbursts of anger, disputes, dissensions, factions, envying, drunkenness, carousing, and things like these" (5:19-21 NASB). The warning, which Paul gives at the close of the sordid list, is this: "they which do such things shall not inherit the kingdom of God" (5:21b KJV). If you claim to know Christ as savior, and yet your life shows only evidence that you respond solely to your old nature, it may be that you are not a Christian at all. If, when it feels good, you normally, consistently, habitually do it, even though you know it to be contrary to God's principles, then perhaps you've never truly placed your trust in Christ. Perhaps you have no new nature, and the Holy Spirit has never come to live within. Now is the time to ask yourself where you really stand in your relationship with Jesus. "Test yourselves to see if you are in the faith; examine yourselves! Or do you not recognize this about yourselves, that Jesus Christ is in you—unless indeed you fail the test?" (2 Cor. 13:5 NASB).

The issue is of salvation. Before they become Christians, people live natural lives, lives controlled by the flesh or the old nature. They have no choice. This doesn't mean they constantly do evil things, but the Christ-given potential for holy living simply isn't there because there is no Spirit, no regeneration, no renewing. If you claim to be a Christian and yet continually live a sinful life, then the worst-case scenario is that you are not actually saved at all. You are trying to work your way into heaven all by yourself, and it is impossible. You've never placed your faith in Jesus Christ, and so the good you may do will never be good enough, and the evil will condemn you forever.

CARNAL CHRISTIANITY

Romans 8:12 tells us that it is possible for us to be Christians, saved for eternity, and still be living carnal, or fleshly, lives. How? We could be living under the assumption that Christianity is a performance, and placing ourselves under the bondage of the law. As we've earlier noted, the flesh loves to kick in and respond where the law is introduced, and so we may be defeated in holy living before we even start, because we're desperately trying *to do*, rather than submissively desiring *to be*.

Perhaps more closely relevant to Paul's message in verses 12-13, a Christian can be living a carnal life because he or she is allowing some sin to infiltrate that life on a consistent basis. Perhaps it is dishonesty, greed, abusive behavior. Maybe it is sexual immorality. Perhaps you find yourself snagged in an affair and you're trying either to rationalize or to misinterpret certain scriptural passages dealing with that kind of behavior. You want to have an excuse to continue. Only just the other day I counseled a young man, a leader in his church, who was embroiled in an adulterous relationship. I was shocked by his ability to twist the simple truths of scripture to suit his own desires and to justify his decision to leave his wife and two children for a younger woman. It happens. "Above all else, guard your heart, for it is the wellspring of life" (Prov. 4:23 NIV).

When sin separates us from the Father, our fellowship with him is broken. We go through the motions of reading the word and praying, faking our way and wondering why we experience no dynamic spiritual reality. We find the Bible too convicting, so our desire for scripture wanes. Talking about God becomes awkward because he is the one we are hurting with our lifestyle. We talk about weighty concepts and blow billows of theological smoke, but we never say anything personal about our walk with the Lord. We can't! If that is true of you, I caution you to take Romans 8:13 to heart now. The truth is you just may be on your way to eternity a little sooner than you expect. You may be in grave danger of forfeiting your earthly life because of your constant lack of obedience. God may call you home to prevent you from sullying his name on earth any more through your refusal to allow the Spirit to energize your new nature. You'll never lose your salvation, but you may well lose your life!

We're not talking about brief lapses from the proper path either. When we slip up, God is there to forgive, cleanse, and restore fellowship, when we acknowledge our guilt and honestly repent (1 John 1:9). But when we refuse to "fess up" and instead independently proceed with carnality in our life, we're asking for trouble. We're asking for physical death.

Scripture records various instances in which carnal Christianity has led to physical affliction, even death. 1 Corinthians 5 contains the account of a man living in immorality with his father's wife. "I have decided to deliver such a one to Satan for the destruction of his flesh, that his spirit may be saved in the day of the Lord Jesus," declares Paul in the chapter (5:5 NASB). This believer's immorality was a serious matter, and his flagrant display demanded judgment. Paul said that the Christian in question was going to be surrendered to the devil, that he might suffer severe affliction, "the destruction of his flesh," or even death. Evidently carnal Christianity was common among the believers at Corinth, for Paul tells them that there are many among them who "are weak and sick" because they have refused to deal with sin and the manifestations of the old nature (11:30 NASB). Many in fact had already died (see also 11:30).

I imagine many of you reading this may be appalled at the severity with which God can deal with us. From the moment we come to know Christ as savior, we have a responsibility, in love, to answer the new nature. Every time we choose the flesh over the Spirit, we are living in the flesh, and we come closer and closer to the day of our physical demise. We forfeit the right to the good life that the Lord has given us by our persistence in living carnally. The Lord is not willing that any unsaved person perish, but when we are born again by the Spirit of God into his family, we've entered a new arena. We've got to desire to be an asset, a tribute, to the God we worship. He's going to begin a good work of making us like Christ. To resist that by persisting in answering the call of the old nature instead, is to take the chance that physical death is going to come sooner than we think. God may be blowing the whistle or pulling the chain, and calling, "Come on home," before we're ready. Then the party will be too soon over.

First John 5:16 states, "If anyone sees his brother committing a sin not leading to death, he shall ask and God will for him give life to those who commit sin not leading to death. There is a sin leading to death; I do not say that he should make request for this" (NASB). With these words, John addresses believers, and his subject matter is much the same as Paul's in Romans 8: physical death. What is the "sin not leading to death"? That refers to the words you used on the freeway the other day when you responded to the old nature and hollered at another driver. That's the glance you gave your secretary. That's the time you were disrespectful to your spouse. That's the time you lied about your age, slammed the door, exceeded the speed limit, neglected your time with the Lord, criticized the preacher, gossiped, exaggerated, kept the extra money when the clerk at the store made a mistake. When these things happen, we stop and say, "Lord, forgive me for being such a poor representative of you and such a poor witness of your great love. I'm sorry. I want your forgiveness and your cleansing. And please help me make restitution where possible." The Lord will respond to the fact that we're learning. He'll forgive and cleanse and, in all likelihood, we won't suffer physical death as a result of our sins.

What is a sin leading to *death*? For believers, it's willfully continuing to pursue a path of disobedience we know is wrong. It's responding to that old nature, living in it, rationalizing away sins, justifying a sin pattern to ourselves, excusing ourselves time and time again, searching the scriptures for passages taken out of context which seem to excuse our conduct. It's knowing something is not right, but doing it anyway, over and over and over again. It's refusing to let the Spirit of God work because of our stubbornness. It's consistently settling for even less than mediocrity. It's living a life of glaring hypocrisy and disobedience in which our own obvious lack of godliness causes others to lose interest in the kingdom.

God is all-powerful and perfectly capable of maintaining his reputation in the world. When we believers, because of habitual patterns of disobedience, hurt that reputation, we'd better watch out! God can say, "Time's up," in the twinkling of an eye, the squeal of some brakes, the tremor of an earthquake, the shattering of a windshield, the sudden silence of a heart monitor. The brain waves go flat, and that very night, your soul is required of you.

What should we do when we view a fellow Christian on the road to self-destruction because of the disobedience in his life? We can be there to plead, pray, and persevere in hope that he will come to his senses and escape from the snare of the devil who has captivated him (2 Tim. 2:26). James 5:20 says, "let him know that he who turns a sinner from the error of his way will save his soul from death, and will cover a multitude of sins" (NASB). We go to that man or woman and urge him to clean up his act, for the sake of the savior. Usually the best results come if we've first spent time with the person, earned the right to confront, earned the right to point out areas of spiritual need. But regardless, God's word is our standard and we can use it as a measure to gauge the carnality we see in another Christian. We must go to him or her in love—that is crucial. The meekness and gentleness of Christ must prevail. If we offer loving correction and the other fellow says, "Yes, you're right. I've got to ask God to deal with that area of my life," then what have we done? We've turned him from the "error of his way," and we have "covered a multitude of sins" (James 5:20). Together we make the commitment that a disobedient life will become open to the Lord's healing, correction, and direction.

John 15:2 depicts the master removing branches that do not bear fruit. Only those bearing fruit are carefully pruned so that they'll produce all the more. The unproductive ones are permanently cut away. The account depicts the Christian life. Like the worthless branches, so may we be removed if we do not take to heart the principle of responding to the new nature.

Besides, the far-reaching effects of sin may damage us the rest of our life. David and Bathsheba tried for a year to live in disobedience, until God used Nathan the prophet to confront the king. David's brokenness and confession brought restoration of fellowship through forgiveness, but David was still scarred for the rest of his life by the consequences of his sin. David had been an adulterer. What legitimate words of counsel and correction could he later give to his son Amnon, in the smoldering days of desire before Amnon raped his own half-sister, Tamar? David himself had been a murderer, arranging the death of Bathsheba's husband Uriah. How could he hope to restrain Tamar's brother Absolom from slaying Amnon in revenge? Even today, when the world thinks of David, recollections of the account of his affair with Bathsheba loom large on the horizon—they are the stuff of movie ads! David's one-night stand on the roof of the palace cost him dearly and has affected his reputation for centuries now. Satan is so seductive in blurring the outcome and pointing only to the pleasure of the moment. How deftly he obscures the agony of an unwanted pregnancy, a fractured family, a substance addiction.

TAPPING THE ULTIMATE POWER SOURCE

As Paul tells us in Romans 8:13, if we live according to the flesh, we may soon die that way. The alternative is to put "to death the deeds of the body" by the Spirit (8:13b DAV). Reliance on the Spirit for his control and his power means that missteps won't total us! We've been taught by the world that we're adequate by ourselves, we're okay without God's constant presence, but that simply isn't so. Romans 7 depicts an exercise in futility as Paul strives to fulfill the law on his own. It doesn't work. Yet one of the biggest obstacles in attaining spiritual maturity is that we want to do it ourselves. Instead, we must focus on the Lord Jesus Christ and on the indwelling Holy Spirit. God's way is the only way.

"You are putting to death the deeds of the body," Paul urges. Notice that the verb tense suggests a continual action. We cannot put to death the deeds of the flesh all at once. It's an ongoing process: moment by moment, day by day. Satan will bombard us every single hour on the hour. He's ready to interfere with us by using our old nature. He's waiting!

Paul warns the Corinthians, "in order that no advantage be taken of us by Satan; for we are not ignorant of his schemes" (2 Cor. 2:11 NASB). Satan studies our game films, and he knows our tendencies and weaknesses. He also has home field advantage. He also has a band and drill team of demons who cheer like mad when we fall or fail. Satan is the master of distraction.

How do we put to death the deeds of the body? Remember, as Romans 6:11-13 taught us, it's a matter of adopting the attitude that we're dead to sin. Then it involves a willful decision not to let sin reign in us. Finally, it's presenting our members to God daily for his use. It's giving our arms, eyes, hands, ears, to him as tools of righteousness. It's a minute-by-minute thing, demanding constant vigilance and care. The moment we realize we can't have victory alone, and we allow the Spirit to be in control of our life, then we begin to discover victory. We begin to tap the power God has given us in the person of the Spirit—supernaturally charged power that is wholly his. We're not talking about emotional outbursts or strange utterances. We're talking about the quiet capacity we have, in Christ, to live a life under the control of the Spirit of God.

Our children's friends, Larry and Eileen, come to mind. Their life story is the gripping account of a couple in the process of putting to death the deeds of the body through the energizing power of the Spirit. Larry, rebelling against his parents and his godly upbringing, left school with only an eighth-grade education. His road was rough and rugged. Eileen was working as a bartender when they met. "I was on one side drinking, and she was on the other side, serving," Larry recalls. But when she reached her early thirties, Eileen received Jesus Christ as her savior. Larry rededicated his life to the Lord. It was then that the quiet, gradual process of transformation began. Things didn't change overnight. Patterns of a lifetime aren't usually forsaken in an emotionally charged moment of decision. But Larry and Eileen did begin to change. Under the direction of the Holy Spirit, they made the choice to change. No one told them to do it ... no one but the Lord, as he revealed more of his character and they came to love him with increasing intensity.

What changed for Larry and Eileen? Their use of profanity, their excessive drinking—the evidences of a worldly lifestyle—all fell by the wayside. It was slow going, step by step, full of both times of discouragement and incredible grace. As they matured, remembering the wasted years of the past, Larry and Eileen refused to glory in the present or the possible. Even when their progress wasn't as rapid as some would have liked, the Father showed his love and acceptance, and provided them with opportunities to use their gifts. As their responsibilities in the kingdom increased, so did Larry and Eileen's awareness of the importance of being godly examples. The process of Christ-likeness was accelerated. Both sought relationships with other believers to whom they could be accountable spiritually.

Today they set goals for themselves, not because they have to, but because they yearn to deepen their relationship with God. It's amazing ... this quiet transformation occurring in the lives of those who love the Lord and want him to work!

OUR SONSHIP IN HIM—ROMANS 8:14-17

Paul's statements in Romans 8:12-13 show us that God means business concerning the carnal Christian, but before we start quaking in our boots, we mustn't lose sight of the fact that he is also merciful and loving. The possibility that he may call us home because of the habitual sin in our life is simply that—a possibility. He is sovereign and generous and good and committed to making us more like his Son. And may I also hasten to add this: just because an individual dies, what to us is a premature death, does not mean that God has taken him because of the sin in his life. Far from it! Godly people have died very young, very unexpectedly ... and Christians constantly answering the call of their old nature have been known to live well into their 90s. God's judgment on the carnal Christian is a possibility, but he alone knows whom he'll snatch home.

THE SONS OF GOD

"For as many as are being led by the Spirit of God, these are sons of God," writes Paul in verse Romans 8:14 (DAV). John 1:12-13 says of Christ, "But as many as received Him, to them He gave the right to become children of God, even to those who believe in His name: who were born not of blood, nor of the will of the flesh, nor of the will of man, but of God" (NASB). When you became a Christian, you became a child of God. You entered his eternal family. As Paul tells us, the fact that you are a son or daughter of God is proved as you are "led by the Spirit of God" (8:14).

Notice Paul does not say that *we must follow* the Spirit, but that *he will lead us*. At the moment of our salvation, the

Spirit entered our life in order to lead us. When we have a power failure, and operate in the flesh, it does not mean the Spirit has vacated the premises. He is still there, but we have not chosen to yield to him and let him work. The Spirit will not take over as long as the old nature is in control. The Spirit and the flesh will dwell within, and we'll respond either to one or the other all the days of our life.

With our sonship come incredible rights, but there is also a flip side. With the privileged relationship comes the responsibility of being a child of God. When our own children left the house for school trips, summer camp, and college, we always told them, "You're an Anderson; remember who you are and whom you represent." The same thing goes for Christians. We belong to Jesus. We represent him. We must conduct ourselves accordingly by allowing the Spirit to work in us. He can handle anything that is thrown our way.

There is a necessary balance in the Christian life. "For you have not received a spirit of slavery to cause you to fear," continues Paul in Romans 8:15, "but you received the spirit of adoption by which we are crying out, Abba! Father!" (DAV). The Holy Spirit is powerful, but it is important to understand that he is not a "spirit of slavery" to cause us to fear. We did not receive a Spirit to tell us, "Do this," or "Do that," "Live by this," or "Live by that."

A spirit of slavery would cause us to fear. Think about it. If the Spirit were to expect us to perform in certain ways, every time we didn't perform too well we'd get scared, just like disobedient children awaiting the moment of reckoning when Dad gets home from work. The Spirit isn't Big Daddy who walks in the door with belt in hand ready to wallop us for somehow messing up. Many, many Christians allow themselves to live under a spirit of bondage, their lives gripped by the utter fear of falling short. They never experience the freedom available from the Holy Spirit. They may even prepare to go to heaven, fearful and frightened because they've lived in the slavery of trying to perform righteous acts in the flesh. They're terrified that God will skewer them because they've fallen so short and slipped up so many times.

The simple truth is that, as a believer, you're a child of God. Nothing will change that status. You're loved unconditionally and permanently. Yes, the warning flags are there so that you'll turn to the Spirit for conquering specific sin patterns in your life, and in the process, please the Father and deepen your relationship with him. What is more, you've received a spirit of adoption whereby you can address God in the most intimate terms possible: "Abba!" or "Daddy!," the cry of a child first learning to talk, the words of a child, certainly not those of a slave. You may have an ex-wife or an ex-husband, but you can never have or be an ex-child.

When I originally wrote those words, I was in the home of Mike and Jane Rodgers in San Antonio, Texas. Jane edits much of my work, and I had flown down for several days to put the finishing touches on this manuscript. Little Carrie, Mike and Jane's then eight-month-old daughter, was lying in her crib in the next room, jabbering. "Abbabbabba." It sounded like, "Abba!" Daddy Mike was supposed to respond—and he did. It's a reminder of how sensitive our heavenly Father is to us. He hears us. He cares for our needs, even though we his children are as helpless as tiny babies in his sight. We needn't be afraid.

THE SPIRIT OF ADOPTION

What does it mean to have a "spirit of adoption"? In order to understand what Paul is saying here, we must understand the Jewish and Greek mind. To the American, adoption means taking someone who is not of your immediate family and bringing him or her into the family. To the Jew and the Greek, adoption referred to the practice of taking someone who was already in the family and giving him the rights of inheritance. It was an act of official recognition whereby a flesh-and-blood son became a legal heir. The Jewish ceremony of adoption takes place when a youngster reaches 13. Then he becomes an heir as well as a son.

In the miracle of God's provision for us, there is no waiting for position in his family. At the moment of our new birth in Christ, we instantly receive status as children of God, and we also are instantaneously adopted into his family, becoming his heirs. In fact, as we'll soon see, we become joint heirs with Christ, and our mutual inheritance awaits us in heaven. In glory, we'll receive the honor and reward that Christ gets!

We are children of God. The Spirit himself testifies to this. Writes Paul in Romans 8:16, "The Spirit Himself is bearing witness with our spirit that we are children of God" (DAV). Within our innermost being, we are assured by God's Spirit that we are highly treasured, fully adopted sons and daughters. The transaction has been made for all time.

To paraphrase John Wesley, we have exchanged the faith of a servant for the faith of a son and discovered the reality of Christ. Do we truly realize the implications of our sonship, our daughterhood? Think about your relationship as a parent to your own children. Isn't your love unconditional, your devotion unlimited? How much more then does God care for you, his son, his daughter? Don't you give good things to your children? How much better then are the things of eternity, which God is preparing to give us! "Do not be deceived, my beloved brethren," writes James, "Every good thing bestowed and every perfect gift is from above, coming down from the Father of lights, with whom there is no variation, or shifting shadow" (1:16-17 NASB).

Paul writes, "And if children (we are) also heirs; on the one hand heirs of God, on the other fellow-heirs with Christ, if indeed, we are suffering with Him in order that we may also be glorified together" (8:17 DAV). Part of being a son or daughter of God involves accepting the discipline that he allows. Earthly parents discipline their own children in order to encourage the development of certain qualities such as faithfulness, loyalty, obedience, humility, respect, maturity. As we'll see in later verses of Romans 8, and in the next chapter of this book, the heavenly Father does likewise in us. He has the amazing wisdom and knowledge to use our disobedience as a stepping stone when we properly respond in brokenness and submission. The point is, he does whatever he does, and he permits whatever he permits because we are his children and because he greatly loves us!

So then, are we living in the light of our sonship or our daughterhood? Are we realizing that we'll spend eternity with our fellow Christians? Are we ashamed of those relationships? Are we aware that our "greater brother" is Jesus Christ, our joint heir to the glories of heaven? Are we spending time now getting to know him? It's the most important assignment we have while waiting for heaven. The more we know him, the more comfortable will be the transition from here to there.

Christ is indeed our greater brother. We are fellow heirs with him and will also inherit the riches of heaven. 1 Peter 1:3-4 speaks of our inheritance, which is imperishable and undefiled and which will not fade away. Ephesians 1:11 likewise addresses this. John 17:24 records Jesus' prayer, "Father, I desire that they also, whom Thou hast given Me, be with Me where I am, in order that they may behold My glory, which Thou hast given Me; for Thou didst love Me before the foundation of the world" (NASB). I ask you, are you truly living today in light of those great riches and in anticipation of your coming inheritance? God's Spirit in us is not a badge of slavery, but of sonship, of a beautiful unending relationship.

I recall reading a news article years ago in our local paper about woman named Maddalena Borella from the village of Gorduno, Switzerland. This wretched, elderly creature lived in a filth-encrusted hovel. She slept on a straw mat on the floor of her hut and wore dirty clothes, which she neither washed nor changed. One day she collapsed in the middle of a road and was taken to a nearby hospital. It was diagnosed that Maddalena suffered from malnutrition. Apparently she had eaten only one small meal per day for years. From the hospital, the authorities placed Maddalena in a home for the indigent aged. She died soon thereafter.

Officials sealed the Borella hut and began a search for the woman's only relative, a nephew living in the United States. Once he was located, the authorities inspected Maddalena's tiny home to see what, if anything, was of value. To their sheer amazement, they found a savings passbook showing that Maddalena had over three hundred thousand dollars in an account. They also found a key to a safety deposit box, which when opened proved to contain gold coins worth $1.25 million dollars! Maddalena was a millionaire, and yet she chose to ignore the great wealth and vast riches that were hers. Perhaps she never understood. Instead she lived and died a pauper, in the very midst of her plenty.

The account of Maddalena Borella parallels the spiritual experience of far too many children of God. We have at our disposal the power of God's Spirit to produce Christ-likeness in our life, yet we choose to live in abject spiritual poverty by resisting him. We keep our relationship with God on a performance basis. We never tap the power he has provided to make us victorious; we never discover the excitement that his blessings and his strength can bring.

Make no mistake about it. With sonship comes suffering, and that we'll especially see as we continue to consider Romans 8. But our identification with Jesus Christ involves more than the sufferings of the present time. It also involves the coming glory, for suffering here reminds us of glory ahead (1 Peter 4:12-13).

IN PIGPEN OR PLENTY?

Now is the time to ask yourself some penetrating questions about your sonship in Christ. Are you really living like you are a child of God? Do you truly realize that you are on equal footing with even Christ himself concerning eternal rewards? Are you acting like a loving child? Are you, out of love for him, incorporating the principles of scripture into your life as you become aware of them? Are you spending time in communion with him and in meditation on his word? Does your heart yearn for closeness with God? Is your appetite for the word intensifying with exposure? Do you find yourself turning conversations with others toward the subject of Christ, your first love? Is it easy to follow in his steps because wherever he leads is where you want to be? Does talk of heaven create a feeling of longing because you desire to see him face to face?

Jesus tells the story of a son who didn't live in the light of the privilege of his sonship. This boy rebelled against his dad. He demanded his inheritance, converted it to cash, and left home to live the high life in a foreign land. In that far country, he squandered everything his father had given him. His pockets were empty, his clothes ragged, his stomach aching with hunger. Unable to find steady work, he finally agreed to slop the hogs and clean the pigpen of a farmer. Then his circumstances finally slapped him in the face with the weight of good sense. He looked around him and wondered why he had ever left the security of his father's house for the husks of a pigpen. He picked up his meager belongings and headed for home.

As the young man approached, did his father ignore his arrival? Had the boy ceased to be a child in his father's family? No! Instead the devoted dad ran out to greet the wayward lad. A fresh, clean robe was placed on the boy's back, clean sandals slid on his feet, a new ring set on his finger. The prodigal had come home (Luke 15:11-24).

If you're a Christian, you're a child of God. Are you a prodigal? Are you asking your heavenly Father to give you everything so you might squander his abundance? Are you living a carnal existence, enmeshed in habitual sin, having forgotten whose eternal family you represent? Is God perhaps dealing severely with you at the moment just to get your attention? Are you stuck eating the husks of a pigpen instead of experiencing God's rich provision?

If so, God desires that you, like the prodigal, return to him. He would have you know of his unconditional love. Nothing in the character of God should cause you to hesitate a single moment longer! You must admit that you've got a spiritual need which you cannot handle yourself. You must acknowledge that the disobedience characterizing your life can only be dealt with by the Spirit. It's not enough just to come to your senses, either. The prodigal could have sat in the pigpen for weeks reminding himself that even his father's servants had more than he did. It wasn't until the prodigal was willing to rise up from the pigpen and head back home that he discovered the joy of a parent who was already watching in the window. On that dusty road, God was reflected in an elderly father who rushed outside to throw his arms around his once-lost son and to restore him to the sweetness and abundance of a right relationship within the family.

Where are you today spiritually? If you're a believer, you're in God's family, but are you in a far country? Are you living in carnality? Are you living under the power of the old nature, or are you living in the control of the Spirit? You know if your lifestyle is pleasing to God. You know if your heart is submissive to him. You know if you're a prodigal or a son of obedience willing to present yourself to him daily for his use. You know. And God knows.

May I suggest that you lay this book aside right now and run to make it right. If you are not yet his son or daughter, envision yourself running into the arms of Jesus. You'll hear him say: I love you and I have made provision for your every need. Honest! The price has been paid. If you are already his child: Come on home! You are missing so much. Crawl up in his lap and tell him where it hurts! He'll restore you and make every provision to get you safely home!

Questions to Consider

1. What does Paul mean when he says that we as Christians have received "a spirit of adoption" into God's family (8:15)? What privileges does adoption involve?

2. According to verse 13, what is dangerous about a Christian's willfully persisting in a pattern of sin? According to 1 John 5:16, what steps must we take when we view a fellow believer on the road to self-destruction?

3. At this moment, you are either living under the control of the Holy Spirit or under the control of the flesh. Which is it?

CHAPTER 10

"I have heard Israel saying, 'You disciplined me severely, but I deserved it. I was like a calf that needed to be trained for the yoke and plow. Turn me again to you and restore me, for you alone are the Lord my God" (Jer. 31:18 NLV).

Suffering in the Relationship

Romans 8:18-28

Wave upon wave of human tragedy crashed on the shore of Job's life. Within minutes of one another, messengers arrived to tell him that his livestock had been stolen or destroyed, his servants slain, and his ten beloved children cruelly crushed to death in the collapse of his oldest son's house. Before Job could absorb the shock of each tragedy, news of another horror had assailed him, and as we read of his gut-wrenching losses, we long to raise our hands and cry, "Stop! No more! He's had enough!" But from the lips of the shattered man, no such protest issued. Instead, after learning that his world had been wiped away, Job fell to the ground and worshiped God with these words:

> Naked I came from my mother's womb,
> and naked I will depart.
> The Lord gave and the Lord has taken away;
> may the name of the Lord be praised.
> (Job 1:21 NIV)

With the scalpel of suffering, the master surgeon cuts away those things which hinder the manifestation of his Son in us. Layer upon layer is scraped away, and the brightness of Christ's glory begins to be seen in us. We are called for that purpose, and for that purpose we sometimes have to suffer. The apostle Peter writes:

> For what credit is there if, when you sin and are harshly treated, you endure it with patience? But if when you do what is right and suffer for it you patiently endure it, this finds favor with God. For you have been called for this purpose, since Christ also suffered for you, leaving you an example for you to follow in His steps. (1 Pet. 2:20-21 NASB; see also 1 Thess. 3:3-4; Phil. 1:29; 1 Pet. 1:6, 4:12-13, 5:10)

"O Father," we might cry, "cut away that I might show forth the beauty of your Son!"

Suffering is an inevitable part of the Christian life, a foregone conclusion. Joyfully enduring it is one of the results of knowing Christ, as Paul tells us in Romans 5:3. Suffering is going to happen to us, and yet suffering comes with a promise. We learned in Romans 8 that our status in God's family is that of adopted sons and daughters. Paul also tells us that we are heirs of God and fellow heirs with Christ. Part of that inheritance involves suffering. As Paul writes of Christ, "we are suffering with Him in order that we may also be glorified together" (Rom. 8:17 DAV). Notice, we are suffering *with* him! The promise is that, although we shall suffer, we'll never suffer alone.

Remember when Saul of Tarsus walked along the Damascus road? Desire burned in him to see any who followed Christ killed. He began the journey to Damascus so that he might seize believers and bring them to Jerusalem for judgment. Yet along the dusty Damascus road, Saul was forever stopped from his murderous mission. The bright light of heaven flashed about him, blinding him, and Saul, prostrate on the ground, heard these words from the Lord Jesus himself, "Saul, Saul, why are you persecuting Me?" (Acts 9:4 NASB). Saul, later to be known as the apostle Paul, had no part in Jesus' death and crucifixion. He persecuted Christians, but not Christ, on earth. Yet Jesus asked him, "Saul, why are you persecuting Me?" Why? It's because Jesus shared the sufferings of the early Christians. He shares our suffering today! He suffers with us as we are mistreated for his sake. He is with us in the fiery furnace, the lion's den, the prison cell, the hospital corridors. He takes us through the turmoil and trouble. "Even though I walk through the valley of the shadow of death, I will fear no evil; for Thou art with me" says the psalmist (Ps. 23:4 NIV).

If having a relationship with Christ means suffering, perhaps you're beginning to wonder if it's worth it. I'm reminded of an old oil filter commercial. A mechanic in greasy duds stands amid the junkyard skeletons of rusted, broken-down, old cars. Smiling broadly, the mechanic holds up an oil filter, and with a sly grin, says, "See me now, or see me later." For the person debating about receiving Christ, the issue is: suffer now, or suffer later! And believe me, hell has more permanent fury than anything we can imagine here.

Why is it inevitable that we suffer in this life? It's because we've still got a nature within us that is rebellious against God. We're proud; we're stubborn; we're egotistical;

we're self-centered. We like to do things our way. We've all got progress to make spiritually. There is no gain without pain, no growth without sorrow. One of the main tools God uses to produce the qualities he desires in our life is suffering. He molds us and shapes us in the crucible of trial. He teaches us the lessons of becoming more Christ-like. The Lord speaks to this issue in Isaiah 48:10-11: "See, I have refined you, though not as silver; I have tested you in the furnace of affliction. For my own sake, for my own sake I do this. How can I let myself be defamed? I will not yield my glory to another" (NIV). Whatever the nature of our suffering, we must remember that we are never alone. Christ is there to share and to sustain.

The furnace of affliction in Isaiah reminds me of Shadrach, Meshach and Abednego, who were thrown into a furnace prepared by the king because they refused to bow down and worship the image of gold. We read that God did not abandon them in this fiery ordeal: "Then King Nebuchadnezzar leaped to his feet in amazement and asked his advisers, 'Weren't there three men that we tied up and threw into the fire?' They replied 'Certainly, O king.' He said, 'Look! I see four men walking around in the fire, unbound and unharmed, and the fourth looks like a son of the gods'" (Dan. 3:24-25 NIV).

Our good friends David and Nona Jackson were involved in our lives for many years, serving on the board of the Ministries and the board of the church I pastored. These two dear friends have had more physical afflictions than we can record here. It all kind of peaked a few years ago when their oldest son Larry was called home, a victim of cancer. Just a few weeks ago, David, also in the final stages of cancer, sat up in the bed and said, "Larry, I'm coming." This announcement was followed a bit later, I am sure, with, "Lord, I'm coming home!" as the earthly sufferings of this saint finally ended.

The portion of Romans 8 we're about to consider fills us in on what we can expect as life continues. We learn how the heavenly Father uses suffering in the program of spiritual development he has designed for us.

LIGHT SUFFERING ... HEAVY GLORY—ROMANS 8:18-22

At times suffering gets to us. Paul could have told us all about that. He underwent his share of trouble. His second letter to the church at Corinth gives us a little insight into what he had endured. Let's read his description of when the going really got tough:

> Five times I received from the Jews thirty-nine lashes. Three times I was beaten with rods, once I was stoned, three times I was shipwrecked, a night and a day I have spent in the deep. I have been on frequent journeys, in dangers from rivers, dangers from robbers, dangers from my countrymen, dangers from the Gentiles, dangers in the city, dangers in the wilderness, dangers on the sea, dangers among false brethren; I have been in labor and hardship, through many sleepless nights, in hunger and thirst, often without food, in cold and exposure. (2 Cor. 11:24-27 NASB; see also 12.7-9)

Paul's troubles weren't exactly small potatoes. I shudder to think of going through what he did. But the apostle tells us he has a very definite opinion about the presence of suffering in the life of a Christian. "For I am of the opinion that the sufferings of this present time are not to be compared with the glory which is about to be revealed to us," he states emphatically in Romans 8:18 (DAV). No matter what we've been through, it'll pale in comparison to the wonders and marvels, of eternity with God. In other words, "we ain't seen nothin' yet!" Paul looks beyond the present into the fascinating future, realizing that the tape at the finish line and the trophy to follow will make the stress and strain of the track completely worthwhile. It's almost as if he has a scale in front of him. On the one side he places every ounce of suffering; on the other he sets each pound of glory, and what is ahead tremendously outweighs what is found in the here and now.

The question is, do you believe the apostle? Are you living in anticipation of the glorious future that is yours as a believer? You know you're a child of God, in loving relationship with him. You have an incorruptible, undefiled inheritance that will never fade in glory. In the words of 1 Corinthians 2:9, "Eye hath not seen, nor ear heard, neither have entered into the heart of man, the things which God hath prepared for them that love him" (KJV). Heaven is a fabulous place! Are you allowing your suffering to do its work and point you toward heaven, intensifying your yearning to be at home with the Lord? The travail of the present is, in the eye of eternity, merely the birth pangs of something pretty special. No woman enjoys labor and delivery—yet after cradling the pink, sleeping baby in her arms, few would deny that each agonizing hour was worth it. Our youngest daughter, Julea, just gave us a precious gift in our tenth grandchild. Little Ella Grace is already a treasure, but she did not arrive without causing her mom significant pain.

Why should Christians have to suffer? The reasons are many, but among the most obvious is that we're encased in a human, mortal body. Nothing can change the fact that we're getting older. We're realizing that we aren't what we used to be or even what we thought we were! There are aches and pains. Things hurt now which didn't used to hurt. We get to where we have to think twice before bending down. Aging hurts, physically and mentally. The difficulties will continue until we walk through the valley of the shadow of death, or until the Lord comes for us in the clouds of the rapture.

The members of our body are the instruments Satan can use in the performance of sin, and it is sin also which ensures that we'll suffer. Our sin nature ensures that we'll continue to sin until we go to glory, and there will be consequences of that sin. Just talk to David or Moses, Demas or Diotrophes (2 Tim. 4:10, 3 John 9). We are also probably going to suffer because of the sin that other people do. It's unlikely that we'll escape the wrath of someone else's temper or the irresponsible behavior of others under the influence of alcohol or drugs. We may be faced with abuse from others who are selfish, stubborn, and unbroken ... or just warped enough to want everyone to share in their misery.

Within us a continuing warfare will rage, too. There will be a struggle between the old and the new nature until the very day we go home to be with the Lord. The internal warfare will constantly produce in us an unsettled sense of strife and suffering, but we must always remember that Paul also assures us that our "momentary, light affliction is producing for us an eternal weight of glory far beyond all comparison" (2 Cor. 4:17 NASB). Our problems may seem impossible now, but seen through the lens of eternity, they're light and momentary—not *insignificant*, but from God's perspective, brief and manageable. We must keep in mind what my wife always observes: this too shall pass. And it does!

In the midst of it all, we must never forget that we have "the glory which is about to be revealed" (8:18) to anticipate eagerly. Rather than a term life insurance policy, one whose benefits decrease with time and age, the believer has a whole life policy. The death benefits are beyond belief. Each moment of the suffering of human existence is building toward the climax of perfect peace, matchless beauty, and complete freedom, when there will be no more dying and when the Lord will wipe away every tear. This is one job that God will not delegate. We read in Revelation 7:17: "For the Lamb (the Lord Jesus) who stands in front of the throne will be their Shepherd. He will lead them to the springs of life-giving water. And God will wipe away all their tears" (NLV).

CREATION'S CRY

We suffer, but not alone. As we've discussed, Christ shares our suffering, and even he is not the only one to do so. As we suffer, all of creation suffers, too. "For the anxious longing of the creation is awaiting eagerly for the revelation of the sons of God," says Paul in Romans 8:19 (DAV). As we await the trump to sound and the heavens to reverberate with the shout of the Lord, we are not alone. The created world awaits the same glorious moment. The earth strains for the sound of that voice which thousands of years ago commanded, "Let there be light" and there was light; that same voice which formed a baby's cry in Bethlehem; that same voice which shouted, "Lazarus, come forth," and a dead man arose; that same voice which cried from the cross, "It is finished." Now creation anxiously awaits with us the shout to be heard 'round the cosmos of the returning savior, coming for his own. Even so, come Lord Jesus! is the cry of creation and Christian alike.

You see, the world around us, as Paul tells us in Romans 8:20, has been "subjected to frustration" (DAV). When Adam disobeyed in the garden, not only was mankind cursed, but also the entire creation. A curse was pronounced on the created world (Gen. 3:17-19). The appealing serpent became a slithering, ugly creature. Rose bushes sprouted thorns, and the earth produced not just grass but thistles and weeds as well. Today, environmental scientists try frantically to preserve the balance of nature, desperately working to keep what we've got, but the Bible tells us that ultimately such efforts are futile. Science merely forestalls the inevitable. Man wreaks havoc on nature, yes, but it's also true that nature frustrates itself with tornadoes, ice storms, avalanches, floods, and less dramatic things like weeds, dry rot, and crabgrass.

The crown of thorns hammered down on Christ's head, cutting into his scalp at his crucifixion, indicated that on the cross he bore creation's curse, as well as mankind's curse. Creation and Christians have the same thing to look forward to: freedom from the curse of sin and death. When will that freedom come? For believers, it will be at our graduation, the rapture, the "revelation of the sons of God," mentioned by Paul in Romans 8:19. At least that will be the beginning. Ultimate release from the curse will issue when a new heaven and a new earth are established, as described in chapters 21 and 22 of the Revelation.

Paul also tells us that creation was subjected to frustration "not of its own free will, but because of Him who subjected it, in hope" (Rom. 8:20 DAV). The created world didn't want to be subjected to the curse that had befallen man. Instead, the lion wanted to lie down with the lamb. Survival of the fittest wasn't in the original game plan. Creation longed for love and cooperation, symbiosis rather than conflict and struggle. God allowed creation to suffer the curse that fell on man.

Paul tells us that God did so "in hope, that the creation itself also will be set free from its slavery to decay into the liberty of the glory of the children of God" (Rom. 8:20-21 DAV). The created world can expectantly hope that its frustration will one day be removed. The Bible tells us that the physical world is going to be re-created in two stages. The first part of this re-creation will come as the Lord ushers in his millennial kingdom; the process will be complete at the creation of the new heaven and earth described in Revelation 21:1 (see also 2 Pet. 3:7-13). Creation's mortal yoke will also be thrown off, and the perishable will become imperishable.

Isaiah 66:2 records the Lord's words: "'Has not my hand made all these things, and so they came into being?' declares the Lord. 'This is the one I esteem: he who is humble and contrite in spirit, and trembles at my word'" (NIV).

One commentator has said that creation cursed is like the bride, draped in white satin, lace, and decked with garlands of fresh flowers, who at the moment she is fully attired for the wedding, witnesses the death of her bridegroom. She stands, her eyes awash in tears, her garments and garlands already fading in life and luster. Thus nature, like every Christian, awaits expectantly that day of liberation from the curse. Nature awaits, as we do, that shout which shatters shackles and signals the fall of Satan's kingdom. At his voice, the gates of hell will tremble; the foundations will crack and crumble. The king of darkness will be bound by a chain and cast into the abyss.

This glorious hope makes me cry with Jeremiah in 32:17: "O Sovereign Lord! You have made the heavens and earth by your great power. Nothing is too hard for you!" (NLV). The Lord responds in 32:27: "I am the Lord, the God of all the peoples of the world. Is anything too hard for me?" (NLV).

In the meantime, as Paul continues in Romans 8:22, "We are knowing that the whole creation is groaning together and suffering the pains of childbirth together until now" (DAV). Do you get the big picture? The suffering is undergone *together*! The Lord Jesus suffers, we suffer, creation suffers. There will not be total healing until the Lord comes, and we're set free from this sin nature and from the curse of the world around us, liberated to the glory that is yet to be ours. Our earthly woes, those "pains of childbirth" mentioned by Paul, will dissolve into dim memories as the reality of God's glory shines about us in all its intensity. All our pain will give birth to something pretty precious.

Think of the caterpillar, spinning his threads, weaving a

tapestry of silk around itself. Round and round the silken thread goes, and inside the spinner becomes increasingly restrained and finally, apparently, dormant. It seems he has woven a coffin about himself. But there comes a day when there is a movement, and then another. The silken cocoon tears a bit, and a wing protrudes. Then appears another wing, and with the sunlight's warming rays, the wings expand to reveal a brilliance of color and design. What was once a mottled, hairy, worm-like creature becomes a floating, fluttering, brightly hued butterfly. So shall we be changed someday, and the suffering that we endure in the meantime is but a cocoon in which we're becoming more and more like Christ. In the words of Solomon, God makes "everything beautiful in its time" (Eccles. 3:11 NIV).

THE FIRST FRUITS—ROMANS 8:23-28

Along with us, creation groans and strains with the labor pains of suffering, awaiting the moment when God will again intervene in natural and human history. The natural world is our fellow sufferer, but, as Paul goes on to tell us in verse 23, we have an advantage over the creation. "And not only this," writes Paul, "but also we ourselves who are having the first fruits of the Spirit, even we ourselves are groaning within ourselves, waiting eagerly our adoption, the redemption of our body" (Rom. 8:23 DAV).

Like creation, we await our adoption—in this case, meaning the moment of the "redemption of our bodies." This will occur at the rapture, when we are given a new, glorified body. We've already received a "spirit of adoption" (8:15); what Paul speaks of in verse 23 is the full realization of our inheritance as sons and daughters in Christ. But, unlike the creation, we already have the "first fruits" of the Holy Spirit, because the Spirit dwells within us.

It's like when you men asked your girlfriend for her hand in marriage. Soon after you popped the question, you probably sprang for a diamond ring. Sliding the ring on her finger was a way of officially saying, "Honey, I want this to be forever. I am committing myself to you." When God answered our faith in Jesus Christ, the Holy Spirit was given as an engagement ring, permanently betrothing us to Christ, our bridegroom-to-be. The Spirit may also be considered the earnest money (Eph. 1:13-14). He is the down payment on the redemption and reward that are to come. He is the seal reminding us that our relationship with the Lord will become ever richer with the passage of time.

In the meantime, we're still "groaning within ourselves" (8:23). We still suffer. We still have that mortal body; we haven't been physically glorified yet. We're not completely like the Lord Jesus. We still shed tears; we still hurt; we still have accidents; we still have problems. Paul, in 2 Corinthians 5:2, says that "in this house we groan, longing to be clothed with our dwelling from heaven" (NASB). The psalmist David writes, "I am weary with my groaning; all the night I make my bed to swim; I water my couch with my tears" (Ps. 6:6 KJV). Christ even groaned within himself as he came to Mary and Martha on the occasion of the death of their brother Lazarus. Their obvious pain and intense grief caused his sobs to spill forth (John 11:33-35).

"Who shall set me free out of the body of this death?" exclaims Paul in Romans 7:24 (DAV). For now, the Spirit enables us to conquer some of the sinful manifestations of our dead body. Ultimately, the Lord Jesus will do the final act of deliverance, resulting in our shedding this old wretched shell in favor of an immortal one. What hope we have in Christ!

IN PATIENCE, HOPING

"For in hope we have been saved," writes Paul in Romans 8:24, "but hope that is seen is not hope; for why is one also hoping for what he is seeing?" (DAV). The promises of God enable us to have that precious commodity: hope. But hope is not hope if we see what we're hoping for! The hope of the Christian faith, the hope of God's glory, is not something we can see. It's something we've just got to believe. As we read scripture, that hope calls for us to lift our eyes from the pages and gaze heavenward. "For this is what the high and lofty One says—he who lives forever, whose name is holy: 'I live in a high and holy place, but also with him who is contrite and lowly in spirit, to revive the spirit of the lowly and to revive the heart of the contrite'" (Isa. 57:15 NIV). By the Spirit of God, we must begin to discern, and to anticipate, the glories of the future. We can't literally see what is ahead, but we must place our hope in what God says it will be. "Blessed are they," the resurrected Christ tells Thomas after allowing the disciple to touch his wounds, "that have not seen, and yet have believed" (John 20:29 KJV).

With the kind of glory we believers may anticipate, what are we supposed to do with our suffering? Should we try to get out of it? Should we try to avoid it? No! We're called to suffer, and much of overcoming really involves patient perseverance (5:3-5). We're called to *patiently persevere* what's there, because a sovereign God is weaving together everything with a twofold purpose: to make us more like his Son and to enrich our anticipation of that which is ahead for us in glory. "But we are hoping for that which we are not seeing, with patience we are waiting eagerly for it," says Paul (Romans 8:25 DAV). The word he uses for *patience* suggests a quality of endurance, of keeping on keeping on, of spiritual survival against incredible odds. Suffering shouldn't adversely affect our relationship with God if we're responding properly to the crucible of trial. We shouldn't become bitter or angry at him, but instead submissive to the discipline that he feels necessary to use to make us more like his Son. Suffering should draw us closer to him, as we realize that he is the only truly constant, dependable, unchangeable person we know.

THE SPIRIT

Besides, God gives us help and companionship to survive the suffering. "And in the same way the Spirit also is helping us in our weakness; for we are not knowing how to pray as we should, but the Spirit Himself is interceding for us with sighs too deep for words," writes Paul in Romans 8:26 (DAV). Not only does the Spirit dwell within us as the engagement ring—the first fruit to remind us of our coming heavenly inheritance—not only does he live in us to energize our new nature to victory over sin—but he also is a helper. He understands with the fullness of God. There are times when suffering may grow so intense that we're brought to silence. We hurt so badly we can't say anything. We can't pray; we don't even know what to ask God. The words won't come. These are the times when the Spirit intercedes for us.

Paul tells us in 8:26 that the Spirit intercedes for us with "sighs too deep for words." The verse has been used many times by Christians to justify the practice of speaking or praying in tongues. The "sighs" with which the Spirit intercedes for us are not the garbled, unintelligible syllables of ecstatic utterance. The intercessory language used by the Spirit is not some mysterious prattle. It is a method by which the Spirit communicates to the Father the needs of our heart. It is the assurance that, even when we don't know how to pray for ourselves, we have a helper who can and will take over.

I remember when a very dear friend of mine, a minister, suffered horribly from a painful form of cancer. When his condition deteriorated markedly, a member of our Ministries board and I went to visit his wife and him. From the cold, sterile hallway outside his hospital room, the man's wife accompanied the two of us to a nearby waiting area, and there we prayed. First I prayed, and then the friend who had come with me. Last, it was Eunice's turn. There was only a long silence, as this godly woman could find no words to speak to her heavenly Father. "I'm sorry," she finally said. "I can't pray." She wasn't angry at God. But the hurt was too deep, speech too difficult, and she had no idea even what to ask of the creator. When it hurts too intensely and it all seems too confusing, then the Spirit takes over and intercedes for us. He knows how to pray when we don't. My ailing friend lived only a few months after that bleak day in the hospital. In those final days, he came to grips with the Father's plan and was fully ready for the call home. The additional months he enjoyed were clear evidence of answered prayer, prayer his wife couldn't even utter: the intercessory prayer of the Holy Spirit.

How comforting it is that God knows exactly how we feel and precisely what we need. Although we often don't know what to ask for ourselves, he provides the helper to communicate our needs and express our longings. In fact, we're often praying through the Spirit when we don't even know it. Prayer can be the shedding of a tear, the upward glance of an eye, the subtle surrender of our own ability. Prayer happens when words refuse to come, because the Spirit is doing the praying. He translates the desires of our heart and the heart-cries of our soul. Like a mother who understands that her baby's wail means tiredness, a shrill cry means hunger, a brief whimper indicates a desire to be held, the Spirit takes the longings we cannot clearly express or do not truly understand ourselves and reveals them to the Father.

And the Father? Paul tells us, "He who is searching the hearts is knowing what the mind of the Spirit is, because according to God. He is interceding on behalf of the saints" (8:27 DAV). God understands the intercession of his Spirit. The Father picks up the requests translated by the Spirit and acts on each one of them, knowing fully what is needed, in the end, to produce glory. There is great comfort in knowing that the Lord Jesus is at his post interceding for us 24 hours a day. "Hence also He is able to save forever those who draw near to God through Him, since He always lives to make intercession for them" (Heb. 7:25 NASB).

Just think, the whole Trinity is involved in our salvation. The Father planned it, the Son purchased it, and the Spirit points us to Calvary and the empty tomb. You've got to say: "It just doesn't get any better than that!"

WORKNG FOR GOOD

When things seem to grow cold and circumstances enshroud us, we have the promise of Romans 8:28, where we read, "And we are knowing that for those who are loving God, all things He is working together for good, for those who are called in accordance with His purpose" (DAV). It's a well-known verse, one that is often quoted at times of great need, one which, frankly, others sometimes throw in our face if we're showing how we hurt. It's sometimes used as the spiritual band-aid supposed to cover every wound and relieve every hurt. But the verse is not meant to deny us the pain—it won't make the hurt evaporate to know that all things are working together for good when our lives seem to be falling apart.

The truth of Romans 8:28 brings comfort. Let's look closely at the verse.

And we are knowing: Our knowledge is part of our present experience.

That for those who are loving God: This is not a truth for somebody who is an unbeliever, but one who knows and loves the Lord.

All things He is working together for good: God is currently, continually, combining the circumstances of our life for his good, the good that he with his omniscient perspective sees. He already has glimpsed the finale so he knows how it all fits together.

For those who are called in accordance with His purpose: We are called to glorify God for now, and throughout eternity. Each temporary trauma fits into that purpose. Each is part of his plan.

What Paul is telling us is that when we enter into a relationship with Jesus Christ, we can know that in our present experience, all the things the Lord has permitted in our life are working together for good, in God's overall plan. Everything is Father-filtered; it has crossed the desk of the divine director before we ever see it (Job 1:6-12). There are no limitations. Every trial, every joy, every delay, every green light—all work together for good. Nothing is excluded—not the good, the bad, the bright, the dark, the bitter, the sweet, the easy, the hard, the happy, the sad, the prosperous, the poverty-ridden, the sick, the healthy, the calm, the stormy, the comforting, the suffering, the life-giving, or the death-bringing. Whatever happens to us happens with God's good in view, and his ultimate goal for us is somehow to make us more like Christ. This very minute, we're in the process of becoming new men and women. Suffering is part of God's fitness program to shape us up from the inside out.

Notice, Paul does *not* say that all things are good. Tornadoes are not good; car accidents are not good; cancer is not good. We shouldn't feel like we ought to look forward to the tough times. Many people enter into a round of suffering with a sort of martyr's delight. Sometimes this attitude manifests itself at the funeral of a loved one. People whose hearts should be breaking and eyes overflowing decide they have to be tough, resigned, and stoic to demonstrate their triumph. They are only delaying the inevitable. The grief will come and do its work. Nobody ought to *enjoy* suffering. We shouldn't revel in misfortune, relishing each ache and pain as a hypochondriac would a common cold, milking each sniffle for all its worth. We shouldn't feel guilty when we're less than ecstatic about whatever new trial pops into our life.

There is a balance. We need to remember that we're in a relationship with God! He loves us intensely. We've got to understand that God himself understands what we're going through when trials hit. He understands that in a sin-laden world, we're going to face some incredibly tough things. He knows that heart-wrenching tragedies are on their way. He also knows that it's all right for us to cry; it's all right to hurt; it's all right to feel the emptiness and the loss. We mustn't pretend that the hurt doesn't hurt. Denying the reality of pain doesn't make us super spiritual—just less than honest.

THE ETERNAL PERSPECTIVE

When the going gets rough, we can, indeed we must, take comfort in the fact that God's perspective is not our own. He's working it all together for good, in his time and in his way and with his limitless knowledge and wisdom. We can trust him in it! But all too often, we really don't. With Jacob we cry, "Everything is against me!" (Gen. 42:36 NIV). When he made that statement, Jacob was mourning the loss of his son Simeon and the impending loss of his youngest son, Benjamin. His favorite boy, Joseph, had evidently been viciously killed by wild animals years before; Simeon was now held captive in Egypt by a suspicious foreign ruler. The only way the other sons could secure Simeon's release was by fetching baby brother Benjamin from his doting dad. Although he eventually submitted to the plan, Jacob saw only gloom and doom on the horizon at the outset. He protested the surrender of Benjamin, but finally relinquished control. How limited Jacob's perspective was! He had no idea that the "suspicious" foreign ruler was really his long-lost Joseph. The whole dozen of his boys would be miraculously reunited within a matter of weeks—but only God knew that at the time. Jacob simply saw the limitations, the trouble, not the overriding purpose and matchless love of the Lord.

Think again of the prodigal son. Picture the prodigal's father on the eve of the boy's departure from home. Because of the young man's insistence, every penny his dad had earned over a lifetime had been divided between his two sons. The younger was so irresponsible. Surely he would waste each dime. Surely he would come to ruin in a foreign land, so far away from home. And this he did. What pain the father must have initially felt as he divided his boys' inheritance between them! What worry! And what of the son? He started out like a blazing comet, only to have his fire snuffed out. Hunger pangs forced him to a pigsty. What good could possibly come out of such a set of circumstances? And yet the father's grief, his forced release of his boy, the son's abject poverty—all eventually worked together for good. At the end of the account we see an old man running to embrace a once-lost son; we observe the birth of a new relationship of forgiveness. Had he never left home, never lost his money, never been cast on the dunghill of humanity, the rebellion in the heart of the boy might never have been quenched. The relationship of love and forgiveness and commitment between father and son might never have developed. Surely it was worth every ounce of heartache.

Still, we often look at the initial event in suffering and our hearts throb with horror, hurt, and dismay. "Oh, what a tragedy! What a disaster!" we cry. "Why me? Why this? Why now?" we beg God to tell us. We drown in despair, instead of trying to look beyond the present ills to see the big picture. We won't always be able to know why the things happen that do. The fact is, we won't totally understand all the reasons *why* until we reach eternity. Then, in the very presence of God, I don't imagine we'll even care any longer why we lost a young child to leukemia, why a drunken driver slammed into a friend's vehicle, why a daughter became pregnant out of wedlock, why a favorite nephew committed suicide, why a business failure left us bankrupt. In the here and now, we are left with the fact that each event of life happens with God's knowledge and perspective. And always, we have the opportunity to trust (1 Cor. 13:12-13).

Joseph lived long enough to have that perspective. In his words, "You intended to harm me, but God intended it for good to accomplish what is now being done, the saving of many lives" (Gen. 50:20 NIV).

TOGETHER

A single word Paul uses in Romans 8:28 should reach out and grab us. The word is *together* "All things He (God) is working *together* for good," says the apostle (DAV italics mine). A single event of sorrow—say, the death of a loved one, the loss of a job, the failure of a business, the foreclosure on a house—may seem like nothing for which to be thankful. God doesn't expect us to jump with joy when we're at the brink of disaster. "Oh good! My finances are in a shambles!" is hardly a statement any sane person could make. But the fact is that God is working every circumstance together in an entire production package called earthly life. He is weaving the circumstances—good, bad, and in between—to accomplish his purposes.

Think of each event in your life as an ingredient in a recipe. One of my favorite desserts is cracker pie. Do you know what goes into cracker pie? A cup of pecans, 24 crushed Ritz crackers, a teaspoon of vanilla, three beaten egg whites, a cup of sugar, and a teaspoon of baking powder. It sounds unlikely that those ingredients could be mixed, poured into a piecrust, baked, and turn into something tasty. But cracker pie is good! Top it with a dollop of whipped cream, and you have a delicious dessert. The baking soda by itself would taste bitter. The vanilla alone would be hard to swallow. The twenty-four crackers would stick in your throat without something to wash them down. But together, the ingredients form a dish fit for company. So it is in our lives. Some events will be bitter, others very hard to swallow; others will stick going down. But everything is working together toward the very good goal of making us and those around us more like Christ.

Our friends Dick and Ethel Knarr illustrate the great truth that triumphant Christianity can come from terrible tragedy. The Knarrs lost their youngest child at age three in a drowning accident. I have watched from the sidelines of their life as God has used this hurt to make Dick a far more compassionate physician and Ethel a beautiful Christ-like witness. Ethel's enthusiasm for the Lord knows no bounds. Her words on the fourteenth anniversary of Amy's death told of how she looked forward to seeing her little girl in heaven. She is fully ready to go home whenever the Father calls her.

RIVERS RUNNING UPHILL

Take one tragic event by itself, and it's easy to blame God. It's easy to build a case against him and his wisdom. When we're pressed against the wall, we often can't fit the shattered pieces of experience together to make a pretty picture of anything. God didn't intend us to. He has revealed that we but see through a glass darkly now. We know in part, but someday we'll know in full, when we see him face to face (1 Cor. 13:12). We've just got to trust. God says to us, essentially, "Love me more and realize I'm using it all for good, although you don't understand it." We can take him at his word.

When Pearl and I make our annual journey to the Pacific Northwest for a Bible conference there, we love to drive through the mountains. Often we'll gaze out the window, sometimes to view a most unusual sight. From the perspective of the mountain road, it seems some creeks actually run uphill. It looks like the water flows up, rather than down. But that's only from the perspective of the road. From the perspective of the mountaintop, the creeks are running the right way after all.

God is on the mountain of our life. He sees the way things are running, and believe me, no matter what happens, it's always in the direction he chooses, and it's always for our own great good. That, more than anything, is the message of Romans 8:28.

While we await the "redemption of our body," and wade through the struggles of earthly life, let's ask God to help us maintain the hope expressed by the prophet Habakkuk, who long ago uttered these words:

> Though the fig tree does not bud
> and there are no grapes on the vines,
> though the olive crop fails
> and the fields produce no food,
> though there are no sheep in the pen
> and no cattle in the stalls,
> yet I will rejoice in the Lord,
> I will be joyful in God my Savior.
> The Sovereign Lord is my strength;
> he makes my feet like the feet of a deer,
> he enables me to go on the heights.
> (Hab. 3:17-19 NIV)

Charlie and Marie, dear friends from our Hide-A-Way Lake congregation, could tell us all about rejoicing in a sovereign God in the midst of adversity. One sunny afternoon several years ago, this precious couple drove to Dallas to pick up an elderly aunt at DFW International. On the trip back, the aunt sat in front with Charlie, while Marie read in the back.

A large truck passed them on the highway and cut in on them sharply, forcing Charlie to steer into a guardrail and bridge abutment. The aunt was instantly snatched home.

Marie broke both legs and an arm. Charlie's lung collapsed, and he suffered other internal injuries plus a gaping nose wound. For several days, his survival was in question.

Marie remained conscious throughout the whole ordeal, and her first remarks in the emergency room were words of quiet confidence: "All I could think of was that God is working all things together for good." In the wake of an aunt's death and a husband's critical condition, this child of her heavenly Father could still speak words of trust.

In my office, four days later, this couple's son came to know Jesus Christ personally. Eight days later, Charlie and Marie celebrated their fiftieth wedding anniversary in separate hospitals. The aunt's death, the excruciating injuries of those remaining alive—were they worth it? In view of a son's salvation, the answer is an emphatic yes. The answer is always yes, even when the whys are not clear. Oh, to learn the simple trust of a child holding the parent's hand in the dark and exclaiming, "My daddy knows where we are!"

Questions to Consider

1. What is the "redemption of our body" described in verse 23? Do you eagerly await the moment when the trumpet will sound and the Lord will call for his children in the rapture? Why or why not?

2. According to Romans 8:26, what function does the Spirit perform for us when we cannot pray for ourselves? Have you ever been aware of an episode in your life or in the life of someone you know where it has been obvious that the Spirit has prayerfully interceded? Share the incident, if you wish.

3. For whom do all things work together for good? (see Rom. 8:28). Can you think of an event in your life where a tragedy eventually resulted in triumph?

CHAPTER 11

"The Lord is my light and my salvation—whom shall I fear? The Lord is the stronghold of my life—of whom shall I be afraid?" (Ps. 27:1 NIV).

Security in the Savior

Romans 8:29-39

"Aw, come on Dad, you'll love it!" Andy pleaded as we stood at the bottom of the amusement park ride. Famous last words!

Get the picture. I'm in my early fifties at this time. Everyone in the enormous snaking line around me looks nineteen at the most. Plenty are junior high age or younger. Soaring above us rises a twisted mass of miles of steel track called the Shock Wave. It was billed as the largest double-loop roller coaster in the world (a distinction it has long since had to give up). I should have known better.

"Okay," I meekly assent. Then I have at least a half hour to wait in line and contemplate my decision. Stupid. Finally I am strapped into a car, and it is too late to back out.

Up, up, up the car climbs, and then swoosh, it plunges down the first immense drop. I'm lifted slightly off my seat;

my neck is thrown back; my stomach crowds my esophagus. Swoosh—the coaster seems to hurtle out of control. Probably into eternity, I think ... but actually, we're only headed for the loops. When we're upside down, midway through the first loop, things start falling out of my pockets. I don't even try to pry my hands loose from the safety bar to grab for my comb and keys. In seconds, the final loop is history, and I feel like I am, too. The car glides to a stop and I jump out as fast as my weak knees will let me. I tell Andy and the Lord that one of those rides is enough for a lifetime.

"Come on, Dad, let's go again. You'll get used to it!" Andy replies with a grin. Ha! Some things I can do without.

When I rode on that roller coaster, it seemed like the whole machine was an uncontrolled metallic beast plunging and plummeting and jerking me around with incredible speed. It looked like a maze of snarled steel designed by some maniac. It lasted only a few fearsome seconds, then it was all over. But you know, as I looked over the Shock Wave after surviving it, I saw that it was constructed with care. The steep ascents and sudden descents of the track were designed so that the cars could build up enough speed to make it around the loops. The cars themselves were equipped with safety features: they fit securely onto the tubular tracks, and an attendant, presumably with a brake of some sort, looked on from a control booth. What appeared totally out of control wasn't really out of control at all.

How much life sometimes resembles that roller coaster. It seems as if we're senselessly hurtling along, speeding toward the conclusion with no logical pattern or design to the process. With incredible speed, the years melt, one into the other. Adolescence becomes young adulthood, then middle age. Far too soon it's time for the gold watch and retirement reception. What we often forget is that everything in life is really preconceived. God the Father sees it all clearly. We aren't hurtling out of control. He knows the direction, and he is worthy of our total trust. As Christians, we are completely secure in a loving relationship with him, and that is the incredibly rich and liberating thought which Paul leaves us with in the closing verses of Romans 8.

THE WORK OF THE FATHER—ROMANS 8:29-30

Remember Paul's words in Romans 8:28: "And we are knowing that for those who are loving God, all things He is working together for good, for those who are called in accordance with His purpose" (DAV). With the idea in mind that believers are "called in accordance with (God's) purpose," the apostle next says of God, "Because whom He foreknew, he also decided upon beforehand those who were to be like His Son in appearance to the end, that He might be the firstborn among many brethren" (Rom. 8:29 DAV). Paul continues in verse 30, "Now those whom He decided upon beforehand, these He also called; and those whom He called, these He also justified; and those whom He justified, these He also glorified" (DAV). Before we go any further, let's tackle a few of the tough theological concepts brought out in verses 29 and 30. Maybe you've heard some of the ideas Paul presents before, and possibly you're wondering about the meaning and relationship of these terms. Hopefully this will help.

Because whom He foreknew. Foreknowledge is a quality that only God has. Only he knows ahead of time what's going to happen. I often wish I did! Then I could stand before a crowded room of hungry investors and predict stock market fluctuations, and more people would listen to me than to their brokers. But only God accurately fore-knows the future. Even before the beginning of the world, he knew us, how long we would live, and what decisions we would make. He knows, but he will never violate our free-dom of choice. If you've accepted Christ as savior, you did so out of your own free will, yet God has known since the beginning of time the decision you'd make.

He also decided upon beforehand those who would be like His Son: Predestination is the concept described here; it goes hand in hand with foreknowledge. On the basis of his foreknowledge, God is able to make some predeterminations about his children. A loving God, he knows beforehand the choices you'll make and what is necessary to bring into your life so that you'll eventually reflect his Son and ultimately end up in glory. That is the destiny he predetermines for each believer. (Incidentally, he provides opportunities for everyone to come to him in faith, even those he knows won't respond; see 2 Peter 3:9.) On the basis of knowing ahead of time, he has decided beforehand those who would be like his Son in appearance. The picture is that of a sovereign God working all things together for good in your life, with the final goal that of glory to the Father throughout eternity.

Now those whom He decided upon beforehand, these He also called: God's call is the next idea broached by Paul. The Lord foreknows who will respond to him; he predetermines where and how he'll draw you to himself and make you like his Son. He then issues a call. What is involved in that call? It's impossible to fathom it all, but here are some ideas. Perhaps you'll sense God's call in a church service. You don't usually make it on Sunday morning—your attendance is spotty. Yet here you are. God knows that, and he knew that at your age on this day at this time, you would be provided with an opportunity to get to know him. You sense, through the words perhaps of a teacher or preacher, that the Lord is speaking to you about your eternal destiny. You know that you are being convicted of the reality of your sin. That's God calling. You may be called while reading the pages of a Christian book or while listening to a speaker give his or her testimony or while simply conversing with a friend. You may be called during a bout with a serious illness or following a brush with death. God's call is an invitation tugging at your heartstrings and penetrating your soul. If you're a Christian, you probably remember the moment when the reality of your own sinfulness devastated you, and the need for the savior overwhelmed you, and you said to God, "I believe."

These also He justified: justification is the next concept mentioned by the apostle. It is the act of being made perfectly righteous. Once we respond to God's call in faith, we are justified. We are made perfectly righteous in his sight. The righteousness of Jesus Christ is applied to us in a single, perfect, finished transaction. Our standing before God is then one of complete holiness. It's not *who* we are, but *whose* we are. It's not what we do, but what God through Christ has done. In God's eyes, it's just as if we'd never sinned, for all eternity (see also Rom. 5:9).

Those whom He justified, these He also glorified: After foreknowledge, predestination, calling, justification, what's left as far as God's work is concerned in us? Glorification remains to be accomplished. It happens when the work is done and we are like his Son. John said it well: "Beloved, now we are children of God, and it has not appeared as yet what we shall be. We know that, when He appears, we shall be like Him, because we shall see Him just as He is" (1 John 3:2 NASB). Someday we'll be completely sanctified, possessors of immortal bodies, dwelling in the company of the Lord forever. Oh, that will be glory for you and for me and for God!

IN THE PAST TENSE

Let's put it all together. God the Father foreknew who would come to him in faith; he predetermined the circumstances so that we'd have the opportunity to respond to his call; he justified us once we did; and he also glorified us. Notice, Paul uses the past tense to describe each one of these actions. Something is missing, isn't it? A lot of life is lived between the moments of justification and glorification. What about that million-dollar word, *sanctification*? Paul doesn't mention it in verses 29-30, but let's talk about it briefly anyway.

Every Christian, following the moment of conversion until the moment he goes home to be with the Lord, is in the process of being sanctified or set apart. What God does, through the work of his Spirit, is to begin a progressive program of making us more and more like Christ, and less and less like the world around us, with its mangled morality. Positionally, as we've discussed earlier, our standing before God is forever perfect. Practically, in the day-to-day grind, our state is still that of a sinner. The Christian life is an upward climb in the Spirit. It's filled with valleys and deep places of failure, but the movement is a vertical one, toward Christ-likeness. Genuine progress comes not from performance but from relationship, not from fulfilling the law because we think we have to, but from growing closer to God in love and desiring to deal with the things hurting that relationship with him. And this, more than anything, is the theme of Romans 6, 7, and 8.

The desire for the word only intensifies with growth. Feeding on scripture and meditating on its principles are vital parts of a deepening relationship. Just staying in God's presence in prayer brings pure delight. The freedom of awakening and sensing his smile thrills the soul, sparking the deep longing never to let a day pass without time in his word and before him in prayer. Quiet our hearts, Father, while we wait before you! Speak in the stillness! How often he does.

It's interesting that Paul mentions our justification and our glorification but not our sanctification, in verses 29 and 30. Glorification is simply sanctification made complete, so Paul uses one word for the whole process. Along the way to eternity we can begin to reflect Christ, but once we exit this earthly life, the work is done. We're glorified. We're like him, for we see him face to face and know him as he is (1 John 3:2). To be absent from the body is to be instantaneously present with the Lord (2 Cor. 5:8). The old body discarded, the old nature departed, we'll be like Christ.

Do you realize the joyous implications of that? What incredible freedom there is in truly comprehending Paul's message in Romans 8:29-30! Remember, Paul uses the *past tense* to describe the concepts of foreknowledge, predestination, calling, justification, and glorification. The reality is that before the foundation of the world, God in love looked down on us. He had a work of glorification to perform in us, and as far as he's concerned, it's already finished. If you're a Christian, he called you, he justified you, and he glorified you. It's done, from the perspective of eternity! You shouldn't feel compelled to perform to please him. Nothing you do or fail to do will change the glorious end result. You have a responsibility in your relationship with God, but that responsibility is to get to know him and to love him with depth and intensity. Your responsibility is to talk to him, to read his word, and to be open to his leading. The acts of godly service you do will spring from a heart filled with affection and thanksgiving. There's no need to worry about earning his favor, because as far as he is concerned, you already have it. If you persist in undesirable habit patterns, then perhaps he may call you home before you expect, but nothing, not even that, will change the fact that from God's perspective you are already glorified. There's no room for guilt—but plenty of space for gratitude in the heart of a believer!

"The steps of a good man are ordered by the Lord: and he delighteth in his way. Though he fall, he shall not be utterly cast down: for the Lord upholdeth him with his hand," writes David in Psalm 37:23-24 (KJV). What tremendous verses! We get fearful inside that perhaps we might be lost at the last minute. We become guilt-ridden over failure, missed opportunities, blown chances. But God promises always to be faithful. He will complete the good work he has started in us, despite ourselves.

In the allegory *Hinds Feet on High Places*, Hannah Hurnard writes of Much-Afraid, a pilgrim wanderer on the journey to the High Places. In the book, Much-Afraid slips and stumbles through a misty wilderness. Resentment, Bitterness, and Self-Pity incessantly whisper and jeer at her from the midst of the clinging fog. From behind, the Good Shepherd, the character representative of Christ, notices her dilemma. "Much-Afraid," he gently counsels her, "don't you know by now that I never think of you as you are now but as how you will be when I have brought you to the Kingdom of Love and washed you from all the stains and defilements of the journey?"[1]

The Shepherd's response to Much-Afraid succinctly sums up God's view of his children today. In Christ, we have that perfect standing, and while we're struggling in the intervening years between now and our point of departure to be with him, he is not embarrassed by us. He is not ashamed of us. He is not disappointed in us. He sees us as we already are—in him! Yes, fellowship with him is broken at times because of the offenses we allow to remain in our life, but God sees even that as contributing together for good. He can and will work it all out because he views our glorification as an accomplished fact. The Lord finishes what he starts: "And I am sure that God, who began the good work within you, will continue his work until it is finally finished on that day, when Jesus comes back again" (Phil. 1:6 NLV).

In the meantime, we must recognize that we're dealing with an all-powerful, all-knowing God. He is in control of every event. The Bible says that all things were made by the Lord and without him was not anything made that was made (John 1:3). Colossians tells us that by him all things are held together: the seasons, the times, the weather (Col. 1:17).

The movements of the created universe are clockwork in his hands, and thus is your life. Every sweep of the hand of time brings something to make you more like his Son. The road will never be completely smooth; the detours will often be surprising, sometimes shocking. But in all and through all, there is the heavenly Father who keeps his promises and in whose eyes we have already put on the golden cloak of immortality

SECURITY IN THE RELATIONSHIP—ROMANS 8:31-39

From the vantage point of eternity, God sees us as we already are: glorified. It is no wonder that the apostle Paul bursts forth in verses 31-39 with a hymn of high praise and a benediction of resounding joy because of the blessed hope we have in Christ. The culminating verses of our study reassure us again of God's desire for relationship rather than performance. Again we see that all which we'll become is thanks to everything that he is. "Lord, you establish peace for us; all that we have accomplished you have done for us" (Isa. 26:12 NIV).

IF GOD IS FOR US

"What then shall we say to these things?" Paul asks at the beginning Romans 8:31 (DAV). These "things" to which he refers are the mighty acts of God mentioned earlier: the foreknowing, the predestining, the calling, the justification, the glorification of believers, and the Lord's work of making all things fit together for good in our life.

"If God is for us, who could be against us?" next exclaims Paul (8:31 DAV). God is sovereign! He reigns over all. He foreknew us ... who can possibly threaten us when he's in our corner? But let's be honest. It seems that there is quite a bit against us in the world. Our old nature may rear up nearly every time we endeavor to allow the Spirit to have victory. Satan, the master of distraction, seems to lurk around every corner. Even so, the answer to Paul's question in verse 31 is *nobody*. Nobody can effectively oppose us. We may hit a few snags or get stuck in a couple of ruts on life's road, but the ultimate victory will be God's. He has laid claim on us for eternity.

"Who could be against us?" Paul begins to answer that question with other questions, gradually showing his readers that God is wholly in control. Let's look briefly at a rundown of the questions posed in the next few verses:

- "Will He not also ... graciously give us all things?" (DAV 8:32).
- "Who will bring a charge against God's chosen out ones?" (DAV 8:33).
- "Who is the one who is condemning" (DAV 8:34).
- "Who shall separate us from the love of Christ?" (DAV 8:35).

The answers? God gives us all things. No one can bring a charge against his chosen ones. No one can condemn, because God has justified us. No one and nothing can permanently separate us from the love of Christ. God makes an unending commitment to us when we enter a relationship with him. Salvation is an act of God, and we are secure in him. How God would be praised if we could today simply and sincerely thank him for that fact. Even when we face life's final moments, all we need do is to rest in the confidence that God means what he says, that his promises are true, that when we step out of this shell we'll be with him. He is greater and mightier than anything or anyone else, and he is permanently on our side.

Who is this God on whom we can so completely depend? Reaching the end of Romans 8, Paul tells us volumes about the Lord. Let's look briefly at verses 32-35 and remind ourselves exactly why, since God is for us, no one can effectively, eternally, oppose us. As Paul's text comes alive on the page, we'll see the Lord for who he really is, reaffirming the reasons we can solidly depend on him.

The Lord is the God of the gospel. "Indeed," writes Paul in verse 32, "He who did not spare His own Son, but delivered Him up for us all, how will He not also with Him graciously give us all things?" (DAV). God the Father sent the Son who, as Paul tells us, "though He was rich, yet for your sake He became poor, that you through His poverty might become rich" (2 Cor. 8:9 NASB). Of Jesus Christ, the prophet Isaiah writes:

> Surely he took up our infirmities
>   and carried our sorrows,
> yet we considered him stricken by God,
>   smitten by him, and afflicted.
> But he was pierced for our transgressions,
>   he was crushed for our iniquities;
> the punishment that brought us peace was upon him,
>   and by his wounds we are healed. (Isa. 53:4-5 NIV)

Paul, expounding the great truth of the gospel, says this in 2 Corinthians 5:21, "He made Him who knew no sin to be sin on our behalf, that we might become the righteousness of God in Him" (NASB). God didn't spare his own Son, he whose sacrifice was absolutely necessary for us to have salvation. He's already done the ultimate work. Surely he will freely fulfill the rest of his promises. His doing the greater assures us that he will complete the lesser. He has made salvation available to a world of sinners; of course he will finish the work in us he has started. What God has done seals what he will do (see Phil. 1:6).

With our acceptance of Christ as savior, we've received the full fare to glory. We know our final destination. Along the way, we can trust him to take care of life. It's almost as if we're first-class passengers on a cruise liner. When we book passage on such a vessel, included in the price are all the meals we'll need. Now, we can ignore that, and stock up on peanut butter, crackers, and jam before we set sail. We can be content with our own humdrum fixings ... or we can take advantage of the fact that everything we need for the voyage comes with the ticket. We've got full fare! In this life, Christ is that paid ticket assuring us of both our final destination and our complete provision along the way.

He is the one who justifies. "Who will bring a charge against God's chosen out ones?" continues Paul in verse 33. "God is the one who justifies" (DAV). When God does something, he does it "real good," as our kids used to say. When he forgives us of our sins, we're forgiven. When he cleanses us of unrighteousness, we're reckoned completely clean. The slate is blank, not just partially erased, because God doesn't do things halfway. Colossians 1:14 says that in him "we have redemption, the forgiveness of sins" (NASB). The word for *forgiveness*, which Paul uses here, suggests the act of stamping "paid in full" on an invoice. When we face the eternal throne, none can challenge us because the debt has been paid by someone far greater than we. In fact, as Paul puts it in Colossians, God "has qualified us to share in the inheritance of the saints in light"; he has also "delivered us from the domain of darkness," and "transferred us to the kingdom of His beloved Son" (Col. 1:12-13 NASB).

It is he who is our supreme advocate. "Who is the one who is condemning" asks Paul in Romans 8:34. "Christ Jesus is he who died, yes, rather who has been raised, who is at the right hand of God, who also is interceding for us" (DAV). Indeed, who can condemn us? The law convicts us of our sins; it condemns us before we are saved. After our salvation, we have no fear of condemnation. According to Hebrews 9:22, "Without shedding of blood there is no forgiveness" (9:22b NASB). Christ's death on the cross was the ultimate blood sacrifice. The blood-spattered cross of Calvary took care of our condemnation when we come to Christ in faith, just as we are. In the words of hymnist Charlotte Elliott, "Just as I am, Thou wilt receive,/ Wilt welcome, pardon, cleanse, relieve;/ Because Thy promise I believe,/ O Lamb of God, I come! I come!"[1]

Just think of that scene when we arrive in glory. The Lord Jesus meets us and assures us that everything is ready and in order. He has paid the ransom in full. He is our redeemer, because he has purchased us not with silver and gold, but with his own precious blood.

It's important to remember that Jesus did not stay in the grave. The Father raised him again, and what assurance there is in that! If God were not satisfied with the sacrifice of his Son, he would never have permitted the resurrection. The Father was fully satisfied with what Jesus did, and he stamped his seal of approval on the atonement by raising Christ from the dead.

There is also comfort in knowing where Christ is right now. He is seated at the right hand of the Father. He is our advocate there, watching over his interest in you and me. He protects his property. We couldn't ask for a better defense attorney than one who has already served our sentence himself. When the evil one hurls accusations our way and proposes that we be condemned to hell, Christ will be able to say, "No, I paid for that already. It's been taken care of by my death on the cross." And we'll escape the judgment.

He'll never be separated from us. "Who shall separate us from the love of Christ?" exclaims Paul in verse 35. "Shall tribulation or distress or persecution or famine or nakedness or peril or sword?" (DAV). The answer is no. Nothing can permanently separate us from God once we're in a relationship with him. Christ's love transcends all. No tribulation is too serious, no distress too great, no persecution too intense, no famine too severe, no nakedness too revealing, no peril too frightening, no sword too sharp, to sever us from the love of Jesus Christ.

Laurentius, also known as Saint Lawrence, was a deacon of the early church who taught and preached under Sextus, Bishop of Rome, in the middle of the third century. The emperor Valerian had begun his reign tolerant of Christianity, but by 257 A.D. had been influenced to launch a severe persecution of the Christians. Laurentius soon met his fate. He was scourged and beaten with iron rods, then his limbs were dislocated. Because he bore these punishments with perseverance and amazing serenity, his torturers were ordered to fasten him atop a large gridiron, under which a slow fire burned. His astonishing calmness continued, his peaceful countenance giving no clue that he was suffering an excruciatingly painful, slow death. Many of the onlookers gave their lives to Christ as they witnessed what could only be Laurentius's God-given strength in the ordeal. Finally, after he had lain on the gridiron for some time, he lifted his eyes toward heaven, and with a serene smile on his lips, he died. Not even the horrors of a torture chamber could separate Laurentius from the love of Christ. One of the most terrifying ordeals imaginable proved bearable because of the peace of God, and culminated in Laurentius's ultimate union with his Lord.

VICTORY IN THE RELATIONSHIP

Nothing can separate us from the love of God in Christ Jesus. God uses the negatives of life to conform us to the image of his Son. There is security. And there is victory. "Even as it stands written, 'For your sake we are being put to death all the day long. We were considered as sheep to be slaughtered,'" writes Paul in Romans 8:36 (DAV).

How does verse 36 convey the victory of the Christian life? A sheep being led to the slaughter can hardly be considered a winner! And yet that is exactly what Christ was—a sacrificial lamb led to the cross, whose cry, "Tetelestai" or "It is finished," (John 19:30) signified a death to performance as a means of obtaining righteousness. We are secure in the fact that his work was sufficient.

"But in all things we are winning a most glorious victory through the one who loved us," continues Paul in Romans 8:37 (DAV). What words of encouragement and reassurance these are! Again we see that all things, including the tribulation, distress, nakedness, peril, and sword mentioned in verse 35, are working together for good. We are more than conquerors through him who loves us so! The captain of our faith, Jesus, will fight beside us when the enemy is great. Even in death we win a glorious victory.

We win. When the Dallas Cowboys won their last Super Bowl (ages ago, now it seems), everyone I knew in the state of Texas hip-hoorayed with joy, "We won!" So closely identified were we with the Cowboys it didn't matter at all that we weren't present at the actual game. In a similar manner, so identified with Christ's death on the cross are we Christians that we can taste the victory. We can shout, "We have won!" And the victory in this case is an overwhelming one over sin and death because of whom we know and what he did at Calvary. We didn't have to be at the cross, because he was there instead.

SINGING THE DOXOLOGY

We are secure, eternally secure, in a relationship with our unchangeable savior. With that thought overflowing, Paul bursts forth with a doxology, ending the chapter with words of praise, thanksgiving, and assurance.

"For I stand convinced," writes the apostle, "that neither death, nor life, nor angels, nor principalities, nor things present, nor things about to come, nor powers, nor height, nor depth, nor any other created thing, shall be able to separate us from the love of God, which is in Christ Jesus our Lord" (Rom. 8:38-39 DAV).

Are you still not convinced that you're secure? Look at the list given by Paul in verses 38-39. What could possibly have been excluded? Nothing can separate us from the love of the Father made so evident by the Son and the Spirit! In Paul's words, none of the following will sever our connection with God:

Not death: It's just the consummation of the relationship. Death is when we'll be united with God. There is no separation in that. It's only the anesthetic while we're changing bodies!

Not life: With its temptations and uncertainties, traumas and trials, life sometimes makes it more difficult to live than to die! But nothing life throws at us can cause us to lose the relationship we share with our Lord.

Not angels: Here Paul probably refers to the angels fallen from grace. It's Satan and his gang, as described in Isaiah 14. Nothing they do will be able to separate us from the love of the Father either.

Not principalities or powers: These unseen satanic forces are well-organized in rank and authority under the evil one's leadership, but Satan's power and authority wane and crumble beneath the omnipotence of God. As the apostle John reminds us, "greater is He who is in you than he who is in the world" (1 John 4:4 NASB).

Not things present: No present circumstance is able to separate us from Christ's love.

Not things to come: Nothing in the future will do so either.

Not height: As far as the eye can see, and even beyond in the uppermost regions of the atmosphere, nothing can cause God to stop loving us. "If I go up to the heavens, you are there," David sings to the Lord in Psalm 139, "If I make my bed in the depths, you are there" (139:8 NIV).

Not depth: Neither is there, even to the very bottom of the ocean, anything to keep us from the love of the Father.

Not any other created thing: In other words, nothing in the created universe can drive a wedge between the Lord and his children.

As we meditate on the categories given above, we see that Paul mentions four definite spheres which may concern us. First is the sphere of existence, of life and death. We sometimes fear that something will happen to us in life to keep us from maintaining a relationship with God, and we sometimes are afraid that death will be an end to it all, rather than a beginning. It isn't so.

Paul also deals with the sphere of created things. Thoughts of angels, principalities, and powers may frighten us. We're scared of the satanic, and also of the natural world of hostile governments under his leadership. Yet no fallen angel and no enemy nation can change the fact that when we've received Christ, God commits himself to us in an unending relationship. Perhaps foreign terrorists will plant bombs in our shopping centers; perhaps Satan will consistently seek to do us harm. None of that will change the fact that God will never go away, and that our eternal destiny will be with him.

Paul next talks about the sphere of time. The things present and the things to come often terrify us. Depressing current events deeply disturb us. The uncertainty of the future fills us with apprehension. "What if?" we wonder. God doesn't mean for us to fight tomorrow's battles today. And he has always been faithful to carry us through.

Finally, Paul discusses the sphere of space: the height and the depth to which Christ's commitment to us extends. That covers it all—nothing within or outside the realm of human comprehension can do anything to keep us from the love of God through our Lord Jesus! From the uppermost reaches of outer space to the deepest depths of the ocean, he is there (Ps. 139).

PROMISES, PROMISES

God is always there. My friend Dub knew him well. Dub walked with Christ for many years, and together we often shared things of the Lord. Once Dub told me a story about his father, a circuit-riding preacher in the Texas panhandle. Towns are few, small, and far between in the panhandle, and Dub's dad frequently rode his horse back and forth between those communities. One time a cowboy and he were caught in a surprise winter storm. The snow blew so hard that they lost their way. Dub's father became frightened at the prospect of freezing to death and started to panic. It was then that the experienced cowboy said, "Reverend, you just lay your reins on the neck of that horse, and he'll take you all the way to the barn. He knows how to get there." Dub's father did as he was told, and the horse led him safely home.

When Dub himself faced open heart surgery, I asked him if he could depend on God in the same way, in the blizzard of uncertainty that was roaring about him. It did not surprise me when he answered yes.

Dub knows, and I know, and the apostle Paul knows, that it's the relationship with God which counts. Nothing can change that. Nothing can keep us from the love of the savior once we know him. Nothing can cause him to change his mind or reverse his position. He cannot and will not be shaken.

I purchased a plaque for my parents with Romans 8:38-39 engraved upon it. I noticed the plaque hanging on the wall in their home and know that it must have been read often by my father during the final days of his journey on earth. I hope he made a positive response. He and Mr. Elliott, Jane Rodgers's dad, were both performers for many years. Before Mr. Elliott died, I had a chance to talk with him about Calvary and a personal relationship with God's own Son. He later confirmed his faith to Jane.

I love the way Lisa Beamer begins her book and the way she ends it:

> To Todd, my husband, my everyday hero. Thank you for loving God, loving us, and always playing hard. Thank you for teaching me patience and mercy. I love you and promise to finish our journey well. See you later. ...[2]

As Lisa ends the book, we need to remember that she now has a stewardship of three young children, the youngest born in January following the tragedy:

> Of course the three sweetest gifts are often gathered on my lap. To them, "Let's roll!" is not a slogan, a book, or a song; it's a lifestyle. A lifestyle Todd and I began together ... and one my children and I will carry on. Each time I hear those words, Todd's voice calls out once again to the children and me, letting us know it's time to set out on another adventure. Our journey is different now, but it's still one of hope, faith, and a knowledge of our ultimate destination.
>
> One day shortly before Christmas, just a few months after Todd's death, I was halfheartedly unpacking some holiday decorations. Evidently I wasn't moving fast enough for David, who was excited to put the stockings up on the fireplace. So he looked at me and, in a playful voice reminiscent of his

father, said, "Come on Mom! Let's roll!" I fought back the tears for a moment, and then said with a little grin, "You're right, David. Let's roll!"

It is well ... it is well ... with my soul.
Are you ready? Okay. Let's roll.[3]

Questions to Consider

1. Read verse 30. Describe in your own words what it means to know that God already sees us as glorified? What comfort can this knowledge bring to someone trying to please God through performance?

2. What do we learn in Romans 8:29-29 about our security with God? How do we know that nothing can separate us from his love?

3. Have you discovered the wonder of a relationship with God through Jesus Christ? If you're a new Christian, begin reading God's word, starting with the gospel of John. Find a solid, Bible-believing church to attend, or get involved with an organization like Bible Study Fellowship, where you can learn more about your heavenly Father and his word. If you've been a believer for a while and are already doing such things, examine your life to make sure you haven't slipped onto a performance kick. And begin praying for someone you know who is not a Christian.

CHAPTER 12

"Brethren, I do not regard myself as having laid hold of it yet; but one thing I do: forgetting what lies behind and reaching forward to what lies ahead. I press on toward the goal for the prize of the upward call of God in Christ Jesus" (Phil. 3:13, 14 NASB).

Pressing on the Upward Way

Once we're convinced that God longs for a deepening relationship with us, not some kind of power performance from us, what's next? How do we transfer that knowledge onto the treadmill of human life? How can it make a difference in us and to us?

I think that we must first look honestly at ourselves and evaluate exactly where we stand with the Father. Do we know Christ as savior, or are we somehow trying to work our way into heaven? If God thought for a moment that we could do it ourselves, he would not have bothered to send Jesus.

If we are sure of our salvation, however, then we'd better look closely at the things we are doing, and more importantly, at the motivation behind them. How are we spending our time? Are we doing things with God, instead of just for him? Are we often on our knees, talking with him? How rich is our fellowship with him in his word? Does our life focus on getting to know him better and better, or has our schedule become so jam-packed with Christian activities that we've just about forgotten Christ? Are we burying ourselves in busyness because we feel guilty about the dryness of our relationship with the Lord? Are we striving to stick to the subsections of the law instead of basking in the freedom of his grace? Is our obedience forced or willing, grudging or grateful, engendered by obligation or enkindled by love?

Everyone must peer into his own heart and answer these questions for himself. Only you and God truly know your motives, practices, and the depth of your shared relationship. "I the Lord search the heart and examine the mind, to reward a man according to his conduct, according to what his deeds deserve" (Jer. 17:10 NIV).

HARD DRIVING AND SPIRITUALLY DEAD

It is time for us to call to mind again the five folks we met at the front end of this study: Joe, Daniel, Sondra, Frank, and Julia. Each, remember, is hung up on *doing* instead of *being*. In some way or another, each is ensnared in the trap of trying to perform to please God. Now is the moment for each to begin evaluating the whys of his or her life.

Joe, remember, is the hard-nosed, hard-driving, relatively ethical businessman. He has no use for organized religion. He is convinced that God helps those who help themselves, and he is singing with Sinatra, "I did it my way," as he bulldozes through life, meeting sales quotas and achieving goals. He is directed, determined, and unfortunately, also eternally lost because he is dead in his trespasses and sins, although he thinks of himself as a pretty decent guy.

A man like Joe is probably only going to respond to God's message of salvation when he sees the gospel effectively lived out in the life of someone he respects. The challenge is there for his Christian friends to model the master, to honestly admit mistakes, and to vigorously pursue integrity in their dealings with Joe. They should actively pray for opportunities to discuss the gospel with him, and they must be ready to seize whatever moments arise.

Even if his Christian friends are never able to penetrate his armor with their talk of Christ, the reality of God is all around Joe, and he is without excuse. God's person and presence are seen in the order and design of creation—in the tides of the sea, in the sun and the moon and the stars, in the seasons of the year (Rom. 1:20). The amazing order of the universe should appeal to a logical man like Joe, a man who deals daily with facts and figures. Behind it all is the great designer himself who, out of love, longs for a relationship with Joe.

Joe desperately needs to understand that faith is always on the winning side, because receiving Christ now makes life worthwhile and wonderful here, and fantastic in the hereafter. Someday Joe's struggle up the corporate ladder is probably going to give him a sense of emptiness. It may spark a search for meaning in life, as he either realizes that he'll never make it to the uppermost rungs, or if he should achieve the top, he recognizes that the view wasn't worth the climb. He'll conclude that there must be something deeper, more meaningful, and lasting, for him out there. Perhaps then he'll be ready to pursue the relationship that will change his life.

Perhaps you are thirsting for purpose and relevance in life. Right now, the knock of Jesus Christ is resounding at your door, awaiting your invitation for him to enter and take over. Let me leave you with some verses to ponder:

For He says,
"At the acceptable time I listened to you,
And on the day of salvation, I helped you;
behold, now is 'the acceptable time,'
behold, now
is 'the day of salvation.'" (2 Cor. 6:2 NASB)

Do not boast about tomorrow,
for you do not know what a day may bring forth (Prov. 27:1 NIV).

How shall we escape if we neglect so great a salvation? After it was at the first spoken through the Lord, it was confirmed to us by those who heard (Heb. 2:3 NASB).

And the Spirit and the bride say, "Come." And let the one who hears say, "Come." And let the one who is thirsty come; let the one who wishes take the water of life without cost (Rev. 22:17 NASB).

Yet you do not know what your life will be like tomorrow. You are just a vapor that appears for a little while and then vanishes away. Instead, you ought to say, "If the Lord wills, we shall live and also do this or that." But as it is, you boast in your arrogance; all such boasting is evil. Therefore, to one who knows the right thing to do, and does not do it, to him it is sin. (James 4:14-17 NASB)

AFRAID IT'S TOO LATE

Daniel started out in his Christian life like a house afire, wholeheartedly focusing his energies on learning more about the Lord and in doing as much as he could for God. When he was in college, Daniel witnessed, taught, discipled, counseled, and involved himself in every opportunity for ministry that came along. Now that he is in his thirties, married, with two small children and a hefty mortgage, Daniel feels a sense of spiritual emptiness. He loves his family but is afraid he's becoming hopelessly caught in the corporate squeeze. How deeply he regrets not entering fulltime Christian service when he was younger. The nagging fear that he has missed the will of God for his life plagues him. He wonders how he could have been so blind. And now it's too late!

There are scores of Daniels out there. Each needs to realize that it is wrong to look back, and that the Lord is waiting to begin right now. God always meets us where we are and takes us on from there. Fantastic opportunities abound for young, godly families to minister effectively in local church fellowships and Christian groups. Daniel will see these opportunities if he is sensitive, and the key to becoming sensitive involves deepening his relationship with God. Praying for refreshment, renewal, and illumination, Daniel must again plunge into personal study of God's word and focus on his communion with the Lord. As he gets on intimate speaking terms again with God, Daniel will become sensitized to the possibilities the Lord is bringing across his path.

One thing Daniel will probably soon realize is that God is actually desiring to use him in the "fulltime Christian service" he longs for. Daniel may never be on the staff of a Christian organization, but he is a fulltime dad and husband. He has the twenty-four hour a day job of providing for his family, loving and encouraging his wife, and unselfishly modeling the heavenly Father for his children so that they too will come to know and love the Lord. With our society's alarming divorce rate and the frightening statistics on child abuse and neglect, Daniel's solid Christian marriage and family life are striking witnesses for the power of Jesus Christ to a world that is spiritually dead.

Not only is Daniel in fulltime service as far as his family is concerned, but God has also placed him in a work situation where he has the chance to be the light of Christ to the lost. It's likely that most of Daniel's co-workers have no relationship with Jesus. As Daniel prays for opportunities to witness for Christ, those chances will come. In fact, he'll have some opportunities to touch others for Christ that he would not have had as an employee of a Christian organization. Who knows? Maybe Daniel works for someone like Joe, a man who will probably only respond to the gospel when he sees it lived out in flesh and blood, making a difference in the life of someone he respects.

Besides Daniel's job, the neighborhood in which he and his family reside is full of folks who desperately need Jesus. What a witness a godly husband and father can be to people searching for solutions to life! Don't get me wrong—Daniel's desire to enter professional fulltime ministry is commendable; the opportunity for him to join a ministry staff may well come some day too, but regardless of his occupation, God can use him mightily wherever he is.

It has been said that when the past quarrels with the present, there can be no future. God is ready to meet Daniel, and us, at any time and at any place to enrich our life with a growing relationship with him. Out of that will naturally flow opportunities for service. And so the call of the master is, "follow Me, and I will make you fishers of men" (Matt. 4:19 NASB). Paul tells the Corinthians: "For the love of Christ controls us, having concluded this, that one died for all, therefore all died; and He died for all, that they who live should no longer live for themselves, but for Him who died and rose again on their behalf" (2 Cor. 5:14-15 NASB). My message to Daniel is two-fold: it isn't over till it's over, and bloom where you are planted.

NEVER QUITE SURE IT'S ENOUGH

And then we come to Sondra. She grew up in a church that taught her to obey the commandments and to regularly ask God's forgiveness. Guilt over her failures and worry about her eternal destiny assailed her constantly. Would she, could she, be good enough to get into heaven? Finally she heard a clear presentation of the gospel and responded in relief and release to the invitation of Jesus. For a time, she flourished in the freedom of God's forgiveness! Yet the weight that was momentarily lifted soon returned as she realized that even as a Christian, she still sinned. Uncertainty gripped her and turned to guilt and fear. Was she even really saved at all?

One of Sondra's problems is that apparently either no one followed up with her after she accepted Christ, or she resisted the efforts of any who did. Sondra desperately needs to establish a friendship with someone who has matured in the faith who will help her understand the ramifications of God's plan of salvation.

First of all, Sondra must be reassured that her salvation and her relationship with God truly did begin the moment she received Christ. 1 John 5:11-12 states, "And the witness is this, that God has given us eternal life, and this life is in His Son. He who has the Son has the life; he who does not have the Son of God does not have the life" (NASB). God said it; Sondra believes it; that settles it.

Next, Sondra must learn that when she came to know Jesus Christ, she entered into a relationship that was permanent. It will exist for all eternity. In the words of Jesus himself, "and I give eternal life to them [believers]; and they shall never perish, and no one shall snatch them out of My hand" (John 10:28 NASB).

Finally, Sondra must recognize that even as a Christian she is still going to sin because she still possesses an old nature. She shouldn't be shocked when she responds to that old nature and sins. Her failures will be humbling, but they will not signal the end of her relationship with God—only the interruption of her fellowship with him. 1 John 1:9 says, "If we confess our sins, He is faithful and righteous to forgive us our sins and to cleanse us from all unrighteousness" (NASB). Sondra must learn that when she knows she has sinned, she needs to acknowledge the disobedience, agreeing with the Father that what she has done is wrong. That's the heart of confession. Doing so should be a daily thing with her, and with us. And she must be willing to pray that her heart might be open before God, searched by him, so that she would be made aware of the areas of disobedience. It's all part of God's process of making her—and us—more like his Son.

The guilt and worry Sondra experiences are sorrows that just shouldn't be. God loves her intensely, and as Romans 8:30 assures, he sees her as she is going to be: glorified for all eternity!

NOT INTERESTED

Remember my good friend Frank, a very successful businessman and family man? A personal relationship with Christ was not a matter of importance to Frank because he was a church attender, and on top of that, a master Mason and Shriner. They take good men and make them better.

The issue is not what one does with and through an organization, but what one does in and through Jesus Christ! Jesus said, "I am the way, and the truth, and the life; *no one* comes to the Father, but through *Me*" (John 14:6 NASB, italics mine). A trip to heaven must pass by the cross and the empty tomb. The only way I have been successful in leading men like Frank to the savior is by avoiding a discussion of the merits of their involvement in certain organizations. A two-fold strategy based heavily on relationship may work. First, lovingly accept them where they are and live Jesus before them every day. Show them what they are missing, in other words. And second, present them with a balanced verse-by-verse exposition of the scripture so that they can make up their own minds. Continually point them to the lamb of God who takes away the sins of the world. The following verses could be helpful to you:

- "Therefore if any man is in Christ, he is a new creature; the old things passed away; behold, new things have come" (2 Cor. 5:17 NASB).
- "For by grace you have been saved through faith; and that not of yourselves, it is the gift of God; not as a result of works, that no one should boast. For we are His workmanship, created in Christ Jesus for good works, which God prepared beforehand, that we should walk in them." (Eph. 2:8-10 NASB)
- "But now in Christ Jesus you who formerly were far off have been brought near by the blood of Christ" (Eph. 2:13 NASB).
- "How much more will the blood of Christ, who through the eternal Spirit offered Himself without blemish to God, cleanse your conscience from dead works to serve the living God?" (Heb. 9:14 NASB).

My wish for you is happy fishing!

SELF-RIGHTEOUS AND SELF-DECEIVED

Finally, we come to Julia. You may recall that she's a churchgoer, but not a Christian. She is consumed with causes, political and personal, and confident that her humanitarianism qualifies her for heaven. She brags that she lives her religion and is sure that she is concretely working for world peace, understanding, enlightenment, and brotherly love. In fact, she even figures that God—whoever he is—is lucky to have her on his side!

The Julias of the world are hard to reach because they are convinced of their own worth. They're rather like the Pharisees, smug in their self-righteousness, yet completely off base spiritually. Luke 18:10-13 gives the account of an ancient-day Julia of sorts, a Pharisee who went to the temple to pray. In Jesus' own words:

> Two men went up into the temple to pray, one a Pharisee, and the other a tax-gatherer. The Pharisee stood and was praying thus to himself, "God, I thank Thee that I am not like other people, swindlers, unjust, adulterers, or even like this tax-gatherer. I fast twice a week; I pay tithes of all that I get." But the tax-gatherer, standing some distance away, was even unwilling to lift up his eyes to heaven, but was beating his breast, saying, "God, be merciful to me, the sinner!" (Luke 18:10-13 NASB)

Hypocrisy is Julia's problem. Like the Pharisee above, she has deluded herself into thinking that she can actually be righteous as God is righteous. She is only fooling herself. It is of the tax-gatherer, not the Pharisee, in the parable above that Jesus says, "I tell you, this man went down to his house justified rather than the other; for every one who exalts himself shall be humbled, but he who humbles himself shall be exalted" (Luke 18:14 NASB).

If she is to avoid a very rude awakening when she crosses the bridge into eternity, Julia must realize that it is not our work for God, but his work in us, that qualifies us for heaven. She must honestly agree with Isaiah that all men's works are but as "filthy rags" to the Father (64:6). She must become broken in spirit, convinced of her own inadequacy, and aware of her need of a personal relationship with Jesus. She must admit the truth about God that Paul writes to Titus:

> He saved us, not on the basis of deeds which we have done in righteousness, but according to His mercy, by the washing of regeneration and renewing by the Holy Spirit (Titus 3:5 NASB).

It's the same message Paul also conveys to his co-laborer Timothy:

> Therefore do not be ashamed of the testimony of our Lord, or of me His prisoner; but join with me in suffering for the gospel according to the power of God; who has saved us, and called us with a holy calling, not according to our works, but according to His own purpose and grace which was granted us in Christ Jesus from all eternity. (2 Tim. 1:8-9 NASB)

There's no place for the self-righteousness of a Julia in our relationship with Christ. As John tells us in his first epistle: "If we say that we have no sin, we are deceiving ourselves, and the truth is not in us ... If we say that we have not sinned, we make Him a liar, and His word is not in us" (1 John 1:8,10 NASB).

Those are serious words, and the Julias of the world should beware. They've been given fair warning. All the magnanimous, philanthropic, and humanitarian things they do, apart from Christ, may make life on earth a little easier but will carry no weight in the next world. As with Joe and Frank, now is the day Julia must consider the claims of Christ ... for who knows what tomorrow may bring.

ONE ON ONE

The Joes, Daniels, Sondras, Franks, and Julias of the world are out there. You won't have to look very far to find one. Perhaps you can already think of someone who resembles one of the characters. Perhaps the description of one or the other seems uncomfortably like a portrait of yourself.

Do you feel in some way that you are focusing on doing for God as opposed to being with him? Are you a believer at all? If so, has your spiritual life begun to be tedious? Do God and his word still seem new and fresh and inviting to you? Or are you spiritually stagnant and desperately desiring to climb out of the sludge and return to the richness and vitality of a growing, deepening relationship? It is never too late!

My friend Les is a case in point. As a relatively new believer, formerly an outspoken agnostic, Les's newfound relationship with Jesus Christ was a source of excitement to him. And he was exciting to behold as he came to know the Father better and better.

Something else equally exciting, in my mind, happened as a result of Les's conversion. He and I started meeting together weekly for one-on-one study and prayer. I can't tell you how encouraging and thrilling these sessions were for me. Watching a new believer grow in his relationship with God, seeing scripture with the fresh eyes of someone who is only just discovering it, joining in prayer together with a brother who was teaching me so much even as I taught him—all this opened new vistas for me. What refreshing insights the Lord gave us into his word!

One of the best ways of shifting your spiritual life into

overdrive is to begin meeting with and discipling a new believer. And I'm sure the same could be said for meeting regularly with someone who has walked with the Lord for sometime. Mutual accountability, encouragement, one-on-one sharing in the truths of scripture make for a spiritually enriching experience, no matter how many years as believers we have under our belt!

Relationship—or performance? Where are you? My friend Les became a brand-new believer, although he had been attending church for forty years. I give you one of his reflections to chew on:

For four decades I looked at God through the lens of the law and was ripped apart by my miserable performance. Now I see him through the lens of his grace and the gift of his Son, and it has all become clear. I've missed it for forty years. Thank God that I found him, and that he paid it all.

HIGHER GROUND

"Won't you please come to Jesus?" Les also asked an older man at church some years ago. The words echoed in our thoughts one parched September when Pearl and I and the Ministries staff enjoyed our annual retreat. The summer's camps were over, it wasn't yet time to gear up for the classes of the fall, and we took a few days to rest, relax, evaluate the year, and prepare for the coming crunch of activities.

Our retreat that fall was held at the lakeside East Texas home and property of some gracious friends. In this oasis of elegance, manicured lawns and immaculate flowerbeds surrounded us. The landscape was surprisingly lush, especially considering the harsh late-summer sun.

The porch of the home overlooked Lake Cherokee. As we explored the property, we delighted in continually discovering new things: a patch of bright flowers, a hidden boathouse, an inviting swimming hole.

"Isn't this something?" remarked Pearl. "We are enjoying

the fruit of the labor of another!" And we certainly did.

The beauty of a lakeside resort only reminds us of another place prepared for us by the labor of another: God himself The pleasures of a green rolling landscape, a gentle breeze off a blue lake, a swift white sail moving on the horizon, pale in comparison to the joys of eternity, the joy we'll only know when, like Les, we come to Jesus.

I want to scale the utmost height,
And catch a gleam of glory bright;
But still I'll pray till heaven I've found,
"Lord, lead me on to higher ground."

Lord, lift me up and let me stand,
By faith, on heaven's tableland,
A higher plain than I have found;
Lord, plant my feet on higher ground.

Romans 5, 6, 7 & 8
Author's Translation

Romans 5

v. 1 Therefore, having been made right by faith, we are
having peace with God through our Lord Jesus Christ,
v. 2 through whom also we have obtained our introduction
(entree) by faith into this grace in which we stand; and we
are rejoicing (exulting, glorying) in hope of the glory of
God.
v. 3 And not only this, but we also are rejoicing (exulting,
glorying) in our tribulations, knowing that this tribulation is
producing endurance;
v. 4 and this endurance, character; and this character, hope;
v. 5 and this hope does not disappoint; because the love of
God has been poured out in our hearts through the Holy
Spirit who was given to us.
v. 6 For when we were still helpless, at the right time Christ
died for the godless.
v. 7 For one will hardly die for a righteous man; though
perhaps for the good man someone would even dare to die.

v. 8 But God is demonstrating His own love to us, because while we were yet sinners, Christ died for us.
v. 9 Much more therefore, having been justified now by His blood, we shall be saved through Him from the wrath.
v.10 For if while being enemies, we were reconciled to God through the death of His Son, much more, having been reconciled, we shall be saved by His life.
v.11 And not only this, but we also rejoice in God through our Lord Jesus Christ, through whom we have now received the reconciliation.
v.12 Therefore, just as through one man sin entered the world, and through this sin, death, and so death spread to all men, because all sinned—
v.13 For until Law sin was in the world; but sin is not put to one's account where there is no law.
v.14 But death reigned from Adam to Moses, even over those who had not sinned in the likeness of Adam's offense, who is a type of the One who was to come.
v.15 But the gracious gift is not like the transgression. For if by the transgression of the one the many died, much more the grace of God and the gift by grace of the one man, Jesus Christ, abound to many.
v.16 And the gift is not like that which came through the one who sinned; for on the one hand the judgment was out of one transgression, resulting in condemnation, but on the other hand the gracious gift was out of many transgressions resulting in justification.
v.17 For if by the transgression of the one, death reigned through that one, much more those who are receiving the abundance of grace and of the gift of righteousness will reign in life through the One, Jesus Christ.
v.18 So then, as through one transgression to all men there resulted condemnation; so also through one act of righteousness, to all men there resulted justification of life.
v.19 For just as through the disobedience of the one man the

many were constituted sinners, so also through the obedience of the One the many will be constituted righteous.
v.20 Now Law entered in alongside in order that the transgression might multiply; but where sin multiplied, grace was present in greater abundance,
v.21 in order that just as sin reigned in death, so also grace might reign through righteousness, resulting in eternal life through Jesus Christ our Lord.

Romans 6

v. 1 What then shall we say? Are we to continue in sin in order that grace might increase?
v. 2 May it never be! How shall we who died to sin still live in it?
v. 3 Or do you not know that all of us who have been baptized into Christ Jesus have been baptized into His death?
v. 4 Therefore we have been buried with Him through baptism into death, in order that in the same manner as Christ was raised up from the dead through the glory of the Father, so also we too might walk in a new life.
v. 5 For if we have become united with Him in the likeness of His death certainly we shall be also in the likeness of His resurrection;
v. 6 knowing this, that our old self was crucified with Him, in order that the sinful body may be done away with, that we should no longer be slaves to sin;
v. 7 for the one who died has been freed from sin.
v. 8 Now if we died with Christ, we are believing that we shall also live with Him,
v. 9 knowing that Christ, having been raised from the dead, no longer is dying. Death no longer is exercising lordship over Him.

v.10 For the death He died, He died to sin once for all; but the life He lives, He lives to God.
v.11 So also you consider yourselves to be dead to sin, but alive to God in Christ Jesus.
v.12 Therefore do not let sin reign in your mortal body so that you are obeying its desires.
v.13 Moreover, stop presenting the members of your body to sin as tools of wickedness; but present yourselves to God as those who are alive from the dead, and your members as tools of righteousness to God.
v.14 For sin shall not exercise lordship over you, for you are not under law, but under grace.
v.15 What then? Shall we sin because we are not under law but under grace? May it never be!
v.16 Are you not knowing that when you present yourselves to someone as slaves resulting in obedience, you are slaves of the one whom you are obeying, whether of sin resulting in death, or of obedience resulting in righteousness?
v.17 But thanks be to God that though you were slaves of sin, you obeyed from the heart to that form of teaching, for the learning of which you were given over,
v.18 and having been set free from sin, you were made slaves to righteousness.
v. 19 I am speaking in human terms because of the weakness of your flesh. For just as you presented your members as slaves to uncleanness and lawlessness, resulting in lawlessness, so now present your members as slaves to righteousness, resulting in holiness.
v.20 For when you were slaves of sin, you were free with respect to righteousness.
v.21 Therefore, what fruit were you having then from the things of which you are now ashamed? For the outcome of those things is death.
v.22 But now, having been set free from sin and having been made bondslaves of God, you are having your fruit, resulting

in holiness, and the outcome, eternal life.
v.23 For the wages of sin is death, but the free gift of God is
life eternal in Christ Jesus our Lord.

Romans 7

v. 1 Or do you not know, brethren, for I am speaking to
those who are knowing the law, that the law is ruling over
the individual as long as he lives?
v. 2 For the married woman has been bound by law to her
living husband; but if her husband dies, she has been
released from the law of her husband.
v. 3 So then, if while her husband is living, she is joined to
another man, she shall be called an adulteress; but if her
husband dies, she is free from the law, so that she is not an
adulteress, though she is joined to another man.
v. 4 Therefore, my brethren, you also were put to death to
the Law through the body of Christ, resulting in your being
joined to another, to the One who was raised from the dead,
in order that we might bear fruit to God.
v. 5 For when we were in the flesh, the sinful passions were
at work in our members through the Law to bear fruit for
death.
v. 7 What therefore shall we say? Is the Law sin? May it
never be! On the contrary, I would not have known sin
except through the Law; for I would not have known evil
desire except that the Law was saying: "You shall not desire
evil."
v. 8 But sin, grasping an opportunity through the commandment, called forth within me every kind of evil desire; for
without Law, sin is dead.
v. 9 And I was once alive without Law; but when the
commandment came, sin became alive, and I died;
v.10 and this commandment, which was to result in life, I

discovered to result in death for me.
v.11 For sin, grasping an opportunity through the commandment, deceived me, and through it killed me.
v.12 So then, the Law is holy, and the commandment is holy and righteous and good.
v.13 Therefore, did that which is good become death for me? May it never be! Rather it was sin, in order that it might be shown to be sin by accomplishing my death through that which is good, in order that through the commandment sin might become sinful in the extreme.
v.14 For we are knowing that the Law is spiritual; but I am fleshly, having been sold under sin.
v.15 For that which I am doing, I am not understanding; for I am not practicing that which I am desiring to do, but I am doing that which I am hating.
v.16 Now if I am doing that which I am not desiring, I am agreeing with the Law, that it is good.
v.17 So now, no longer am I the one doing it, but sin which indwells me.
v.18 For I am knowing that nothing good is dwelling in me, that is, in my flesh; for the being desirous is present in me, but the doing of the good is not.
v.19 For the good which I am desiring, I am not doing; but I am practicing the very evil that I am not desiring.
v.20 Now if I am doing the very thing I am not desiring, I am no longer the one doing it, but sin which dwells in me.
v.21 I am finding then the law, that evil is present in me, the one who is desiring to do good.
v.22 For I joyfully agree with the law of God concerning the inner man.
v.23 But I am seeing a different kind of law in my members warring against the law of my mind, making me a prisoner of war to the law of sin which is in my members.
v.24 Wretched man that I am! Who shall set me free out of the body of this death?

v.25 Thanks be to God through Jesus Christ our Lord! So then, on the one hand I myself with my mind am serving the law of God, but on the other, with my flesh the law of sin.

Romans 8

v. 1 Therefore now there is no doom for those who are in Christ Jesus.
v. 2 For the law of the Spirit of life in Christ Jesus freed you from the law of sin and death.
v. 3 For what was impossible for the Law, because it was weak through the flesh, God, having sent His own Son in the likeness of sinful flesh and concerning sin, He condemned sin in the flesh,
v. 4 in order that the requirement of the Law might be fulfilled in us, who are not walking according to the flesh, but according to the Spirit.
v. 5 For those who are according to the flesh are setting their minds on the things of the flesh, but those who are according to the Spirit, on the things of the Spirit.
v. 6 For the way of thinking of the flesh is death, but the way of thinking of the Spirit is life and peace;
v. 7 because the way of thinking of the flesh is hostile toward God; for it is not subjecting itself to the Law of God, for it is not even able to do so;
v. 8 and those who are in the flesh are not able to please God.
v. 9 But you are not in the flesh but in the Spirit, if indeed the Spirit of God is dwelling in you. But if anyone is not having the Spirit of Christ, he does not belong to Him.
v.10 Now if Christ is in you, on the one hand the body is dead because of sin, but on the other hand the Spirit is alive because of righteousness.
v.11 And if the Spirit of the One who raised Jesus from the

dead is dwelling in you, He who raised Christ Jesus from the dead will also give life to your mortal bodies through His Spirit who is dwelling in you.
v.12 So then, brethren, we are those under moral obligation, not to the flesh, to live according to the flesh—
v.13 for if you are living according to the flesh, you are about to die; but if by the Spirit you are putting to death the deeds of the body, you will live.
v.14 For as many as are being led by the Spirit of God, these are sons of God.
v.15 For you have not received a spirit of slavery to cause you to fear, but you received the spirit of adoption by which we are crying out, Abba! Father!
v.16 The Spirit Himself is bearing witness with our spirit that we are children of God.
v.17 And if children, also heirs; on the one hand heirs of God, on the other fellow-heirs with Christ, if indeed, we are suffering with Him in order that we may also be glorified together.
v.18 For I am of the opinion that the sufferings of this present time are not to be compared with the glory which is about to be revealed to us.
v.19 For the anxious longing of the creation is awaiting eagerly for the revelation of the sons of God.
v.20 For the creation was subjected to frustration, not of its own free will, but because of Him who subjected it, in hope,
v.21 that the creation itself also will be set free from its slavery to decay into the liberty of the glory of the children of God.
v.22 For we are knowing that the whole creation is groaning together and suffering the pains of childbirth together until now.
v.23 And not only this, but also we ourselves who are having the first fruits of the Spirit, even we ourselves are groaning within ourselves, waiting eagerly our adoption, the

redemption of our body.
v.24 For in hope we have been saved, but hope that is seen is not hope; for why is one also hoping for what he is seeing?
v.25 But if we are hoping for that which we are not seeing, with patience we are waiting eagerly for it.
v.26 And in the same way the Spirit also is helping us in our weakness; for we are not knowing how to pray as we should, but the Spirit Himself is interceding for us with sighs too deep for words;
v.27 and He who is searching the hearts is knowing what the mind of the Spirit is, because according to God He is interceding on behalf of the saints.
v.28 And we are knowing that for those who are loving God, all things
He is working together for good, for those who are called in accordance with His purpose.
v.29 Because whom He foreknew, He also decided upon beforehand those who were to be like his Son in appearance to the end, that He might by the first-born among many brethren.
v.30 Now those whom He decided upon beforehand, these He also called; and those whom He called, these He also justified; and those whom He justified, these He also glorified.
v.31 What then shall we say to these things? If God is for us, who could be against us?
v.32 Indeed, He who did not spare His own Son, but delivered Him up for us all, how will He not also with Him graciously give us all things?
v.33 Who will bring a charge against God's chosen out ones? God is the one who justifies;
v.34 Who is the one who is condemning? Christ Jesus is He who died, yes, rather who has been raised, who is at the right hand of God, who also is interceding for us.
v.35 Who shall separate us from the love of Christ? Shall

tribulation or distress or persecution or famine or nakedness
or peril or sword?
v.36 Even as it stands written, "For your sake we are being
put to death all the day long. We were considered as sheep
to be slaughtered."
v.37 But in all things we are winning a most glorious victory
through the one who loved us.
v.38 For I stand convinced that neither death nor life, nor
angels nor principalities, nor things present nor things about
to come, nor powers,
v.39 nor height nor depth, nor any other created thing, shall
be able to separate us from the love of God which is in
Christ Jesus our Lord.

Endnotes

Preface—"I Never Got To Know You"

1. Bill Butterworth, "What Does It Take," © 1976 Singspiration Music (ASCAP) (admin. by Brentwood-Benson Music Publishing, Inc.) All Rights Reserved. Used by Permission.

Chapter 2

1. Unger, Merrill F. 1966. *Unger's Bible Dictionary.* Third edition. Chicago, Illinois. Moody Press, 1065. Used by permission.
2. "Finally Home" words by L. E. Singer & Don Wyrtzen. Music by Don Wyrtzen. Copyright © 1971 by Singspiration Music.
3. "He's Still Workin' on Me," © 1980 Bridge Building Music, Inc. / Family & Friends Music (BMI) (admin. by Brentwood-Benson Music Publishing, Inc.) All Rights Reserved. Used by Permission.

Chapter 3

1. "Frank & Ernest" cartoon by Bob Thaves has been reprinted by permission of Newspaper Enterprise Association, Inc.

Chapter 4

1. Alan Jackson "Where Were You (When the World Stopped Turning)" (administered by EMI Music Publishing)
2. Dunn, Ronald. n.d. *Victory*. Flower Mound, Texas: Rita Kaye Dunn, 49. Used by Permission.
3. Dunn, 57-58

Chapter 5

1. "I Want To Be Like Jesus" by Thomas O. Chisholm. © 1945, Renewed 1973, Lillenas Publishing Co. (admin. By The Copyright Co., Nashville, TN) All rights reserved. International copyright secured. Used by permission.
2. Chip Ingram, *I Am With You Always: Experiencing God in Times of Need.* Grand Rapids, MI: Baker Books. © Chip Ingram, 2002. 35-38. Used by Permission.

Chapter 6

1. Lisa Beamer, *Let's Roll*, Wheaton, IL: Tyndale House. © Lisa Beamer, 2002, 232-233. Used by Permission.

Chapter 7

1. Lane Adams, "How Come It's Taking Me So Long?" 24-25

Chapter 11

1. Hannah Hurnard, *Hinds Feet on High Places*, 164. Used by Permission.
2. Lisa Beamer, *Let's Roll*, dedication page.
3. Lisa Beamer, *Let's Roll,* 312.

Select Bibliography

Adams, Lane. 1975. *Home Come It's Taking Me So Long?* Living Studies edition. Wheaton, Illinois: Tyndale House Publishers, Inc., 1986.

Barclay, William. 1957. "The Letter to the Romans." In *The Daily Study Bible.* Edinburgh, Scotland: the Saint Andrew Press.

Barnhouse, Donald Grey. 1961. *God's Freedom.* Vol. 6, *Exposition of Bible Doctrine.* Grand Rapids, Michigan: William B. Eerdmans Publishing Company.

- - - . 1959. *God's Grace.* Vol. 5, *Exposition of Bible Doctrine.* Grand Rapids, Michigan: William B. Eerdmans Publishing Company.

- - - . 1963. *God's Heirs.* Vol. 7, *Exposition of Bible Doctrine.* Grand Rapids, Michigan: William B. Eerdmans Publishing Company.

- - - . 1958. *God's River.* Vol. 4, *Exposition of Bible Doctrine.* Grand Rapids, Michigan: William B. Eerdmans Publishing Company.

Beamer, Lisa. 2002. *Let's Roll.* Wheaton, Illinois: Tyndale House Publishers, Inc.

Bruce, F.F. 1963. *The Epistle to the Romans: An Introduction and Commentary.* The Tyndale New Testament Commentaries. Grand Rapids, Michigan: William B. Eerdmans Publishing Company.

Dunn, Ronald. n.d. *Victory.* Flower Mound, Texas: Rita Kaye Dunn.

Epp, Theodore H. 1960. *Salvation Needed and Provided.* Vol. 1, *Romans.* Lincoln, Nebraska: Back to the Bible Publishers.

- - - . 1959. *Victory Imparted and Tested.* Vol. 2, *Romans.* Lincoln, Nebraska: Back to the Bible Publishers.

- - - .1959. *Victory Triumphant and Practiced.* Vol. 3, *Romans.* Lincoln, Nebraska: Back to the Bible Publishers.

Godet, Frederic Louis. 1883. *Commentary on Romans.* Reprint. Grand Rapids, Michigan: Kregel Publications, 1977.

Halverson, Richard C. 1973. *God's Way Out of Futility.* Grand Rapids, Michigan: Zondervan Publishing House.

Hurnard, Hannah. 1977. *Hinds' Feet on High Places.* Living Books edition. Wheaton, Illinois: Tyndale House Publishers, Inc., 1985.

Ingram, Chip. 2002. *I Am With You Always: Experiencing God in Times of Need.* Grand Rapids, Michigan: Baker Books.

Ironside, H.A. 1928. *Lectures on the Epistle to the Romans.* Neptune, New Jersey: Loizeaux Brothers, Inc.

Johnson, Alan F. 1974. *The Freedom Letter.* Everyman's Bible Commentary. 2 vols. Chicago, Illinois: Moody Press.

Lange, John Peter. n.d. *Commentary on the Holy Scriptures: Romans.* Grand Rapids, Michigan: Zondervan Publishing House.

Lenski, R.C.H. 1936. *The Interpretation of St. Paul's Epistle to the Romans.* Minneapolis, Minnesota: Augsburg

Publishing House.
Lloyd-Jones, D.M. 1972. *Romans: Assurance.* Grand Rapids, Michigan: Zondervan Publishing House.
- - - .1976. *Romans: The Final Perseverance of the Saints.* Grand Rapids, Michigan: Zondervan Publishing House.
- - - . 1974. *Romans: The Law: Its Functions and Limits.* Grand Rapids, Michigan: Zondervan Publishing House.
- - - .1973. *Romans: The New Man.* Grand Rapids, Michigan: Zondervan Publishing House.
- - - .1975. *Romans: The Sons of God.* Grand Rapids, Michigan: Zondervan Publishing House.
MacGorman, J.W. 1976. *Romans: Everyman's Gospel.* Nashville, Tennessee: Convention Press.
Massey, Craig. 1977. *Adjust or Self-Destruct.* Chicago, Illinois: Moody Press.
McGee, J. Vernon. n.d. *Reasoning through Romans, Part I.* Los Angeles, California: Church of the Open Door.
Meredith Corporation. 1988. *Religion, Spirituality, and American Families: A Report from the Editors of Better Homes and Gardens Magazine.* N.p.: Meredith Corporation.
Sandlay, William, and Arthur C. Headlam. 1902. *The Epistle to the Romans.* The International Critical Commentary. Edinburgh, Scotland: t. and T. Clark.
Stedman, Ray C. 1978. *From Guilt to Glory.* Vol. 1. Waco, Texas: Word Books.
Stott, John R.W. 1966. *Men Made New.* Downers Grove, Illinois: InterVarsity Press.
Thomas, W. H. Griffith. 1974. *St. Paul's Epistle to the Romans.* Grand Rapids, Michigan: William B. Eerdmans Publishing Company.
Unger, Merrill F. 1966. *Unger's Bible Dictionary.* Third edition. Chicago, Illinois. Moody Press.

Printed in the United States
1251200004B/49-510

9 781591 609353